The Anteater's Guide to Writing and Rhetoric

COMPOSITION PROGRAM
UNIVERSITY OF CALIFORNIA, IRVINE

FIFTH EDITION

General Editor
Loren Eason

Consulting Editor
Bradley Queen

Contributors
Jonathan Alexander
Bobbie Allen
Emily Brauer Rogers
Libby Catchings
Alice Crawford Berghof
Sue Cross
Keith Danner
Kat Eason
Daniel M. Gross
Lynda Haas
Peggy Hesketh

Leah Kaminski
Ali Meghdadi
Collier Nogues
Cathy Palmer
Tira Palmquist
Abraham Romney
Jackie Way

Cover Art
Photography by
Loren Eason

Director of Composition: Daniel M. Gross
Campus Writing Coordinator: Jonathan Alexander

Hayden-McNeil Sustainability

Hayden-McNeil's standard paper stock uses a minimum of 30% post-consumer waste. We offer higher % options by request, including a 100% recycled stock. Additionally, Hayden-McNeil Custom Digital provides authors with the opportunity to convert print products to a digital format. Hayden-McNeil is part of a larger sustainability initiative through Macmillan Higher Ed. Visit http://sustainability.macmillan.com to learn more.

Printed in the United States of America

10 9 8 7 6 5 4 3 2 1

ISBN 978-0-7380-7462-7

Hayden-McNeil Publishing
14903 Pilot Drive
Plymouth, MI 48170
www.hmpublishing.com

Eason 7462-7 F15 (The Anteater's Guide to Writing and Rhetoric)

Table of Contents

Acknowledgements

This textbook is a collaborative project and a labor of love on the part of those involved in its production. Much of the work has been done on a strictly volunteer basis and no one involved in the writing of this guide is profiting from the proceeds, (which go to fund writing-related activities for the Writing Department. As always, I am blown away by the time and energy that my colleagues have put into making this guide live and breathe for the students in our classes.

I could not have put this book together without the previous work done by all the editors of prior editions of *The Anteater's Guide...* (and the *Student Guide to Writing...* before that). Much of what is good in this volume comes from the work that they did before I took over this project. Thanks to Lynda Haas, Kat Eason, and Tira Palmquist.

My chapter writers and editors put in tremendous work keeping this edition on-time and on-target. Thank you Libby, Kat E., Leah, Jackie, Cathy, Emily, Ali, Kat L., Tagert, Brad, Alice and Lisa.

And thanks to Jonathan Alexander, Bobbie Allen, Francisco J. Ayala, Chieh Cheng, Jeff Clapp, Sue Cross, Keith Danner, Jaya Dubey, Daniel M. Gross, Lynda Haas, Lance Langdon, Jens Lloyd, Writers in Focus: Elizabeth Loftus, Collier Nogues, Joy Palmer, Tira Palmquist, Michael R. Rose, Roger Walsh, Cara Watkins, and anyone else whose writing for previous editions survives on in this book. All works of writing have histories and our work would not be the same without your prior work.

Thanks to all the faculty, Lecturers and TAs, who teach in the Writing Department and whose classroom practices form the backbone of all that is practical in this book.

Thanks to Lin Fantino and the staff at Hayden-McNeil for giving us the tools and professional know-how to put this book together and make it look credible. You shape our ethos in many invisible ways.

Chapter 1

WHY RHETORIC?

*By Loren Eason, Daniel M. Gross,
Abraham Romney (and others)*

I'm Loren Eason, Lecturer in the Composition Program, former graduate student at UCI and General Editor of The Anteater's Guide to Writing and Rhetoric. *I began studying rhetoric when I was a graduate student here in an effort to explain how playing video games shapes our understanding of the world without us even noticing. (Ask me about it sometime…we'll talk.) I've been a rhetorician ever since.*

I'm Daniel M. Gross, Associate Professor of English and Director of the Composition Program. In my professional life I use my middle initial "M." because there's a much more famous "Daniel Gross" who seems like a nice enough guy but who sucks up my air all over the Internet. I have a PhD in rhetoric and I work on the history and theory of rhetoric so I've loved this discipline for a long time now. I feel this way because it provides a unique and powerful methodology for engaging the world from the benign, like consumerism (e.g., why do I prefer Coca-Cola over Pepsi?) to the pernicious, like racism (e.g., How are children systematically convinced that they live in a world where race matters?). Rhetoric helps us see the world anew, and it also helps us get things done.

Abraham Romney left UCI after graduating with his PhD in rhetoric and is currently a professor at Michigan Tech (where he gets to watch hockey and play in the snow).

Rhetoric Is...?

This is the fifth edition of *The Anteater's Guide to Writing and Rhetoric*. Before the first edition, UCI used a book called *The Student Guide to Writing at UC Irvine*.

Why is this information relevant to your life as a student in the Writing Program at UCI? After all, the textbook is required for the course, so from a student perspective this guide is a necessary nuisance that costs approximately ten glasses of boba on the Ring Road (and sells back for only one glass of boba—a horrible rate of exchange). Now, on top of taking boba out of your mouth we are asking you to care about the history of this guide.

Not so much the history of the AGWR as the rhetorical situation of it.

Back up...the rhetorical what? And for that matter, what is this rhetoric thing of which you speak?

Back in 2010 in the First Edition of the AGWR we described rhetoric like this:

> Rhetoric is a comprehensive "art," or set of techniques, for effective communication. Aristotle, the Greek philosopher and teacher whose writings did much to solidify the art, defines rhetoric as "the ability in each particular case, to see the available means of persuasion." Throughout your composition courses, you'll hear this ability called rhetorical knowledge or **rhetorical know-how**, where the former refers to your conceptual understanding of rhetoric and the latter refers to your practical ability.

Here you are, wanting to know what rhetoric is and instead of a clear example of rhetoric we give you information about Aristotle and a sentence about...persuasion? Something, something, persuasion. Definitely underline that persuasion part because it looks important, right?

So why tell you all this about Aristotle and his famous, but not entirely intuitive, definition of rhetoric? And why do this for pretty much every edition of the AGWR, just as we have for every edition of the *Student Guide* before that?

Time for another strategy and another way of explaining. This time we'll go with a story analogy:

You arrive at a party that is already going on and has been going for some time. All around you, people are already deeply engaged in conversations. You listen for a while and piece together what they are talking about and circulate until you find a conversation in which you are interested. You settle in there and pay closer attention to get a feel for the conversation. Soon you hit a point in the talk where you feel you have something to add, so you pick your moment and interject: "That reminds me of something that I heard the other day…"

So, you see, you're like the person who has just gotten to the party and all of us who have been writing this guide are like the people who are already there. That's rhetoric: one big party. And, hey, wasn't Aristotle just here, over by the Doritos, just a few thousand years back? What a guy, that Aristotle. Something, something, persuasion something. Brilliant!

All kidding aside (at least for the moment) the underlying point here is that writing—all communication, really—is a social act. This point often gets obscured or lost in all of the worry that you, your parents, your teachers, your society place on the product of your writing. In the real world, rhetoric gets used to communicate something of some significance to another being and it either succeeds if that communication happens or fails if that communication goes wrong. And, just like at that party, both you and the audience you are communicating with exist within a shared context and at least a partially shared history. Communication only happens when we can build bridges from our own history and context to the histories and contexts of our audience.

That's what Aristotle was attempting to explain with his definition: rhetoric is about seeing opportunities to build bridges between where you are and where your audience is by using the ideas, experiences, texts, etc. that you share in order to persuade your audience to try on your way of seeing these things, at least for a while, and consider what seeing things in this way might add to their own world.

Cue the Fishbowl!

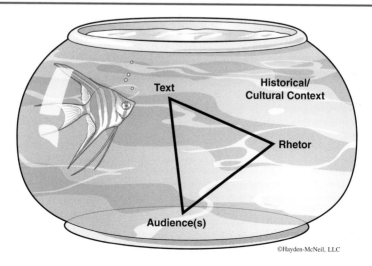

We call this picture "the rhetorical situation," because it illustrates how every act of communication happens in a particular context and moment in time shared between the person who is sending the text, (the Rhetor) and the person(s) receiving the text (the Audience(s)). All communication requires all these elements in order to happen.

To me, though, this fishbowl is not just "the rhetorical situation"; *it's a rhetoric party in a fish bowl.* The picture is misleading because there should not be just one fish; there should be two or more fish talking to each other.

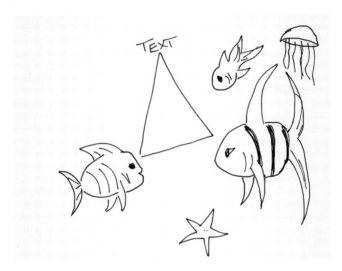

They are hanging out in the bowl talking about whatever people talk about at rhetoric parties. (Go *ahead, draw little party hats on the fish. It's not like you can sell this textbook back for much, anyway.*) But, again, the idea here is that, in order for the two fish to communicate, the rhetor fish needs to be thinking about what bridges s/he can build between the subject and the audience in order to speak to that audience using their own words and ideas and relating the new ideas and meanings to the things that the audience finds significant. And in order to properly understand the message, the audience fish needs to consider where the rhetor fish is coming from and look for clues embedded in the rhetor's text that help us to understand the context in which the rhetor crafted the message. Both sides of the conversation have to do some work to make communication happen.

And that's a big point that we need to remember in all of our writing and all of our rhetoric. Every time we find ourselves wanting to (or called upon to) communicate with the other people in our fishbowl world, we need to think about this triangle—not just to remember that communication is Not Just About Us, but also because that triangle can be a cue to remind us of our purpose in communicating. Rhetoric is "the ability in each particular case, to see the available means of persuasion," (see, there it is again), and persuasion involves effecting some sort of change in your audience through your communication.

The triangle can also be seen as a delta—Δ—and deltas mean "change," (right, math fans?). All acts of communication change the world in some way. The challenge lies in changing the world in the way you set out to change it, and not changing it in some unintended way, either through making mistakes or through choosing poorly considered tactics.

The Rhetorical Triangle in Action

In the previous edition of this book, Daniel M. Gross gave us the following example of one such tricky situation:

> I recently had to teach my 8-year-old son Max some rhetorical awareness.
>
> 2012—Max wrote in a familiar **genre**, the thank-you note:
>
> > "Thank you aunt Jeannie for the generous gift!
> > I'll probably buy some Legos and then put the rest in the bank."

> 2013—Max wrote:
>
> > "Thank you aunt Jeannie for the generous gift!
> > I'll probably buy some Legos and then put the rest in the bank."
>
> Needless to say, mom and dad asked for a revision on rhetorical grounds.
>
> Max's first note was entirely appropriate and said all the things that were expected to persuade his aunt that her gift, and her consideration, were appreciated.

The second note did all of those things again, but made the mistake of repeating the previous note exactly. Using the same words and expressing the same sentiment a second time, however, does not produce the same effect when the rhetorical situation has changed.

The second thank-you note was factually correct and truthful (**logos**), expressly grateful (**pathos**), and technically respectful of the relationship (**ethos**). The genre of the thank-you note had been realized adequately on a formal level. So why in our opinion was the exact same note appropriate the first time but not the second? Why was the first note "persuasive" to Aunt Jeannie, who found it charming enough, whereas the second note would not have been so persuasive?

For one thing, if you're in the domain of the "technically respectful," then something is probably wrong. What would a successful gesture of gratitude and respect—a successful interaction—look like in this case? The second note should look somehow different to acknowledge the passage of time from one year to the next, and the living relationship (not some mechanical gesture) between nephew and great aunt. In other words, rhetoric is about gaining familiarity with the ways in which form—the thank-you note in this case—can be realized in a lived situation that includes an emotional dynamic, classically referred to as **pathos**.

Seems like this rhetoric party is more complicated than it first appeared. Daniel points out, above, three strategies, or "appeals," that people commonly use to build bridges between themselves and their audience:

Logos refers to the way that a communicator reasons with her audience through the use of claims, examples, evidence and the like that are both logically consistent and clearly explained. Both math and science rely primarily upon appeals to logos as an objective standard.

Pathos refers to the way that a communicator appeals to his audiences' emotions or sentiments in order to affect the way an audience feels about the object of that appeal. It's often used in order to sway how much the audience identifies with the subject in question.

Ethos refers to the way a communicator represents herself to an audience. It could refer to the person doing the communicating in a real setting or it could refer to how a particular character in a fictional text represents himself to the audience; in fact, ethos is sometimes translated as "character." It is often used to build trust between the author and the audience or to appeal to the audience's sense of values.

Let's "Unpack" This a Bit

What Daniel is saying is that while Max expresses gratitude in his note, demonstrating that he is thoughtful and conscientious, the fact that he has reproduced his previous note exactly could raise questions about his ethos by leaving the impression that he has not taken time to consider his response and remember his previous exchange with his great aunt, or, worse yet, has merely re-sent his previous thank-you note in order to fulfil an obligation with minimal effort.

Most of us can relate to Max, here—being called upon to write a particular sort of message in an agreed-upon format for a particular type of audience. (You'll read more about this in the next chapter when Libby explains genre to you.) It takes a bit of practice to both learn the sets of expectations that come with this sort of communication and to find a creative way to break out of these expectations in order to say something individual and personal.

Pay attention, because here is where we start to look at the real power of rhetoric and why understanding it can help us to become more effective communicators.

Let's forget about Max and Aunt Jeannie for a moment, though, and think about the larger "rhetorical situation." Max and Aunt Jeannie are not the only fish in this fishbowl. To really understand this fishbowl we also have to think about Daniel's role in this rhetoric party as well.

Daniel is, in some sense, both the secondary audience for Max's letter and a rhetor sending messages to both Aunt Jeannie and Max. He reads Max's note in order to make sure that Max understands things about the rhetorical situation that are not so easy to see at first, like how sending a perfectly factual text can send the wrong message if it breaks the unspoken rule that a thank-you note should be personal and distinct, leaving the receiver to feel less appreciated than the sender intends. So he is acting to help send Aunt Jeannie the message that she is loved. He's also acting to send the message to Max that it is important for us not just to appreciate the gifts we receive, but to communicate that apprecation to the giver. And he's teaching Max that even simple acts of communication can prove more complex than they seem at first glance.

Moreover, by teaching Max to send thank-you notes, he's sending the message to all those who receive a note that Max is being raised to be a considerate person who values those around him. Max's message not only builds his own ethos as a good person—it also builds Daniel's ethos as a good parent.

What About *Our* Fishbowl?

Just as Max's fishbowl was more complex than it first appeared, the fishbowl you are now in has its own complexities. Nearly everything that you write for a Writing 39 class will make you think not only about the rhetorical situation outlined in the prompt, but also about the larger fishbowls the prompt's fishbowl lives inside.

Fishbowls within fishbowls…isn't that just grand?

But seriously, just as Max had to figure out how to write to Aunt Jeannie in a way that made her feel appreciated, he also had to write in such a way that he convinced Daniel that he understands why we write thank-you notes and that he could be trusted in the future to write his own notes and to approach other sorts of social communication with the right sort of rhetorical awareness to send only the messages that Max intends to send and none that he wishes to avoid.

Our purpose in teaching these writing courses, and in focusing on rhetoric within these courses, is the same. We wish to equip you to face all your rhetorical situations in college and beyond.

This fishbowl is way bigger than just this campus. The Council for Writing Program Administrators is a part of the larger conversation that sits behind what you do in a writing class. The people in charge of setting guidelines for writing programs at American universities have agreed that all students who go through a writing program should learn the following during their first year:

Rhetorical Knowledge

Rhetorical knowledge is the ability to analyze contexts and audiences and then to act on that analysis in comprehending and creating texts. Rhetorical knowledge is the basis of composing. Writers develop rhetorical knowledge by negotiating purpose, audience, context, and conventions as they compose a variety of texts for different situations.

By the end of first-year composition, students should

- Learn and use key rhetorical concepts through analyzing and composing a variety of texts

- Gain experience reading and composing in several genres to understand how genre conventions shape and are shaped by readers' and writers' practices and purposes

- Develop facility in responding to a variety of situations and contexts calling for purposeful shifts in voice, tone, level of formality, design, medium, and/or structure

- Understand and use a variety of technologies to address a range of audiences

- Match the capacities of different environments (e.g., print and electronic) to varying rhetorical situations

Critical Thinking, Reading, and Composing

Critical thinking is the ability to analyze, synthesize, interpret, and evaluate ideas, information, situations, and texts. When writers think critically about the materials they use—whether print texts, photographs, data sets, videos, or other materials—they separate assertion from evidence, evaluate sources and evidence, recognize and evaluate underlying assumptions, read across texts for connections and patterns, identify and evaluate chains of reasoning, and compose appropriately qualified and developed claims and generalizations. These practices are foundational for advanced academic writing.

By the end of first-year composition, students should

- Use composing and reading for inquiry, learning, critical thinking, and communicating in various rhetorical contexts

- Read a diverse range of texts, attending especially to relationships between assertion and evidence, to patterns of organization, to the interplay between verbal and nonverbal elements, and to how these features function for different audiences and situations

- Locate and evaluate (for credibility, sufficiency, accuracy, timeliness, bias and so on) primary and secondary research materials, including journal articles and essays, books, scholarly and professionally established and maintained databases or archives, and informal electronic networks and internet sources

- Use strategies—such as interpretation, synthesis, response, critique, and design/redesign—to compose texts that integrate the writer's ideas with those from appropriate sources

Processes

Writers use multiple strategies, or *composing processes*, to conceptualize, develop, and finalize projects. Composing processes are seldom linear: a writer may research a topic before drafting, then conduct additional research while revising or after consulting a colleague. Composing processes are also flexible: successful writers can adapt their composing processes to different contexts and occasions.

By the end of first-year composition, students should

- Develop a writing project through multiple drafts

- Develop flexible strategies for reading, drafting, reviewing, collaborating, revising, rewriting, rereading, and editing

- Use composing processes and tools as a means to discover and reconsider ideas

- Experience the collaborative and social aspects of writing processes

- Learn to give and to act on productive feedback to works in progress

- Adapt composing processes for a variety of technologies and modalities

- Reflect on the development of composing practices and how those practices influence their work

Knowledge of Conventions

Conventions are the formal rules and informal guidelines that define genres, and in so doing, shape readers' and writers' perceptions of correctness or appropriateness. Most obviously, conventions govern such things as mechanics, usage, spelling, and citation practices. But they also influence content, style, organization, graphics, and document design.

Conventions arise from a history of use and facilitate reading by invoking common expectations between writers and readers. These expectations are not universal; they vary by genre (conventions for lab notebooks and discussion-board exchanges differ), by discipline (conventional moves in literature reviews in Psychology differ from those in English), and by occasion (meeting minutes and executive summaries use different registers). A writer's grasp of conventions in one context does not mean a firm grasp in another. Successful writers understand, analyze, and negotiate conventions for purpose, audience, and genre, understanding that genres evolve in response to changes in material conditions and composing technologies and attending carefully to emergent conventions.

By the end of first-year composition, students should

- Develop knowledge of linguistic structures, including grammar, punctuation, and spelling, through practice in composing and revising

- Understand why genre conventions for structure, paragraphing, tone, and mechanics vary

- Gain experience negotiating variations in genre conventions

- Learn common formats and/or design features for different kinds of texts

- Explore the concepts of intellectual property (such as fair use and copyright) that motivate documentation conventions

- Practice applying citation conventions systematically in their own work

Oh...So That's Why We Have to Write All These Papers

Yep. Like Max learning to write a thank-you note in order to also learn how to interact with his family, your year-long rhetoric party here at UCI is aimed at helping you to learn the things that you will need to know to get along in this community. The people in charge of designing these writing courses have been talking to the people at other colleges and universities to see what sorts of challenges you will face in the course of writing papers for college classes and beyond. We also consult with those who have been at this rhetoric party here for a while. I could not have written this chapter if it weren't for the work that all the past editors, instructors, and directors have done. I've learned from this extended conversation. Talking with these people over the last ten years has taught me a lot and parts of what they have written and what we have talked about—parts of the ways in which they have structured their explanations of rhetoric to other groups of students in other years—have shaped the way that I explain it to you now.

Of course we also learn from you—or, at least, from our experience with past groups of students a lot like you. We look at what works and what does not work. We look at your questions and the places in past *Anteaters' Guides* that we have always had to explain in more depth and we make changes based on what we learn about our audience. And we do all of this because we intend to use our rhetoric to change the way you write and the way you think about the act of writing. We do it to help you achieve the outcomes described above.

Back to You, Student

The point of all of these examples and discussions of audiences and rhetoric (at last, a point!) is that real writing is addressed to real audiences with real histories. Sure, you can learn a lot from "answering the prompt," but once you are an experienced and capable rhetor, you will understand enough about the rhetorical situation to see past the prompt and get at the underlying purpose for addressing a particular audience in a particular way at a particular time.

Possible Rhetorical Purposes

- **To persuade** an audience to consider or adopt a particular course of action

- **To inform** an audience of some new piece of information or provide better evidence for a given rhetorical situation

- To provide the audience with **a new narrative** for the rhetorical situation that changes how they see it or who they identify with in that moment

- To **draw attention to your language** or rhetoric (or the rhetoric of others) in order to provoke further reflection on the method of communication

- **(And the list goes on...)**

You will also see each rhetorical occasion—that moment in which you are called upon to use your communication skills to intervene in the larger conversation and change the dialogue in some meaningful and productive way—as something more than just an isolated obligation and find some way to use that opportunity to achieve something real for yourself and for your communities.

Rhetoric is not a series of devices that you use in the same way every time to achieve a particular effect, independent of the audience and the context. Rhetoric is a conscious awareness that we live in a social world and that in order to achieve our largest goals we need to find ways to build common ground and communicate these goals. We need to know what opinions our audiences hold. We need to understand why they hold these opinions. And this means that we need to ask good questions and we need to learn to listen to the answers we are given and test our own reactions to ensure that we are not just hearing what we want to hear.

And, most of all, we are asking you to work hard to develop your rhetorical know-how. To consider what your audience needs and to work with what they value. Rhetoric reminds us that communication is not simply expression. Messages need both a sender and a receiver in order to convey information and change the world. We are all in the middle of a world of rhetorical triangles and messages being sent from the past to the future and our words and rhetorical acts are the bridges that connect the past to the future and ourselves to the rest of the world. We are negotiating what the past means and building bridges to a shared social future. It's up to us to make sure that future is a good one.

Works Cited and Further Reading

Aristotle. *On Rhetoric: A Theory of Civic Discourse.* 2nd ed., Trans. George Alexander Kennedy. New York: Oxford University Press, 2007. Print.

Bartholomae, David. "Inventing the University." *Journal of Basic Writing* 5.1 (1986): 4–23. Print.

Booth, Wayne C. "The Rhetorical Stance." *College Composition and Communication* 14.3 (1963): 139–145. Print.

Burke, Kenneth. "Symbolic Action in a Poem by Keats." *A Grammar of Motives.* Berkeley, University of California Press, 1969. 447–463. Print.

Cicero, Marcus Tullius. *Cicero: On the Ideal Orator.* New York: Oxford University Press, 2001. Print.

Ede, Lisa, and Andrea Lunsford. "Audience Addressed/Audience Invoked: The Role of Audience in Composition Theory and Pedagogy." *College Composition and Communication* 35.2 (1984): 155–171. Print.

Elbow, Peter. "The Teacherless Writing Class." *Writing Without Teachers.* New York: Oxford University Press, 1998. 76–116. Print.

Fahnestock, Jeanne. "Accommodating Science The Rhetorical Life of Scientific Facts." *Written Communication* 3.3 (1986): 275–296. Print.

Fish, Stanley. "Rhetoric." *Doing What Comes Naturally: Change, Rhetoric, and the Practice of Theory in Literary & Legal Studies.* Durham: Duke University Press, 1989. 471–502. Print.

Hesford, Wendy S., and Brenda Brueggemann. *Rhetorical Visions: Reading and Writing in a Visual Culture.* 1st ed. New York: Longman, 2006. Print.

Johns, Ann M. "Situated Intervention and Genres: Assisting Generation 1.5 Students in Developing Rhetorical Flexibility." *Generation 1.5 in College Composition: Teaching Academic Writing to U.S.-Educated Learners of ESL.* Eds. Mark Roberge, Meryl Siegal, and Linda Harklau. New York: Routledge, 2009. 203–220. Print.

Miller, Thomas P. *The Evolution of College English: Literacy Studies from the Puritans to the Postmoderns.* 1st ed. Pittsburgh: University of Pittsburgh Press, 2011. Print.

Phelan, James. "Narrative as Rhetoric: Reading the Spells of Porter's 'Magic'." *Narrative As Rhetoric: Technique, Audiences, Ethics, Ideology.* Columbus: Ohio State University Press, 1996. Print.

Shuger, Debora Kuller. *Sacred Rhetoric: The Christian Grand Style in the English Renaissance.* 1st ed. Princeton: Princeton University Press, 1988. Print.

Sloane, Thomas O., ed. *Encyclopedia of Rhetoric.* New York: Oxford University Press, 2001. Print.

"WPA Outcomes Statement for First-Year Composition (3.0), Approved July 17, 2014." *WPA: Writing Program Administration* 38.1 (Fall 2014): 129–143. Print.

Chapter 2

READING AND WRITING GENRE
Guideposts for Thinking and Acting in the World

By Libby Catchings

Greetings and Salutations! I'm Libby Catchings, a writing instructor here at UCI who's taught everything from the Writing 39 series to drama and literary journalism. In my other lives, I've written grant reports for the Peace Corps, feature pieces for community newspapers, and technical documents for nonprofits in the Bay Area, so for me, genre awareness has been (and continues to be) an indispensable tool for adapting to new rhetorical situations. As you read this chapter, I hope that you'll find that understanding genre can not only help you interpret new texts, but also give you tools to reinvent yourself as a writer, no matter how uncharted the waters.

The weekend is coming up, and your friend has an extra ticket to an Angels game in Anaheim. You've never been to a baseball game before, but you have a reasonable idea of how it works: ball, bat, and bases, nine innings, and "three-strikes and you're out." When you get there, however, you're reminded that baseball is so much more than the equipment and rules to the game—that what the crowd does is just as important as what the players do on the field. There's cheering for the home team, silence when a pitcher is about to throw, hats-off for the national anthem, and standing up with the rest of the crowd for a 3–2 count, with runners on base and two outs, since it means something exciting is about to happen.

What this tells is that baseball isn't just defined by the forms of the game (a grassy diamond instead of an ice-covered hockey rink), or the structure of how it's played (nine innings vs. hockey's three periods). It's also defined by the social practices that surround it.

So, what does baseball have to do with genre, or the writing classroom?

If we think of the game of "baseball" as a text to read, and the activity of the people around the game as the social *context*, it helps us begin understand how genre is not just a "what," but a "how"—a social practice that gives us guideposts for thinking and acting in the world.

Defining Genre

In our everyday lives, most people think of "genre" as a way to sort different kinds of texts into different categories—categories like, "sci-fi dystopia," or presidential address; military-themed FPS (first person shooter) game, or haiku. Through the process of *rhetorical analysis*, we are able to identify the characteristics that give shape to those genres we know, and help us learn those genres we don't—the signs we use to explore new terrain. If we look at the example above, the person knows some of the formal conventions of baseball before the game starts, just like movie-goers know in advance that a new sci-fi dystopia will most likely give you a good environmental disaster, struggle against dictatorship, and a parade of ingenious gadgets that the young protagonist will steal from the clutches of the bad guys to fight for a new world order.

Yet, as the baseball example shows us, genres give us so much more than a set of boxes to put things in. Genres are also *a way to see sets of relations*, in that they help us define different social situations and organize them so that we know how those situations work; moreover, they help us to understand how we ourselves fit in. We only begin to understand baseball fully, for example, when we take part in the rituals and activities around the game; it's not just knowing the form and structure, but knowing how to act that enables us to connect to hundreds if not thousands of people across the country. At the same time, however, genres also enable us to create new relations to fulfill our needs at a given moment. Because genres are communicative activities that help us respond to particular rhetorical situations, they help us accomplish certain tasks—here, genre becomes that moment of connection between our intentions and their desired effects.

This tells us that the person watching the baseball game in the previous example doesn't understand genre just because of the rules or the uniforms. The narrator *participates* in the genre of baseball through the process of cheering and standing with the rest of the crowd—such that it's a way of *acting* in the world with others. The other people in the stadium learned the rules from someone else, and you'll pass along what you know to the next person—whether that's today, or in several years. In this way, the *process* of genre moves and develops over time. Reading new texts works the same way: you learn the rules for how to read certain kinds of writing, whether it's a poem, or an academic essay, and then you know what to expect of other texts in the future—whether those texts are similar to genres of writing you already know, or they're new genres for you to master.

Reading Genre as Social Relation

Use this QR code to watch a YouTube video about a particular genre of activity happening here at UC Irvine, and answer the following questions. You can also type in the following link:

http://www.youtube.com/watch?v=VNcdxTPv6g0

1. What genre is this video about? What are its formal characteristics? What are the social practices connected to that genre?

2. This group is engaging in a genre of activity that responds to a particular rhetorical situation. What is that rhetorical situation (i.e., Rhetor, Purpose, Message, Audience, Text, Context)?

3. List the things the people in the video do or say that explain how their use of this genre connects their intentions to their desired effects.

YOUR TURN:
Think of a genre you use in your everyday life that is defined by the kinds of social interaction you have with other people, to accomplish certain tasks (examples: band practice, or fundraising for a club activity). What kinds of communicative activities can you list to define that genre for an outside observer?

Of course, you can't experience a live baseball game whenever you want—you've got to go to a particular stadium or field, at a particular time, with other people who know what's expected of them. In this way, genre requires *context*. We learned in Chapter 1 that context locates a rhetor, audience, and text in a particular place and time. If you stand and boo and cheer at a ballet, or a scholarly lecture, for example, they might look at you funny, or even just kick you out, since those cultural settings demand that you sit quietly.

So, genre really does a lot of different things ... and yet it's not as complicated as you think. One way to understand genre is through an analogy made available through physics, and applied to language use by linguist Kenneth Pike. Through this analogy, we can see genre as a particle (a thing or object unto itself); wave (a process); and field (context). Just as quantum mechanics shows us that photons can behave as both particles and waves in a field, so does genre function in multiple ways, simultaneously.

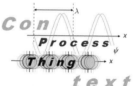

- This means that genres, like particles, can be *THINGS* or *OBJECTS* with certain forms and stylistic conventions, like a Raymond Chandler detective novel;

- Like waves, they can be *PROCESSES* that develop over time and space, such as the development and adoption of social media like Facebook; and

- Like a field, genres exist as part of different social and institutional *CONTEXTS*, like a flash-mob in a shopping mall, or standardized testing in a public school.

Why Genre Matters to You

It's your sense of genre—being able to both identify a text's conventions, and respond to those conventions appropriately—that makes for successful rhetorical engagement in the world. It's like what you learned about baseball at the beginning of this chapter; by understanding what a genre looks like and how to "do" it, you now have the ability to enjoy and maybe even use that genre for your own purposes later on. Part of your task, then, is to become more conscious of the way you use genre to read and respond to a variety of rhetorical situations you'll run into at UCI, and beyond.

In Chapter 1, you learned that UCI's composition course series has been de-signed to give you the practice you need to develop rhetorical know-how. The first step to thinking like a rhetorician is understanding that you are an author, reader, and responder to every "text" you encounter in your own life—whether that be an assigned reading from your psychology book, or email from your mom. No one had to tell you to "read" these two rhetorical situations differ-ently—you already know that their social contexts, objectives, and styles are completely different, just like you know without being told that the style and content of your responses should be different as well. This means you're already pretty good at reading and responding to a rhetorical situation; now, however, you need to make a habit of reading a rhetorical situation *consciously and me-thodically*. For a refresher on how to conduct rhetorical analysis, visit Chapter 8 on Argument.

Summary Questions—Defining Genre

1. How does *rhetorical analysis* help you identify the different parts of genre?

2. What analogy can we use to describe the different *functions* of genre?

3. Why does this analogy help us understand the different ways genre works in a rhetorical situation?

Applying Genre—Your Class

Because understanding genre is an important part of every writing course you take at UCI, here are some questions to help guide your use of genre in your particular 39-series course.

Writing 39A

1. Part of your goal in 39A is to understand other people's writing accurately so that you can respond meaningfully and critically.

   • How does understanding genre as an object, process, and context help you understand other people's writing accurately?

2. Writing 39A encourages you to recognize how writing can be used to accom-plish a variety of purposes, in a variety of rhetorical situations.

   • How does knowing genre help you recognize the different purposes that a piece of writing can have?

Writing 39B

1. One goal of 39B is being able to critically read all different genres of texts to prepare for all of the different genres of writing you'll encounter through your academic career.

- How do you think the concept of genre as an object, process, and context helps prepare you for different kinds of writing you'll be asked to do at UCI?

2. Another goal of 39B is the ability to write a rhetorical analysis essay for an academic audience.

- How does understanding genre help you write successfully for an academic audience?

Writing 39C

1. In 39C, you learn how to analyze the construction of arguments in a variety of sources.

- How might the concept of genre as an object, process, and context improve your ability to understand how different sources are put together in different ways?

2. One goal of 39C is to help you learn how to conduct academic research, both in the library and online.

- How might understanding genre help you conduct more successful academic research, using a variety of different tools in different settings?

Tools for Identifying Genre as Thing, Process, and Context

Four ways to give shape to genre as an *object* or *thing* are through characteristics of FORM (its structure, style), MEDIUM (the means used to transmit the message), AUDIENCE, and CONTENT (its subject matter). Once you know the genre of a text as an object, you will also be able to make some predictions about what to expect from it, since texts from the same genre often have many of the same features or conventions. Later, you can move on to thinking about how those characteristics reflect changes in that genre's role as a social action over time (genre as a *process*), and how the genre operates as part of a larger social system (genre as *context*). Because different genres respond to different rhetorical situations, these tools will also enhance your ability to perform *rhetorical analysis*.

For example: let's say you're trying to describe the genre for Quentin Tarantino's film about slavery, *Django Unchained*. You might first identify characteristics of its FORM by saying that it has the style of "black comedy," and the structure of a "revenge" film, featuring a peaceful protagonist who is provoked by bad men to unleash spectacular violence in order to avenge the injustice done against him and his wife. You might identify the MEDIUM as film, and the AUDIENCE as variously, "fans of spaghetti westerns," "fans of Quentin Tarantino," and "American filmgoers." You might then describe the CONTENT of the film in terms of slavery in the American South. However, when you move on to discussing genre as a *process* and *context*, it gives you the opportunity to talk about how the film's combination of spaghetti western, black comedy, revenge caper, and historical fiction genres not only reflects a history of popular cinema through the eyes of the director, but also holds a mirror up to the audience in a way that challenges us to reevaluate what we think a story about slavery should look like, including the emotions we are expected to feel. In this way, understanding genre as *process* and *content* helps us get a better sense of the film's rhetorical purpose and rhetorical effects. Below are detailed descriptions of the four main types of tools for identifying genre.

Form

Texts within the same genre often share some elements of structure and style. As an example of *structure*, poems are written in lines and stanzas, with a particular rhyme scheme, whereas essays often have an introduction, body paragraphs for development, and a conclusion. Popular songs have a repeating chorus, and plays are divided by scenes and acts. Different kinds of narrative also have distinct structures, such as the particular plot sequences that recur in a Quest narrative. A Quest usually features a hero or heroine whose objective it is to either seek their fortune, or regain something that was taken away. The quest usually involves a harrowing journey featuring tests of strength, cunning, or bravery, and they may discover resistance to their return once the object is obtained. The *style* of each of these genres, however, may differ according to the diction (word choice) or syntax (how phrases are put together) a rhetor chooses to make their language their own; this may affect a genre's *tone*, or the attitude a rhetor uses to convey a message.

YOUR TURN

- Take a moment to think about one of your favorite songs, preferably one with lyrics.

- *Structure:* How is that song put together? Do the lyrics rhyme? How many verses does it have? Is there a chorus?

- *Style:* What is the style of the song? Is it a slow ballad, with words that recall sentimental memories? Is it a hip-hop song, with lyrics that showcase that artist's skill, and reveal their cultural affiliations?

- *Tone:* How does the style of the song reveal its tone? Does the song's choice of words make it defiant? Romantic? Ironic, or playful?

Medium

Part of that stylistic choice may influence the *medium* a rhetor chooses for their message—it may be text on a page, or it may be visual, like a photograph. It might be your favorite novel printed in paperback, or that same novel voice-recorded on a CD, read aloud to you by your favorite actor. It may be performed live, or streamed digitally; or it might even be all of the above—this kind of hybrid genre is considered *multi-modal.* For the moment, however, it's important to remember that medium tells us a lot about genre both as a *process* and as a *context*; because a given text can be shared through a variety of different media—at different times and places, by different people—medium is critical to understanding how a text is socially situated, who it's reaching at a given moment, and where it's going.

 YOUR TURN

- Think back to the genre of melodrama you read about at the beginning of the chapter. Is it a medium you see, hear, or read on the page? Or is it a combination of these?

- How might the medium of a *live* performance in a theater differ from seeing that performance on your computer or phone, posted on YouTube, a year later?

- How might the rhetorical situation of a live performance differ from reading the script of that play, printed as a written text?

Audience

Some genres are born out of the need to communicate within a specific community. For example, the essay, a "short nonfiction literary composition," is a written genre that first appeared in 1597 in the work of Francis Bacon (who was probably imitating Montaigne, a French Renaissance scholar). The academic essay has its own particular conventions for form (including *structure*, *style*, and *tone*) and content because it is written specifically for an academic (scholarly) audience. Thinking about audience also gives us a good idea of how the genre operates in a social and historical context—whether that be the context in which a work was originally composed and published, as was Bacon's 1597 essay in London, or your own context, reading that essay in Irvine in 2013. Moreover, different academic audiences favor different conventions of form and content, depending on their particular disciplinary writing practices; for example, an executive summary for a Business Administration audience will have different formal features compared to a policy statement intended for scholars in Public Health. In your composition courses, part of UCI's general education requirements, you'll learn some of the most prominent features of general academic writing. As you progress into your upper-division "W" courses, you'll begin to learn more about the particular conventions for your chosen discipline.

 YOUR TURN

- Think back to a moment when you had to speak publicly in front of a group of people. It could be an oral presentation for a class, words of encouragement for your team before a big sports event, or a speech at a faith-based community gathering.

- Describe the particular historical or cultural context of that rhetorical situation.

- What are some of the conventions of *form* that you had to use to speak to this particular audience, and why?

- What are some of the conventions of *content* that you had to use to speak to this audience, and why?

Content

Some genres we know by their subject matter or themes, such as country music, or reality shows like *The Real Housewives*. We can expect that a country song will talk about love or hardship in the lives of ordinary people, and that an episode of *The Real Housewives* will serve up healthy portions of luxury living, domestic drama, and complex friendships among women in affluent American neighborhoods. It is helpful to remember, however, that content and form are not mutually exclusive categories; you may find that some genres share common themes, but differ dramatically in structure and style, or medium. Take, for example, the star-crossed lovers Romeo and Juliet; you may know them primarily from the play by Shakespeare, but their story continues to be transposed into different structures, styles, and media, including musicals, rock ballads, films and ballets—some remaining faithful to Shakespeare's original plot, language, and characters, and others that render their story barely recognizable, keeping only the star-crossed lovers theme.

 YOUR TURN

The superhero genre is an inescapable feature of the pop-culture landscape; we see the same characters and themes reimagined in a variety of ways, using different media, forms, and styles—even appealing, at times, to different audiences. One example is the *Batman* story.

- How would you describe the *content* of the *Batman* story; i.e., its themes, characters, setting, or distinct plot features?

- Think of two different interpretations of *Batman* that you know of; they can differ in form, medium, style, audience, or all of the above.

- How do those different choices in *medium* affect the *content* of the *Batman* story? For example, how does a comic book rendering tell the story differently from a Hollywood film?

- How do those different choices in *style* affect the *content* of the *Batman* story? For example, how does Tim Burton's version change the themes and characters compared to the version imagined by director Christopher Nolan?

- Do changes in the *content* and *style* of a *Batman* interpretation affect how different *audiences* will receive that interpretation? In other words, do those changes alter the text's rhetorical situation?

Critical Rhetorical Awareness

So, now you've got a handy set of tools for identifying genre; those tools, in turn, make it that much easier to "read" a rhetorical situation. Equally important to rhetorical awareness, however, is being able to reflect critically on your own rhetorical choices, and on the choices of others, since they can influence social relations and structure shared knowledge about the world. Successful rhetorical awareness means you've managed to see and use the available means of persuasion in a given situation; *critical* rhetorical awareness, however, means being able to *take responsibility* for the consequences of our rhetorical acts, since they have the power to both reinforce and challenge social norms.

Imagine you and your friends decide to write and perform a parody of a well-known TV show and put it on the Web, using highly exaggerated stereotypes of the people you come across at UCI. You have a blast making the video, and a good laugh at the final product, since part of your goal was to show people how ridiculous some of those stereotypes are. The only thing is, you soon discover that some people don't get the joke—some are downright offended, and some use your video to reinforce the idea that those stereotypes are true.

Critical Rhetorical Awareness means understanding the rhetorical power that something like a stereotype can have in different contexts, and considering how that power has the capacity to influence personal relationships, social climates, and even political structures.

 YOUR TURN

WR 39A and 39B

We see this kind of problem all the time in comedy, where a stand-up comic routine, film, political cartoon, or television show takes a stereotype to its logical conclusion for laughs.

1. Think of an example in popular culture where you've seen this happen.

2. What kind of rhetorical appeal did that text use to get a response from its audience?

3. What were the social, economic, or political consequences of that rhetorical act?

WR 39C

In 39C, you encounter sources that characterize individuals, groups, and social issues in particular ways, depending on the rhetorical purpose of the author. It could be an op-ed in the newspaper, or an article from a peer-reviewed academic journal, but there's always the possibility that a writer will give you a very particular slant on the facts to persuade you of their argument. How the reader interprets that text can have social, economic, or political consequences.

1. Find a source related to your class theme where you've seen this happen.

2. What kind of rhetorical appeal did that text use to get a response from its audience?

3. What are the social, economic, or political consequences of that rhetorical act?

Critical Genre Awareness

Critical Genre Awareness is closely connected to Critical Rhetorical Awareness. Because genres are social actions that connect our intentions to their rhetorical effects, Critical Genre Awareness allows us to see how genre helps 1) create shared aims and social relations; and 2) reinforce existing social norms, institutions, and ideologies. But that doesn't mean we just sit back and critique the scene playing out before us, powerless to do anything about it; Critical Genre Awareness also helps us see the potential we have as writers to *use and reinvent* genre to redirect social aims, challenge institutions, and transform accepted wisdom. If you're searching for examples of what Critical Genre Awareness might look like, you might consider *The Daily Show* or *The Colbert Report*; both TV shows parody the genre of a cable news program to satirize the commercialism of the 24-hour news cycle, and make fun of the more ridiculous characters in American politics. We laugh at Jon Stewart and Stephen Colbert for their jokes and sense of irony, but more than that, we appreciate their ability to skewer the cable news industry with the very same tools that cable news uses to shape our understanding of current events. In other words, they're able to not only *identify* the conventions of genre, but also use those conventions to challenge accepted ways of thinking, and maybe even convince their audience to see or do something differently.

Yet, neither structure nor style, medium, nor content exist in a vacuum; because genre is a social process that occurs over time, and in a particular context, it's critical that we look at genre's form-specific features.

Applying Critical Genre Awareness—Questions to Ask

☐ "How did it get that way?"

☐ "How has it grown and changed over time?"

☐ "What other traditions, either historical or cultural, does this genre draw on?"

☐ "What is the social, historical, or institutional context in which this genre is being used?"

☐ "How is it being used to reinforce, critique, or change existing social structures?"

☐ "What does it mean for me to read or use this genre in my own social, historical, or institutional context?"

☐ "What are the consequences if I choose to critique, use, or transform this genre for my own rhetorical purposes?"

Critical Genre Awareness in the WR 39 Series

Because Critical Genre Awareness helps us understand the consequences of our own rhetorical acts, it's an important part of all the writing you will do at UCI and beyond. However, because your writing class addresses a unique set of issues, here are some questions to help think about what Critical Genre Awareness means in your particular WR 39-series course.

Writing 39A: *One goal of 39A is to discover your own writing voice, and make it both effective and versatile.*

- How might Critical Genre Awareness help to make your writing voice more effective?

Writing 39B: *The final assignment for 39B asks you to create your own rhetorical situation, including how to target a specific audience with a certain message, using a certain genre.*

- Why might Critical Genre Awareness be an important skill when creating your own rhetorical situation?

Writing 39C: *In 39C, you'll learn how to write credible essays based on solid academic research.*

- Why do you think Critical Genre Awareness is an important tool for writing strong, credible academic research?

Looking Beyond the WR 39 Series

However, Critical Genre Awareness doesn't stop once you complete your lower-division writing requirement. If anything, this skill becomes even more important as you become a more accomplished writer. As *Marvel Comics* creator Stan Lee writes in the first installment of *Spider-Man*, "With great power there must also come—great responsibility!"; the more skilled and flexible your writing becomes, the more power you have to influence the world around you. So regardless of what your upper-division writing course might look like, just remember that Critical Genre Awareness is still an important part of understanding the relationship between the genre that you choose to write in, and its rhetorical implications for different audiences.

 TESTING YOUR GENRE KNOW-HOW—IDENTIFYING GENRE

1. What are the four kinds of tools we can use to identify a genre?

a. Form, Tone, Audience, and Structure

b. Style, Audience, Content, and Structure

c. Form, Medium, Content, and Audience

d. Style, Structure, Medium, and Content

YOUR TURN

1. Think of a genre that you enjoy, or know well—whether it be a type of film, or fan fiction.

2. Then, list all the identifiers you can think of that give shape to that genre (e.g., different aspects of form, content, medium, etc.).

3. Based on what you know, what are the different social and historical contexts for this genre?

4. Is this genre associated with a particular set of shared social aims, or a particular rhetorical purpose? If so, what might they be?

5. What are the social norms or ideologies that this genre uses to operate? Does the genre reinforce those norms, or challenge them in some way?

Genre and *Ethos*

So, Critical Genre Awareness helps us to see that genre can be used to reinforce or subvert power structures, and even the shape of knowledge itself—suggesting that genre carries with it different kinds of authority. This means that whether you're using secondary sources to explain the historical context of a Dickens novel, or write a bibliographic annotation for 39C, knowing the genre of a text can be a big help for determining not only rhetorical purpose, but also a text's credibility as a source.

Digital non-fiction texts like the following two websites show us how genre-specific characteristics such as form, content, medium, and audience reveal a text's purpose; these characteristics, in turn, show us a text's value as a credible source. How you *use* that information, however, will help determine whether your reader will see you as a reputable source of information—and whether you're qualified to join the conversation already in progress.

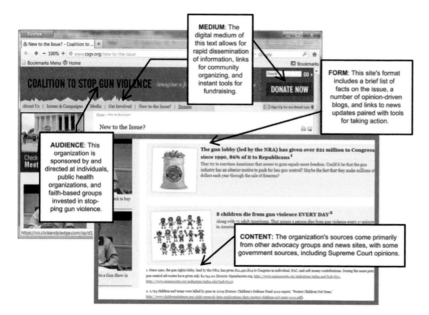

The owner of the website above, the *Coalition to Stop Gun Violence*, is a non-profit organization. They state that their mission is "to secure freedom from gun violence through research, strategic engagement and effective policy advocacy." This particular page is a brief primer on the basic facts the organization wants their audience to know. To explore the site in greater detail, visit http://www. csgv.org.

Another website that disseminates statistics on gun violence is sponsored by the U.S. *Bureau of Justice Statistics*. They say their purpose is "[t]o collect, analyze, publish, and disseminate information on crime, criminal offenders, victims of crime, and the operation of justice systems at all levels of government [toward] ensuring that justice is both efficient and evenhanded." This particular page is entitled, "Homicide Trends in the United States 1980–2008." For more detailed information about this source, go to http://bjs.gov.

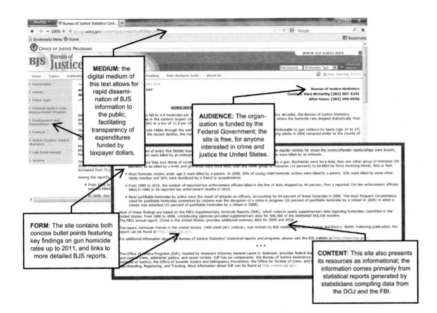

Test Your Genre Know-How: Source Credibility

Based on the call-outs on the screenshots, answer the following:

1. How would you describe the difference between the genres of these two texts?

2. How does the *purpose* of each genre inform its credibility as a source?

3. How does the *medium* of each genre inform its credibility as a source?

4. How does the intended *audience* for each text help determine its credibility as a source?

5. Which genre is more appropriate for providing an impartial analysis of gun violence in recent years?

6. Which genre is a better source for characterizing the political attitudes and cultural movements around gun control in the United States?

Works Cited and Further Reading

Bawarshi, Anis S. *Genre and the Invention of the Writer: Reconsidering the Place of Invention in Composition*. Logan, UT: Utah State University Press, 2003.

Bazerman, Charles. "The Life of Genres, the Life in the Classroom." *Genre and Writing: Issues, Arguments, Alternatives*. Wendy Bishop and Hans A. Ostrom, Eds. Portsmouth, New Hampshire: Boynton/Cook, 1997. 19–26.

Brent, Douglas."Rogerian Rhetoric: Ethical Growth through Alternative Forms of Argumentation." *Argument Redefined: Negotiating Meaning in the Composition Classroom*. Emmel, Barbara, Resch, Paula and Tenney, Deborah, Eds. Thousand Oaks, CA: Sage, 1996. 73–96.

Devitt, Amy. "Teaching Critical Genre Awareness." *Genre in a Changing World*. Charles Bazerman, Adair Bonini, and Débora Figueiredo, Eds. Fort Collins: WAC Clearinghouse, 2009. 344–346.

Lee, Stan, Steve Ditko, and Jack Kirby. "Spider-Man!" *Amazing Fantasy*. Vol. 1, no. 15 (August 1962). Print.

Miller, Carolyn. "Genre as Social Action."*Quarterly Journal of Speech*. Vol. 70 (1984). 151–167.

Prior, Paul. "From Speech Genres to Mediated Multimodal Genre Systems: Bakhtin, Voloshinov, and the Question of Writing." *Genre in a Changing World*. Charles Bazerman, Adair Bonini, and Débora Figueiredo, Eds. Fort Collins: WAC Clearinghouse, 2009. 17–34.

Sung-Gi, Jon. "Toward Wave Rhetorics for Scholarly Communications in Human Sciences." *Advances in the History of Rhetoric*. Vol. 14, no. 2 (2011).

Tarantino, Quentin, dir. *Django Unchained*. Anchor Bay Entertainment, 2013. Film.

Young, R. E., Becker, A. L. and Pike, K. L. *Rhetoric: Discovery and Change*, New York: Harcourt, 1970.

Chapter 3

PRACTICING CRITICAL READING

By Kat Eason and Leah Kaminski

A small note about the personal pronouns: this chapter was not written by a disembodied and distant authority. It was, in fact, written by a we who have used, currently use, and will use the techniques listed herein when we read. The techniques detailed in this chapter have been tested, re-tested, refined, and, dare we say, perfected, over time and a lot of practice. Which is to say, we—authors Leah (speaking to you in the gray text) and Kat (speaking in blue)—have tested all this material ourselves, and survived. So will you.

I'm Kat Eason, and I and the marvelous Leah Kaminski are your guides to the tricks and techniques of critical reading, the primary ingredient of successful reading comprehension (which translates into successful writing and rhetoric!). I've been a teacher for about a decade, the last seven of which have been here, in the Composition Program at UCI, where we've read critically about zombies, cyborgs, and Beowulf (although not all at once).

I teach 39A a lot and assign some "tough" reading in my classes, because I know even the bio majors among us can be persuaded to get animated about books that aren't just TV-on-the-page (much as that's fun too)—and that's important. I'm a poet, too, and creative writers are really nerdy about reading: in my favorite seminar when I was here at UCI as a graduate student, we'd often spend the whole class talking (and arguing) about some of the basic questions (like, Who's speaking? Who are they speaking to?) that we include in our chapter.

A second small note: No students were actually harmed in the writing of this chapter.

Critical Reading: What Is It?

The kind of reading we're talking about in this chapter doesn't come naturally. It requires practice. And time. And effort. And not leaving your 20 pages of *Beowulf* until 3 a.m. Critical reading—also sometimes called close reading—isn't something you can do quickly (if you want to do it well). Learn to treat your reading assignments like your homework from math, bio, or chem. Bring a writing utensil and some paper (or their electronic equivalents).

This sounds like a lot of work, yes, and not a bit like the quick-glance-at-the-page-reading you can use on a Facebook post or a *Twilight* novel. But the kind of reading we describe here is something you'll need, and use, for the rest of your career, both as a student in the university (textbooks, articles, essays), and in your later professional life as well, when you encounter specialized, difficult, formal writing (articles in scholarly journals, books, white papers, lab reports, legal briefs, scientific proposals, etc.).

You may have heard the phrase "critical reading" before (after all, it's in the title of our course "Critical Reading and Rhetoric"). The word *critical* has a somewhat negative connotation, and it sounds like to read critically is to criticize. Well, no. You aren't looking for what's wrong in a text. You are, however, looking to make judgments about the text: what it means. How it means. For whom it is intended. Why it was created. So when we use the phrase "critical reading," we mean to read something carefully, judiciously, thoughtfully. Sometimes you'll see an instructor use the phrase "close reading"—and that phrase also works for what we're talking about here.

No matter *what* you read, if you read critically (and closely), you will be reading *actively*.

What does it mean to read actively? Pay attention. Our brains like to slide over words, filling in what we *think* the words mean, or should mean, rather than focusing on what they *do* mean. Our task, as critical readers, is to keep focused.

We need to be detectives, of a sort, learning to use context and clues from both within the text and from its rhetorical situation, to figure out what it's saying. You can totally dash past a Facebook update and get it. Probably not *Hamlet*, though. Or that chapter in your biochemistry book.

But while it requires close attention and even analysis, here's something important to know about reading literature: there are no secret codes to break. There are no exact formulas to solve. There are certain facts about texts that we can't ignore (see the sections on **What a Text Means** and *How* **a Text Means** for more about that), but there's also a lot of soft science involved in active reading. There's a lot of learning to respect your own impressions and responses (and then being precise and determined to explain how you got those impressions), trusting yourself as a reader and being open to whatever you're reading.

Robots don't write books (yet?). So throw out the oversimplified, one-to-one correlations ("Symbols"? Boo! "Foreshadowing"? Grr!) that made your paper-writing experience so stale and your reading experience so tortured in high school.

So really, to read critically (or closely) means to read attentively and deliberately. Which is to say: with focus and concentration, looking at both *what* a text means and *how* a text works.

Critical Reading: *What* a Text Means

One way to understand a text is to pay attention to small pieces at a time, and asking questions about what you see there. These questions are all related to context *within* the text, details inside a larger story, poem, essay, article, whatever. The answers are more or less concrete, verifiable "facts" about the text. (Either Hamlet is talking to Gertrude, or he isn't. There's not much room for interpretation.)

Round One: Meeting Your Text for the First Time

So you just got your first reading assignment for your writing class, and you're a little freaked out. The instructor seemed to think you'd have no problem just, you know, just getting it. And you didn't either, until you read the first paragraph and realized you have no idea what the author just said. And then you realized exactly how many pages of text were waiting after that paragraph....

Oh, sure, maybe you can go Google up a synopsis some-where; but that's not going to help you *at all* when your instruc-tor expects you to write an essay using specific details. Okay. So let's look at this monstrous text.

What follows are some of the most important steps you can take toward reading more actively.

THE SIMPLE STEPS TO ACTIVE READING

1. Read aloud.

2. Mark the words you do not understand and look them up.

3. Make notes on your copy of the text.

4. Make a note of the main idea of a paragraph or passage, either on a hard copy of your text, or in a notebook or separate file.

So, that all looks pretty basic, right? Maybe even…*too* basic? Here are some thoughts on why these steps are important, and how you can make even the simplest of them powerful. Your teacher might have some other tips for you, too. Tweak these (and the other lists in the chapter, too), until they work for *your* reading and learning style, and make habitual any new strategies you discover along the way.

In this chapter I will be annotating a section from Aristotle's *Nicomachean Ethics*, in which Aristotle concludes that happiness is the final good to which all humans aspire, and attempts to define what happiness must mean. The individual words are not difficult, but Aristotle's ideas are complex and sometimes hard to follow, even nailed as they are to the frame of his logic. That example appears in its entirety at the end of this section to better illustrate both my method and Aristotle's whole argument.

Hamlet, a play by William Shakespeare (you've probably heard of it, maybe even read it), will help me show what it looks like to ask and answer these questions as you're reading. In the following section I'll use one of the central scenes of the play, Act III Scene iv, in which Prince Hamlet talks to his mother Queen Gertrude about her betrayal of his father, kills the nosy advisor to the court, Polonius, and sees his father's Ghost (who causes a lot of trouble because Gertrude can't see him, and is naturally worried about her son's sanity). We get a lot of action in this scene, and a lot of really emotional dialogue.

Step One: Read aloud.

Often our minds will skip words when we read silently, especially if we're tired, distracted, or the word itself is unfamiliar. Reading aloud forces you to concentrate on the text, and to face each word at it comes. It's also a very good way to discover new, unfamiliar words. And when you find such an alien....

Read more slowly than you think you should. Read like a real person, not like your computer's speech function. Have your pencil in hand as you read. Reading out loud will help the text come alive for you; it will force you to slow down and notice words that your brain might slide over on paper—and it will also make the text seem more human. Reading aloud will help you respond and react to the vital, fun communication the author's sending you.

Step Two: Mark any words you do not understand and look them up.

Write down, circle, highlight, or otherwise mark any unfamiliar words. Look them up and make a note of what they mean in the margins of your reading, or on your notebook. Learn them. You'll probably need them later on.

Definitely. I'll also add that it's a good idea to mark words that seem out of place, that are being used more than once, or that are used in a different way than you're used to. This can help you with figuring out *how* a text means, questions we'll talk about a little later in this chapter.

Step Three: Make notes about what you read.

In addition to unfamiliar words, make note of thoughts you have as you are reading. I like to treat my notes as a conversation (admittedly one-sided) with the writer. *Yo, Aristotle, I don't even get this. Final product…? What? Or oooooh, right, the good is that thing that we're all seeking. Gotcha.* This helps me find places I don't understand, and keep track of the Eureka! moments.

See this bit from when I marked up a passage from *Hamlet*. Along with marking words I don't know, I note moments that create tone, moments of characterization, important plot points, and patterns.

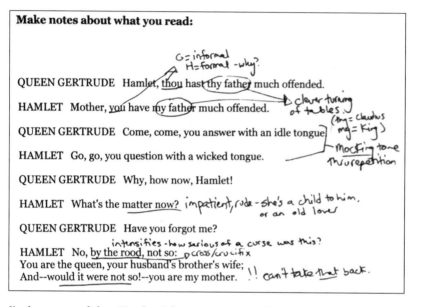

Make notes about what you read:

QUEEN GERTRUDE Hamlet, thou hast thy father much offended.

HAMLET Mother, you have my father much offended.

QUEEN GERTRUDE Come, come, you answer with an idle tongue.

HAMLET Go, go, you question with a wicked tongue.

QUEEN GERTRUDE Why, how now, Hamlet!

HAMLET What's the matter now?

QUEEN GERTRUDE Have you forgot me?

HAMLET No, by the rood, not so:
You are the queen, your husband's brother's wife;
And--would it were not so!--you are my mother.

I'm less personal than Kat, but I do note moments of my own reaction. Feel free to use whatever method, marks, or madness make sense to you. Annotations and reading notes are for *your* purposes, to help you read and later write, not to check off an assignment. The only rule, as far as I'm concerned, is that you do it with care. And that you can read your own handwriting later.

Step Four: Make a note of the main idea of a paragraph or passage.

Finally, jot down any main ideas or key words in the text, or write a quick summary in your notebook or the margins. If you find yourself staring blankly at the page, or realize you've forgotten everything you just read ... do it again.

This is especially useful for difficult-to-read texts. If you make a note of a passage's main idea and other big-picture things (like connections between one passage and another, for example) you'll have a quick reference when you go back to the text. Past-you will tell present-you whether it's important, without present-you having to read it the whole way through again.

This is a full-page example of my annotation of a brief passage from *Nicomachean Ethics*. In it, I attempt to follow Aristotle's argument, point by point, by underlining and making marginal notes. I also remind myself about key terms and arguments from earlier parts of the reading—what Aristotle is referencing when he says "thing" in the first line, for instance.

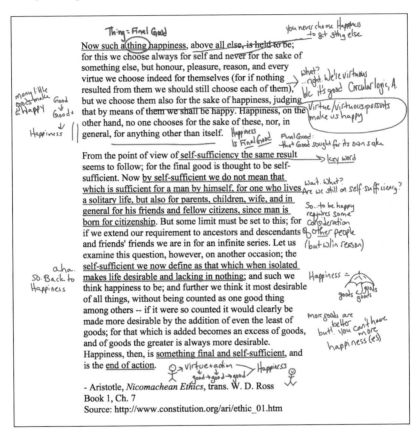

Whatever your method: engage with the text. Talk to it. (Worry if it talks back.) Talk to *yourself*. (It's okay if *you* talk back.) Think of annotating a text as a conversation with your future self.

This might seem like a lot of work, and it is. Critical reading is messy, difficult business. The process gets easier and faster as you practice. And while critical reading does take time, it also saves you work when you return to a text to write an essay or study for a test.

Critical Reading for Creative Works: What's Happening?

Nonfiction, by definition, presents itself as itself. The writer and her words are one and the same, and those words are transparently "what's happening" in the text. Annotating or writing about that in the margins would often mean simply repeating what the writer said. You're not a time-waster, so unless what the writer said is difficult to understand on a literal level (in which case you might write a paraphrase in the margin) you're going to go straight to *responding* to their message.

The "facts" of fiction, drama, poetry, and other creative texts are less straightforward: there's a distance between the writer and her words, and her primary objective is not to speak directly to you, as herself. She speaks instead through characters and action in a play; through narration of fictional events by a fictional character in a novel; or even as a seemingly possessed, hyperreal version of herself, as in much poetry—ask your teacher for some Emily Dickinson if you want to know what I mean. Understanding the situation in this kind of literature will sometimes require a bit of detective work.

You may not record all of this on the annotated page, but you might jot it down in a reading journal or your class notebook. Whatever you do: *ask these questions, always!* They are simple, but they matter a lot. These questions, in fact, should never leave your mind, because the *what* affects meaning, message, and import just as much as the *how* and *why* we'll talk about in a bit.

Here are some questions to start with. Some may be more relevant than others, text-by-text, and there are many possible combinations of these parts.

 HOW TO FIGURE OUT WHAT'S HAPPENING

1. Who is speaking? To whom?

2. What is the situation within the passage?

3. What's happening in the passage?

4. What happened immediately before this part of the text? What do you think will happen right after?

As with our first list, these might seem See-Spot-Run obvious at first, but the more you read critically, the more complex and subtle the answers will become. They can open up a whole lot of new things to think—and then write—about.

Question One: Who is speaking? To whom?

Consider the basics: Is it dialogue, monologue, internal monologue, narration, poetic speech? Are there even characters, or is it pure description? If there are characters, do we know them? Who are they? If it's not dialogue, still ask: who is being spoken to? It could be the reader, or an imagined other person, or the narrator/speaker herself. For example, let's look again at the passage from *Hamlet*:

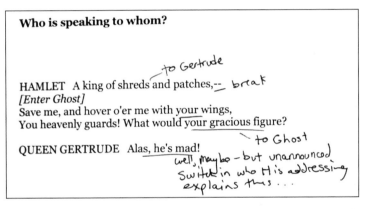

Who is speaking to whom?

HAMLET A king of shreds and patches,-- *to Gertrude* *break*
[*Enter Ghost*]
Save me, and hover o'er me with your wings,
You heavenly guards! What would your gracious figure?

QUEEN GERTRUDE Alas, he's mad! *to Ghost*
well, maybe — but unannounced
Switch in who His addressing
explains this . . .

The idea here is to remember that you are not reading words in a vacuum. Hamlet's "To be, or not to be" soliloquy in Act III Scene i might mean something different to the play if you establish that the evil Claudius and wily Polonius are listening in.

Question Two: What is the situation within the passage?

In what physical location is this passage set? At what time (within the text)? What are the speaker's physical surroundings?

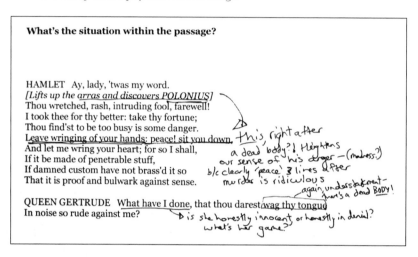

The fact that Polonius's body is in the room with Gertrude and Hamlet is probably important, and might change the way we read the rest of the scene. Instead of a charged, intimate conversation between mother and son, we are unable to forget the larger implications of his actions, which are greatly intensified: he's not just an angry, betrayed son; he's a vengeful and unhinged prince.

Why are the character/s speaking? That is, what was the literal catalyst for this speech or conversation? The reason for speaking, the situation, can alter and shade the meaning.

Question Three: What's happening, and/or what's being said?

Okay. When you're lucky, you should be able to answer this simply. We can complicate it by thinking about surrounding circumstances, catalysts for the action, and so on, but at root it's fairly straightforward. For example, when Polonius says "I am slain," he dies.

But even when you're reading highly experimental work you can boil it down and answer this most crucial of questions. What's happening on a literal level if it's a realist work, or on the level of the reading experience or the writer's experiments, if it's not? What's this text *trying to do*?

So when the immeasurably awesome James Joyce begins the immeasurably crazy *Finnegan's Wake* with this:

Finnegan's Wake:

 comes hard after "fall". ..

The fall of (bababadalgharaghtakamminarronnkonnbronntonner-   _?!?_
ronntuonnthunntrovarrhounawnskawntoohoohoordenenthurnuk) of a   _7 experimental style... ??_
once wallstrait oldparr is retaled early in bed and later on life down
through all Christian minstrelsy!

---

you will of course first look up "bababadalgharaghtakamminarronnkonnbron
ntonnerronntuonnthunntrovarrhounawnskawntoohoohoordenenthurnuk" as a
word you don't know. Google will tell you that Joyce made it up and you'll be
discouraged—_now_ how are you supposed to know what it means? Well, after
much help from your teacher, and reading about what others think about the
book, you will eventually be able to say that it's (probably) Joyce's approximation
of the sound of God's voice dictating the Fall of Adam and Eve.

Reading and writing skills are progressive. You won't always know the entire
answers to the questions that arise as you read, no matter how carefully you
follow our advice in this chapter. So just like in some of your nicer math classes,
allow yourself to take partial credit even for unfinished work. _Engage_, even if
you can't completely understand at first. You can't progress without taking the
first step into the work, even if your first footprint is a question mark.

Question Four: What happened immediately before this part of the text? What do you think will happen right after?

As with "what's happening?" these questions are always answerable in some fashion. And you should always, *always* ask them. Knowing that Polonius and Claudius planned to listen to Hamlet in Gertrude's bedroom makes a difference to how we read the scene I've been using as an example here.

Thinking about how the actions of a text are connected to each other might bring up the term "foreshadowing" for you, and if so, it's great that your synapses are firing. But let's shift the language a bit. "Foreshadowing" is not part of an algorithm that only Kat and I and your teachers know. It's straightforward: what's happening now needs to make sense based on what happened before, otherwise it's going to be a frustrating read (of course, that can sometimes be part of the point—*ahem, Finnegan's Wake*). So *of course* current events are affected ("foreshadowed") by what came before. This happens in real life too: if your friend slams the door after her boyfriend was rude to her on the phone, the phone call isn't "foreshadowing." It's an action that caused another action. The connection is still important, though, even if you have to take off your fortune-telling hat. So look back from what's *happening* to what *happened*, not the other way around.

If you can't tell what's happening and what has happened in a text, and make a reasonable guess about what will happen, one of two things are going on: you're having trouble understanding the text, or there's something about it that is actively resisting the question.

Try two things then: read more carefully and talk to your teacher and peers, or think about why and how the text is trying to make understanding difficult for you. Is there a purpose to the difficulty?

Reading and Rhetoric: *How* a Text Means

So now that we've established the facts of a text, it's time to explore *how* the text communicates. The answer, no surprise, lies in the words: their style, their arrangement. The words are all the writer has, after all, to communicate her message, so she's going to be very careful about how she chooses to deploy them. As you read, you should begin to pay attention to these choices and note them in your text.

Leah will use some more lines from *Hamlet* to show possible annotations based on *how* questions.

You should be able to address the following questions for every—no, really—
every text you read.

HOW IS THE TEXT CREATING MEANING?

1. What is the tone? How can you tell?

2. What kind of language is the author using? Complicated? Formal? Casual?

3. Can you identify markers of style? Note any specific strategies or figures of
   speech that are appropriate to the genre.

4. What do tone, language, and style tell us about the intended audience of the
   piece?

We'll use Aristotle and Shakespeare to show how each question can apply
equally interesting pressure to any genre.

You'll learn a little later to think about *why* a writer chose one thing over another—what effect they meant to have. But since (as we keep repeating) this
isn't an exact science, it could be that in the experience of critically reading you
address the *why* questions before the *how* questions. So if you want to identify important rhetorical (*how*) choices, you can sometimes work backward,
from effect (*why*). What is your immediate response to this passage? What
does it make you think about? What does it make you feel? Now, where are
those feelings coming from—what detail is making you feel it? Our questions
that follow prompt you to work both ways—starting from choice and starting
from effect.

Question One: What is the tone? How can you tell?

Tone is the attitude a writer (or character) takes to her subject matter and, at
least by implication, to her audience.

You can describe *tone* with adjectives: sarcastic, condescending, compassionate,
snarky, pedantic (look that word up!), patient, sad, and so on. Aristotle's tone in
the passage on page 39, for instance, is logical, serious, and objective.

Yes to adjectives! Of course, once you describe Hamlet's tone as prickly, spiteful, and hyperbolic, then you have to describe where you're getting your impressions (for example, from his building rhythm in this litany of a line: "Such an act / That blurs the grace and blush of modesty"). And the next few questions will help you collect that evidence.

Question Two: What kind of language is the author using?

Language is another indicator of the author's attitudes toward the subject, and a clue to both the audience's identity and the context of the piece itself.

Look for both the grammatical structure (how complex are the sentences?) and at the diction (word choice) an author uses. Aristotle's sentences are not particularly complex, taken individually, and his words are simple. But the way in which he strings the sentences together is extremely complex. His language also enacts his thinking patterns: in other words, his writing models his thought processes, which are methodical and logical, and, if you read slowly and carefully, make fine sense.

Shakespeare uses language to enact meaning, too. He often switches between everyday prose and blank verse, and noticing this can add to our understanding. For example, Hamlet speaks in high-flown blank verse in most of his monologues; the unrhythmical, "common," cruelly pun-filled prose he uses in dialogue with Polonius stands out from his usual polished metrical language. The difference in language imparts a different sound and texture to the scene and the characters.

If you're having trouble identifying which language choices matter and what effects they have, try thinking about what *hasn't* been chosen. So, for example, are you seeing an abundance of short sentences? Okay, what would have been different if the writer chose long, rambling sentences? Or a jumble of sentence fragments?

Question Three: Can you identify markers of style?

Now is a good time to use a few remnants of high school English class: **literary terms**.

Where are the metaphors? Similes? Alliteration? Even fancy-shmancy ones like synecdoche and antithesis? Are there any patterns or repetitions of these strategies within the passage or the entire text? You need to learn the arsenal of choices for whatever genre you're reading, though: the same literary terms won't apply to every kind of text.

As we foreshadowed with our "foreshadowing" chat, it's also time to shed some of the terms that oversimplify meaning in creative arts. Symbols have been known to occur (though they're less common than AP English might have had you think), but when they do they're not unchanging, thing-equals-other-thing, rule-bound, press-this-button creatures; they're a lot moodier, more shifty, and more interesting than that.

So don't oversimplify meaning by grasping for "symbol" the second something reminds you of something else. Consider softer verbs like "suggest" and "evoke" over "represents" or "symbolizes." You'll like your books more, and your teachers will probably like your papers more.

Literary Terms:

HAMLET Look here, upon this picture, and on this,
The counterfeit presentment of two brothers.
See, what a grace was seated on this brow;) → personification,
Hyperion's curls; the front of Jove himself;   leading to antithesis
An eye like Mars, to threaten and command; hyperbolic similes
A station like the herald Mercury
New-lighted on a heaven-kissing hill;) rhythm - builds up
A combination and a form indeed,   hymn to dad
Where every god did seem to set his seal,
To give the world assurance of a man:
This was your husband. Look you now, what follows:
Here is your husband; like a mildew'd ear, simile - gross.
Blasting his wholesome brother. Have you eyes? → confrontational -
Could you on this fair mountain leave to feed,   but rhetorical,
And batten on this moor? Ha! have you eyes?   or demanding
                                                    answer?
→ metaphors - high place → low place

Margin notes:
allusions to Greek to emphasize dad's nobility

no allusion, the brevity is telling

Question Four: What do tone, language, and style tell us about the intended audience of the piece?

Tone and **language** are major clues about a text's intended **audience**.

Just because we can all understand a text (eventually) doesn't mean we're the audience for it. Aristotle wasn't writing to 21st-century university students. The thoroughness with which he delivers his arguments, and the seriousness and objectivity of his tone, indicate that he is trying to reach an audience who will be receptive to that kind of address. He's appealing to *logos*, or reason, rather than any sort of *pathos*, and his *ethos* rests on his objectivity and thoroughness. So whoever his audience is, they must value those things.

Kat, that was so clear you've left me with nothing to say. Except: there are practical issues that help us think about audience too—and we'll get to that a little later when we discuss *context* in the section *No Text Is an Island*.

Addressing the Audience: *Why* a Text Means

Contrary to popular belief, Aristotle, Shakespeare, and the authors of your chemistry book did not set out to make you miserable. They had an actual purpose in mind with their writing, and a message to communicate to their readers. The key to uncovering that purpose and message lies in figuring out the ways in which the *how* connects with its particular, intended audience.

You've now learned to identify the specific details of how the text is creating meaning, and you can take the next step now, thinking about the function of those details: what the *how* actually does. Rhetorical choices have particular effects (otherwise, they wouldn't exist; metaphors, for example, don't just exist for fun decoration—writers use them on purpose to create certain effects for certain readers). The choices transmit meaning, elicit emotion, create patterns, resonate with other parts of the text…

So this is getting complicated, right? We're not just *inside* the text anymore; we're also trying to see *out* of it. Here are questions to help you explore purpose, effect, and audience:

 WHY IS THE AUTHOR MAKING THESE CHOICES?

These questions will yield very different answers depending on the type of essay you read—academic, popular, personal, etc. And it can be even more varied when you're dealing with a piece of fiction.

1. What does the author want the reader to understand, believe, or feel by the end? How can you tell? This is the text's *primary message*.

2. What kind of evidence does the author use to support his or her position? Anecdotes? Scientific data? Imaginary examples?

3. What does the kind of evidence tell us about the intended audience? What does the author assume the audience already knows (what information does s/he leave out)? What does s/he assume they still need to understand (what information does s/he deliver)?

4. How does the writer construct his or her *ethos* for the audience?

Question One: What is the text's primary message?

The answer to the question of **primary message** depends on the types of rhetorical appeals the author is using.

Think back to tone and language. Aristotle wants his audience to *think*, yes, but he wants them to follow his reasoning and agree with his logic and by extension, his conclusions. So Aristotle wants to persuade his audience, through an appeal to their logos, to agree with his arguments. This suggests an audience who will be convinced by reason and objectivity.

While the concept of "message" may not be as straightforward in **fiction, poetry,** and **drama** as it is in nonfiction writing, poets, novelists, and playwrights write because they *have something to say.* For simplicity's sake, let's call that something the text's "message." This is a tricky balance. Novels don't have thesis statements, but every writer is trying to reach her reader and effect some change. Consider the message of the whole text, **and** if you're reading a text in parts, you might also ask yourself: how does **one** passage's message resonate with the message of the whole? Does this passage add to, change, or complicate the overall message? Always imagine someone asking, *how can you tell?* A writer's every choice creates immediate effects, and those effects combine to create the text's or passage's message.

Question Two: What kind of evidence does the author use?

The **types of evidence** an author uses tell us a lot about the audience as well.

Subjective evidence appeals to *pathos.* A personal anecdote or narrative can create an emotional connection to the audience. While no author *wants* his readers

to be bored, obviously there are times and places where a subjective appeal would be inappropriate. The TA grading your lab report probably doesn't care what you did over the weekend. She wants to see your data. Objective evidence appeals to *logos.* And by objective, we mean not only evidence like scientific data (like your lab report), but also references to other texts. An academic essay about *Hamlet* will rely on the writer's reason and objectivity, sure, but it needs specific excerpts from the play to have any credibility with its potential readership.

For creative works, evidence usually means something different. A novel's message requires less overt "support" than does your lab report: the writer isn't *proving* anything, per se. She's cajoling the reader into buying her perspective or point of view—or even just coaxing the reader into continuing to read, responding appropriately, feeling involved. So replace "evidence" with "means of seducing/persuading/convincing the reader." Then think of those *how* questions. What's the tone? What kind of images are being used? What level of diction? And how do those things work to evoke a response in you, or keep you on board with the text?

Question Three: What does the evidence tell us about the intended audience?

A writer chooses the evidence to support her arguments based on what she knows about her **audience**.

You're writing about *Hamlet* for your English class? Better use quotes from the play, maybe a secondary article or two, to demonstrate your understanding and support your particular reading…and probably, you know, leave out the account of the time you played Gertrude in a high school production. An astrophysicist writing about stellar life cycles and planetary formation for the *Journal of Geophysical Research* will not waste time talking about what stars are made of; she'll assume that her audience knows that already. But that same astrophysicist giving a planetarium presentation to elementary school children *will* cover the basics.

Again considering "evidence" a little differently, it's still true for fiction, poetry, and drama that different writing choices help us picture the intended audience. Keep thinking about what kind of choices would appeal to certain readers. Shakespeare uses bawdy jokes because the peanut gallery of his time would get and appreciate them. Style—evidence—is the bouncer of literature. If you don't look right for the room, you're not coming in. And, of course, you have some say in it too—you wouldn't go to a club on the Jersey Shore if you liked dressing for museum benefits.

Question Four: How does the writer construct ethos?

You already know what *ethos* means from Chapter 1. In the same way that evidence, language, structure, and tone tell us about a text's audience, they *also* construct the author's ethos.

So, Aristotle's serious, logical, objective arguments establish him as a credible thinker and, whether or not we agree with his conclusions, we have to respect the chain of logic that gets him from beginning to end. We might not much *like* his style, but his authority resonates off the page.

Notice that *ethos*, from our *why* questions, and *tone*, from our *how* questions, are quite similar. Tone is a really useful way for authors to build ethos.

No Text Is an Island: Putting Everything into *Context*

And finally, a word about *context*. We've looked at how words, evidence, tone, and ideas work within the context of a text; now let's think about how the text itself relates to *its* context.

The text's context affected the choices the writer made (*how*) and the effects she tried to create (*why*, and for whom). So thinking about context can give you a lot of insight into what went into the author's choices.

One more list! This time, we want you to consider the historical and cultural situation in which a text was produced.

 QUESTIONS TO ASK ABOUT CONTEXT

1. When and where was the work published?

2. How was it originally delivered? Was it written down? A speech? A performance?

3. What is the cultural background of the writer and audience? Consider geographic location, gender, ethnicity, shared beliefs, and discourse communities.

Some of these questions may require research, especially on texts for which you, O college students, are not the primary audience.

Question One: When and where was the work published?

Considering **publishing context** is pretty self-explanatory, in most cases: all you have to do is check the copyright information at the front of the text (or the website from which it was taken).

But sometimes you might encounter a really *old* text from before the days of the mighty printing press, or a text that you're reading in translation (like our friend Aristotle). In those cases, you will have a publication date for the particular edition or translation, not necessarily the work itself. Don't confuse a translator with the author!

Question Two: How was it originally delivered?

Consider **how the original work was experienced**.

This kind of information can really change your understanding of a text. Thinking about *Hamlet* as **it was** performed in a raucous, rowdy theater, as opposed to something you associate with drooling on your desk and the smell of cheap paper, can remind you to look for the humor and pathos in the play, to react to it as a human beyond your life as a college student, and to fully understand how different the original audience was from you in taste, shared knowledge, and experience.

Question Three: What is the cultural background of the writer and audience?

Which leads us to the **cultural background** part.

With *Hamlet*, for example, it's not just that Shakespeare might not be addressing people who hate plays, or who don't respond to lyricism and intense characterization. There's also the fact that, you know, you don't speak to your mother in allusions to Greek myth: people nowadays don't know Greek myth as well as they used to (because of course, if they did, you'd totally make a speech about it in your next fight with your mom).

But if you could argue with your parents using Aristotle's airtight logic and cool-headed objectivity, you might have a better chance of winning. Something to consider.

So Now What?

You did it. You read out loud. You circled all the words and looked them up. You annotated your copy of the text. And now, at last, you're finished. Time to put the text away and go watch the next episode of *Daredevil*.

Okay, fair enough. Take a break. But you're not done, yet. Your instructor didn't ask you to read Aristotle, or Shakespeare, or Chekov, or fifteen pages of academic argument just because she's mean. She wants you to think about what you read, and then *do* something with it.

If you read a *primary* text, like that *Hamlet* or Aristotle, (Ref. Jackie's chapter) then you can start thinking about the text's place in the rhetorical situation (ref. ch. 1).

But if you read a *secondary* text (ref. Jackie's chapter again)—an article *about* other works, like an academic article about the history of the zombie genre, or an analysis of gender roles in *Hamlet*, or a think-piece about twitter humor, you want to start thinking about connections between that article and other texts.

We've already given you advice on figuring out *what* a given text means. You even know something about its purpose and *why* it makes the choices it does. But now you need to think about the text as part of a larger conversation—fitting into the "story" of your class, or even of your discipline at large.

(Re)Reading with Purpose

You need to have a bit of an agenda when you enter into a secondary text, some questions to keep in mind when reading: for example, does it describe genre conventions in a way that you can apply to your section's main text? Can it help you piece together your argument about the history of hill tribe citizenship in Thailand? Reading with purpose will help you find the best pieces from a variety of secondary texts in order to make your *own* meaning.

Of course, you can't go in hoping to twist a secondary text to fit your own assumptions and preconceptions: as you'll read in the 39B chapter on finding your place in the conversation and acknowledging alternative views, you need to have a give and take with the secondary sources you plan to use. As much as you go in with a purpose, you must still be open-minded.

After all, we don't have riveting (or even useful) conversations when we're inflexible.

Thinking about how to read and *use* secondary texts in that way is going to be useful in all kinds of classes in all kinds of disciplines: for example, in our program, you'll read texts about genre and about primary texts, and texts about a primary event or social problem...and you'll use them for multiple reasons (see source chapter): for background information, for help comprehending the facts of a text or situation, for support for your argument, for illustration of a fact or argument.

So here are some questions to help you use these strange creatures for your own nefarious purposes:

1. How does this article or essay connect to other texts I've read in this class? Does it *support*, or *contradict*, or *challenge* ideas you've already seen?

2. Does this article explain something about the rhetorical situation of another text I've read in this class? Historical context? Genre protocols [see ch. on Genre]?

3. What new information does this text give me?

4. How does this new info help my understanding of another text (secondary or primary) or idea in this course?

5. Note whether and how soon the text begins engaging with other voices, and having conversations with other writers (other than with the text that's their subject).

6. If you think the author(s) make a claim or announce their purpose in writing, underline it. Make note of where it comes in, and what precedes it.

7. How can I apply it to the primary text it references? Does it help me understand the background of the text?

8. Do I disagree with its argument, or can I use a bit of its argument to extend and respond to?

9. Can I find evidence of its argument in a primary text, or use it as a theoretical framework through which to read a primary text?

More than Just Words: Expanding the Meaning of "Text"

Just when you thought it was safe to close the book and check your Facebook and figure out what you're wearing to the movie later…let's ruin things for you. Books and magazines are texts, of course, as are Facebook updates and Tumblr posts. But *text* can mean more than written discourse, including many different kinds of media, as well: television, film, music, speech, art. Essentially, any act of communication—from *Hamlet* to the clothing you choose for a first date—can act as a text, and be "read" accordingly.

Happy reading.

Works Cited and Further Reading

Aristotle. *Nicomachean Ethics*. Trans. W. D. Ross. *The Internet Classics Archive*. Web Atomic and Massachusetts Institute of Technology. Web. 8 April, 2013.

Joyce, James, Robbert-Jan Henkes, Erik Bindervoet, and Finn Fordham. *Finnegan's Wake*. Oxford: Oxford University Press, 2012. Print.

Shakespeare, William, Barbara A. Mowat, and Paul Werstine. *The Tragedy of Hamlet, Prince of Denmark*. New York: Washington Square Press, 2003. Print.

Writers in Focus: *Dr. Roger Walsh*

 Professor, Psychiatry and Human Behavior, School of Medicine
Philosophy and Anthropology, School of Humanities
PhD, University of Queensland, Australia
MD, University of Queensland, Australia

For a list of Dr. Walsh's publications, go to http://www.faculty.uci.edu/scripts/
UCIFacultyProfiles/DetailDept.CFM?ID=2372 or http://www.drrogerwalsh.com/

Why does good writing matter to you?

I suspect that all of us who are here at the university have a shared purpose which
is to make our lives as meaningful and contributory as possible—and that means
communicating effectively. I found it rather paradoxical at a certain stage that I had
spent an enormous number of years acquiring a massive amount of information as one
does in medical school and PhD degrees, and yet I had not learned much about how
to communicate this information. When I came to writing, I found that I was writing
in the style of "academese," which was the writing style that I'd been exposed to in
my professional training, and that "medical-ese" had its purpose—very technical,
very abstract, very precise—which was fine. But if I wanted to get these ideas out to a
larger audience, out to the larger world, I had to know how to communicate in a way
that would get to them.

**Was there a specific moment or event that made you realize that the way you were
writing wasn't appropriate to the task at hand?**

At the height of the Cold War, I, like many others, became horrified when I realized
that there was a high risk that we would destroy the planet … that human existence
now hung by a nuclear thread. So I began looking at how I could make a contribution
to this field, and it eventually became clear that I could write on the psychological
dimensions of this. So I started to write a popular book. I presented my first draft to my
wife, who read the first two pages, and who said, "You know, if you want to save the
world, it would be really nice if people could actually read this."

I realized she was right, and I went back and rewrote it. She read through the first two
chapters this time, and then said, "Well, this is better. Now go and rewrite it." I realized
that if I really wanted to have a larger impact on the world, I really needed to learn to
communicate effectively.

So what did you do to help yourself meet that goal?

It's an ongoing process: firstly, reading people who know how to write well; second,
getting feedback from as many people as I could; thirdly, hiring people to teach people,
paying editors to read my manuscripts and give detailed comments. It's very curious, to
pay someone to insult you, but it's been absolutely invaluable, and I think students at a
university have a remarkable opportunity to have this as part of their education.

Then, there's the process of writing and rewriting, and rewriting: looking for clarity and precision and ease and emotive power—something that will make a piece of writing a dynamic, lively, engaging, emotionally moving piece of work. Learning that has been a kind of counterbalance, learning a whole new art form compared to the abstract academese. That kind of reporting has its value in the scientific world, and it's well worth learning (and I still need to master it). It's also important to learn how to write for not just a narrow professional audience but for a larger audience. All of us will at various times be communicating to multiple audiences.

Chapter 4

CITING AND INTEGRATING SOURCES

By Jackie Way

I'm Jackie Way, a writing instructor in UCI's Composition Program. When I'm not teaching, I research and write about literature and history writing in the eighteenth century, which often requires me to work not only with a broad range of sources, but also with different versions of the same sources. I love piecing together the details of historical debates and investigating how important ideas are formed by different writers responding to each other in printed conversation. During my time here, I've taught writing and research at both the lower and upper-division levels and have helped many students work with sources in all kinds of writing situations. This chapter will explain why and how we use sources in academic writing and give you practical insight on how to cite and integrate sources when you write.

Sources and Academic Writing

The main purpose of academic work at a research university like UCI is to create and share knowledge. No matter your major, your goal as an undergraduate student is to learn the conventional ways in which scholars working in different disciplines create new knowledge and share it with others. From your English classes, you may be familiar with the technique of "close reading" a text: paying attention to the all the choices an author makes in a novel, play, or poem and interpreting the artistic significance of these choices. Historians also create knowledge by interpreting texts—in their case, various types of records and how these records depict or even shape historical events. Anthropologists and sociologists create knowledge by describing and interpreting human behavior by way of observation, surveys, statistical analysis and research studies. Chemists and biologists create knowledge by observing the natural world and interpreting the significance of natural events; physicists and mathematicians describe and theorize these events using mathematical language.

Despite the many obvious differences that separate these disciplines, we can notice two important things that unite them as forms of academic work. First, scholars in all these fields communicate through writing; second, these scholars always refer to sources in their writing. The point "everybody writes" is perhaps a no-brainer; but you may ask yourself: "Why sources?." If the point of academic research is to create new knowledge, why must we keep referring back to "old" knowledge?

The short answer is that we cannot know what knowledge is truly new without familiarizing ourselves with what is already known, and with what others have previously said about what we know. The long answer has to do with something called "information literacy." Information literacy encompasses a broad range of skills that enable you to find information, understand how and why it was created, assess its value, and then use this information to create new knowledge. To practice these skills is to participate as a member of our academic discourse community.

Information literacy is discussed in many other places in *The Anteater's Guide to Writing*, especially in Cathy Palmer's chapter on finding sources and in the chapter introducing WR 39C. Here, it is enough to point out that—no matter which writing course you are currently taking—working with information means working with sources. The aim of this chapter is to explain how you should cite and integrate sources in different writing situations; among others, these include responding to open questions and presenting individual arguments; analyzing a given text's rhetorical situation and effects; analyzing a political or social issue and advocating a position on it; and reflecting on your own writing process. The conventions described here may seem complicated, but once you understand some of the principles behind them, using sources in your writing should become much easier.

Different Types of Sources

Popular Sources

Information resides in sources—check. And of course, different sources contain different kinds of information. For academic writers, the most important distinction between sources involves a given source's rhetorical situation: the kind of authority a source has, based on how and why the source was created and for what particular audience. These elements together help us tell scholarly sources apart from popular ones. It can be easy to confuse popular and scholarly sources when researching predominantly online, but the differences are pretty big and easy to spot, once you know what to look for.

A popular source is any source written for a public audience, in order to share information, shape public opinion, or entertain. Authors of popular sources include creative writers, professional journalists, government officials and agencies, non-profit organizations and think tanks, lobbyists, and scholars.

In your own writing, you already have and will continue to draw on many kinds of popular sources, including:

- Websites, blogs and most other types of online sources

- Newspaper and magazine articles

- Literary texts like novels, short stories, plays and poems

- Nonfiction texts like speeches, essays, and various book genres

- Government documents (intended for the public, hence "popular")

- Think tank reports, policy briefs, and "white papers"

- *CQ Researcher* Reports

Notice the broad range of authority represented in the sources listed above—we consider these sources "credible" for various reasons. In the case of newspaper and magazine articles, the authority of journalists comes from the fact that their job is to report the news as objectively and accessibly as possible and that individual journalists covering specific "beats" for extended periods of time develop reliable expertise in the relevant subjects. In the case of literature like novels and speeches, authority rests in the writer or speaker who has something meaningful to say that audiences care about. Writers like William Shakespeare and Martin Luther King, Jr. have considerable authority as significant historical figures; however, writers like J. K. Rowling and Suzanne Collins also have authority over their stories and their readers. Likewise, the authority of government documents depends on the trust we place in the government itself to make reliable information broadly accessible, and the authority of a given website depends on the credibility of whoever created it.

The takeaway here is that the authority and, hence, the usefulness of popular sources depends on the rhetorical context of the source and your own writing situation. If your assignment is to analyze young adult dystopian fiction, you might use *The Hunger Games* as a source. You probably will not use it if your assignment is to analyze the political significance of ancient Roman gladiatorial games or the social significance of reality television in the 21st century.

What about Wikipedia, you ask? Let's be frank—many people use Wikipedia to learn more about unknown topics and the information they find there is not necessarily suspect for this general purpose. As a crowd-sourced encyclopedia (and depending on the particular article), Wikipedia can be a good resource for gathering background information on a topic and, in many cases, for understanding biased perspectives on a given topic. The editors at Wikipedia do evaluate accuracy and relevance, and enforce standards that privilege objectivity and fairness. However, the ability of Wikipedia contributors to remain anonymous poses a major problem for academic writing, where it's important to know the writer's expertise, as well as who said what.

Feel free to consult Wikipedia, but beware any issues of credibility—often, but not always, described at the top of the page—that may plague the article. Check the entry's edit history to examine how the article has been altered and by whom. In general, you should not cite Wikipedia as a source in your academic writing; however, you can always check the list of references at the bottom of Wikipedia entries for possible sources you *can* cite.

Scholarly Sources

Scholarly sources rely on other factors to establish authority, in addition to the credentials of the writer and the intended audience. Because the purpose of scholarly research is to circulate new knowledge, the authority of a scholarly source also depends on the methods used by the writer to create that knowledge: how data was gathered and analyzed; what previous ideas influenced the analysis and why the writer engaged them; and the intellectual worth of the overall argument. **In the academy, peer review is the standard process scholars use to consider whether new knowledge should be considered reliable and trustworthy.** Before a scholar can publish her research, her work is sent anonymously to other scholars working in her field, who must verify the knowledge and methodology as original and accurate. These peer reviewers must also evaluate the contribution of this new knowledge to what is already known and be convinced of its intellectual value. Only after peer review has been completed does the new research actually appear in the form of a journal article or book, to be read, reviewed, and debated by the academic community at large. You may be surprised to learn that a lot of scholarly research does not pass the peer review process the first time without significant revision before publication.

Sources that pass peer review gain authority by the approval of experts who have the in-depth knowledge to judge a writer's methods and critical thinking, according to the conventional standards of a specific discipline. Non-experts, who may not have the knowledge or experience to assess these factors, depend on academic peer review to help ensure their own arguments are based on sound information, and thereby strengthen their credibility. In the context of your own writing, **a scholarly source is written by a professional academic researcher primarily for an audience of other researchers, cites its sources, and undergoes peer review**. Of all these criteria, peer review is the most important—if the source is not peer-reviewed, you should not count it as scholarly, even if it is written by an expert or includes a bibliography. For example, an op-ed piece in a newspaper written by a university professor is not a scholarly source; the writer's goal is not to produce reliable knowledge, but rather to inform and influence public opinion. Nor is a *CQ Researcher* report a scholarly source, despite the fact that it cites its sources in an extensive bibliography.

So how can we tell if a source has undergone peer review? For a book, check the press that published it—any publisher called something like "X University Press" is definitely in the business of publishing academic research and practices peer review.

However, keep in mind that not all academic presses are associated with a specific university. When in doubt, check the publisher's website to see if they publish academic work and if they practice peer review. Author credentials and the presence of a bibliography alone cannot confirm for certain whether a book is scholarly or popular; however, if the book cites its sources and the author is affiliated with a university or research institution, chances are pretty good it is a scholarly source.

As for scholarly journals and articles, check the journal's website to see if it practices peer review or is "refereed." You can also check the academic credentials of the author of the article and/or the editorial board of the journal, as well as whether the article cites its sources. In physical form, scholarly journals are easy to distinguish from popular magazines: journals are not printed on glossy paper and they do not contain commercial advertisements. Online, scholarly articles tend to appear in .pdf form, not as an HTML website (though there are increasing exceptions). The titles of scholarly journals often have straightforwardly descriptive names and often include the word "journal."

Multimodal Sources

Not all sources you use in your essays will be pure text—sometimes the information contained in your sources will be communicated through image, sound, video, video games, and so on. This chapter is not the best place for an extended discussion of multimodality, which you can find elsewhere in *The Anteater's Guide*. But when it comes to choosing multimodal sources—especially visual elements like images and graphs—keep in mind that, like traditional textual sources, your multimodal sources should communicate specific information that is relevant to your overall argument.

In general, you should avoid generic images like clip art and stock photos, which are unlikely to produce a rhetorical effect beyond a bored "Huh." Graphs, charts and tables should be big enough to read clearly and placed near the paragraphs where you discuss them so that the information they contain is readily comprehensible and contextualized. Sound clips and videos should be queued up to the place where you want your reader to click play, or you should indicate the minute and second where you want your reader to begin listening or watching.

Multimodal elements are a wonderful way to enrich your writing, but they are not merely decorative. To use them effectively, you must also consider them as sources containing information, which you will analyze or engage in order to build your own ideas.

Reading and Understanding Sources

So—you've gathered some sources and your first draft is due sooner than you'd like. At this point in the process, you may well ask yourself how you're supposed to translate all this information into shiny new knowledge and sophisticated argument.

The trick is to read your sources as efficiently as possible. In this context, efficiency is not just about speed; skimming your sources over and over again will not help you understand the ideas contained in them, nor will it help you plan how and where you will use your sources in your essay. Reading efficiently means remembering information after you've read the source, organizing the information in a way that makes sense to you, and understanding the value of that information to your own writing project.

DISCLAIMER: The following techniques are NOT intended to help you tackle the readings assigned by your writing instructor! See the chapter on "Critical Reading" for great advice on how to read to understand literary meaning and rhetorical effect, as well as prepare for class discussion.

How to Read Scholarly Books

It's easy to assume that books are overly complicated sources that won't have much to offer you as you write your essays, or that it's not worth your time to find print sources in the library when so many are available online—both these assumptions are wrong.

First, books that you find in a university library are practically guaranteed to be useful—they go through a lengthy editorial and (depending on the book) peer-review process before publication; after that professional librarians evaluate the texts' intellectual value before adding them to a library's collections. This process of editing, peer reviewing, and evaluating—all before a book lands on a library shelf ready for you to check out—takes years of careful effort intended to ensure that the information you get from it is reliable, credible, and practical for your college writing needs.

Second, books have a lot more information than scholarly articles, all collected in one place. You might think of each chapter of a book as containing a comparable amount of information as is contained an article, and they often contain more details, explanations, and references. In short, books—especially scholarly books—are incredibly rich sources for your research project. The same goes for ebooks you find in the university library, which are searchable and can therefore make finding information much easier. In many respects, ebooks have the same virtues as print books—a lot of information collected all in one place, careful editing and peer review, etc.

Of course, books are also much longer than articles and the prospect of wading through their wealth of information can be intimidating. However, experienced academic writers rely on strategies to help them determine whether a book will be useful before they lug it home. When you're choosing books to spend some time with, don't just start reading on page one or skimming the middle bits. Instead you first should look at:

- The title. It sounds simple but seriously, does the title suggest the book's relevance to your writing project? Pay attention to word choices in the title that may match or even suggest important keywords.

- The table of contents. The book as a whole may not be directly relevant, but it might contain a chapter or two that you can use; this is especially the case for book-length anthologies of essays by different authors. Again, pay attention to keywords in the chapter titles.

- The list of illustrations or figures. If included, this list should appear right after the table of contents. Pay attention to the labels attached to these visual elements to determine if there is valuable information in non-written form.

- The index. After you check the table of contents, always browse the index to see if any keywords for your topic appear there. If so, go directly to those pages and read what the author has to say about your topic. The more keywords that you find and the more relevant the author's ideas about your topic, the more useful the book will be to your essay.

- The bibliography and footnotes/endnotes. Sometimes the bibliography is the most valuable section of a book. Does it include sources you've already found? Find where the author cites them and read what the author says at that point. Does it cite relevant sources you haven't found yet? Note them and look them up too. The more relevant sources you find in the bibliography (whether you've looked at them already or not), the more useful the book is likely to be.

- A summary or abstract of the book. These are not always present, but check the back of the book or the inside of the book jacket anyway for a more detailed description of what information the book contains.

One of the great things about finding books on the library shelves is the opportunity to find other useful books nearby that you may not have found in the online catalog. The Library of Congress catalog system places books on the same or similar subjects next to each other on the shelves. Make sure to check both sides of your chosen book and even the shelves above and below that book—at the very least—to see if there are others that can be helpful.

How to Read Scholarly Journal Articles

Journal articles are published on a faster schedule than books, though they undergo the same process of peer review, and professional librarians similarly evaluate journals for their scholarly value before subscribing to them. Before we proceed, here are a few important definitions:

- Journals are the scholarly equivalent of magazines, and both contain short pieces of writing called "articles"; in the library, you can find the physical copies of journals and magazines described together as "periodicals."

- Both scholarly journals and magazines are published on a regular schedule. Each year a journal is published equals one volume of the journal—for example, Volume 47 of *The Journal of Popular Culture* was published during the year 2014. (We can also infer from this information how long the journal has existed).

- Each volume contains a specific number of issues. Magazines often publish on a monthly or even weekly basis, meaning that each magazine volume could have fifty or more issues. Because peer review takes time, scholarly journals usually have fewer issues—for example, *The Journal of Popular Culture* publishes every two months, for a total of six issues per volume. Some journals publish every three months (or every quarter), for a total of four issues per volume. Some journals only publish once a year, and the one issue equals one volume of the journal.

Though individual journal issues usually have tables of contents, they do not usually contain indexes. However, articles published in scholarly journals often begin with abstracts or summaries, which you should always read first to figure out whether the article will be helpful to your writing project. You can also use the article's titles (and, if present, section titles), illustrations, and works cited section to determine how relevant it is to your topic.

Scholarly articles, no matter what discipline they belong to, always begin with an introduction containing the main idea and, often, a review of previous research that is relevant to that main idea. After the introduction, direct analysis begins. In the social and physical sciences, the authors usually describe an experiment or study and follow with an interpretation of the results. In the humanities, the author describes and analyzes some kind of text, contextualizes that text and applies other people's ideas to create a meaningful interpretation. The conclusion of an article points to larger significance, and the scholarly article ends with a bibliography of sources cited.

Due to their relative brevity, articles are usually easier to read quickly than books. Still, you should begin by reading the abstract at the beginning, checking the section titles, and skimming the bibliography at the end for sources that draw your attention.

Sources About Other Sources

In addition to books and articles, you can also consult sources whose main purpose is to compile and organize other sources. Sources like bibliographies, literature reviews and book reviews can save you time and effort, as well as deepen your understanding of the current scholarly conversation about your writing topic.

A bibliography is simply a list of sources; each source that appears in a bibliography is called a citation. You may be most familiar with bibliographies in the form of "Works Cited" pages that you include at the end of your essays, which list all the sources you used, cited in a particular style format like MLA. As sources in themselves, published bibliographies are curated compilations of sources related to a particular topic or set of related topics; researchers consult these bibliographies to find out what information has been published on a given topic. If the bibliography is annotated, each citation is accompanied by a brief note—or "annotation"—that summarizes what each source contains and comments on the value of that information.

Literature reviews are somewhat similar to annotated bibliographies; these sources are synthesized, analytical summaries of a set of published sources on a given topic. Sometimes, literature reviews may also be restricted by a particular timeframe. Writing a literature review requires a great deal of familiarity with the published arguments on a specific topic; reviews usually serve as reports on the state of current knowledge on a specific topic and may appear on their own or as a section within a book or article.

Book reviews are just what they sound like. However, book reviews that you find in academic journals are more than just a professional opinion about a book; these reviews usually contain some kind of summary of the book's chapters, an evaluation of the argument's strengths and weaknesses, and sometimes a comparison to other books appearing near the same time about a similar subject.

Evaluating Your Sources

When it comes to assessing the value of your sources and planning how you will use them in your essay, you should consider what argumentative goals you want to achieve in your writing and how your sources help you achieve those goals. There are three main categories by which academic writers understand and evaluate a source's relevance to their writing projects:

Primary or exhibit sources: These sources contain information that you will analyze or otherwise interpret in your essay and they usually comprise the most numerous and/or most important sources you use.

- In writing classes that focus on literary or rhetorical analysis, these sources are texts like novels, poetry, films, op-ed pieces, historical speeches, and so on. Essay analysis involves breaking down one or two texts at a time and explaining how each part contributes to the artistic meaning or rhetorical effect of the whole.

- In writing classes that focus on research, exhibit sources are typically scholarly sources that report new research findings and popular sources that report current or historical events and public opinion. Information may be qualitative or quantitative or both. Essay analysis will often bring together multiple exhibit sources and explain how the relationships between different studies, experiments, polls, events, etc. create a meaningful bigger picture.

Secondary or argument sources: These sources contain other people's arguments and commentary about a problem or issue that you will explain, engage or otherwise apply in your essay. These sources are the second most important category of sources you will use, after your exhibit sources. Whatever academic writing situation you find yourself in, argument sources will offer their own analysis or interpretation of the problem, issue, or text you are considering. You may agree or disagree with the author's argument. If you agree, your analysis should show why the author's argument holds up in the situation you're discussing; if you disagree, your analysis should refute the author's argument. You might choose to refine or complicate the author's argument by adding additional context or by applying it to a new-yet-relevant situation.

Tertiary or factual or background sources: These sources offer important, foundational, and generally undisputed information about your topic. This information might be statistical or historical background; a famous saying or quotation that introduces your discussion; definitions of key terms or concepts; any basic knowledge or assumptions that frame current understanding of a topic or issue; or anything else on which you will consider true in your essay or use to contextualize your argument.

As you gather information from different sources, consider the various ways you might use these sources in your essay. Keep in mind that some sources can belong to more than one category, depending on what information they contain and their relevance to your writing project. Consult your instructor whenever you have questions about how to use a particular source in your writing.

Keeping Notes on Your Sources

It's impossible to overstate the vital importance of keeping detailed notes that record and organize the information you glean from your sources. Experienced researchers know—often through trial and hair-tearing error—that most little shortcuts taken while writing notes inevitably prolong the time and effort spent completing the writing project. Re-reading passages to search for that perfect quote, or to verify that small-but-vital-to-your-argument statistic eats up the minutes to your deadline! In moments of fatigue or frustration, it may feel incredibly easy to neglect what seems like extra, unnecessary work. But the truth is that keeping detailed source notes will ultimately save you time, for a number of reasons.

First, simply having detailed, well-organized notes means that you don't need to keep re-reading your original sources because you forgot what information you read in them, which quotes you want to use, the authors' arguments, or any number of other details you want to use in your essay. Reviewing notes automatically helps you make more efficient use of your time.

Second, numerous studies on cognition and note taking show that the process of note taking helps your brain digest your sources more thoroughly, improving your learning. In their review of the scientific literature on note taking, researchers Annie Piolat, Thierry Olive and Ronald Kellogg point out that "taking notes themselves can also increase learning by fostering retention and connections of information, as seen in the generation effect...moreover, students also memorize during note taking, particularly when they engage in deep comprehension of the source" (296). The "generation effect" they mention is the idea that people remember and understand the notes they've written for themselves better than notes created by other people (like lecture notes posted by a professor).

Third, source notes can help you plan various parts of your essay before you start writing, including its organization, potential analysis of quotes and other evidence, your preliminary responses to the ideas contained your sources, and so on. Planning ahead as you take notes not only saves you time, but also tends to raise the quality of your final written work.

So how should you take useful source notes? The good news is that the measure of any system of note taking depends chiefly on the person writing and using the notes—in other words, you are the best judge of what useful notes look like for yourself. You might choose to keep notes in one big Word document, or write notes by hand in your notebook; you might write outlines of each source, or a paragraph summary; you might color code your notes according to how you plan to use each source or which sources are most and least important; if you're a visual learner, you might create a graphic- or image-based system for keeping track of your sources. You might also choose to use bibliographic (or reference) management software like Endnote, Mendeley, Zotero, and so on. Seriously, the sky's the limit here and you should experiment with different strategies to discover what you like best.

Regardless of what system(s) of note taking you adopt, good source notes tend to contain similar kinds of information, including but not limited to the following:

- Citation information: author name(s); titles of the article/journal or book; publication details, etc.;

- Summaries (written in your own words) of the author's main arguments/ideas;

- Paraphrases (again, written in your own words) of the author's rhetorical positions and compelling evidence;

- Quoted passages (in the author's original words) containing significant or striking ideas, expressed eloquently or pointedly;

- Page numbers of important passages and quotations;

- Descriptions of graphs and images you might use as evidence in your essays;

- Related sources—those the author directly engages in the source itself and/or those you've mined from the bibliography;

- Your own preliminary thoughts, feelings, and questions about the author's ideas;

- Your preliminary plans to use (or not use) the source in your essay as an exhibit, argument or background source.

Citing Sources

Citing your sources according to a particular format might seem like a chore—especially if you've left it to the last moment before submitting your essay. However, citations serve an important purpose in academic writing: because they document where the information you've used came from, they enable your readers to track down your sources and verify that your interpretations, analyses, and ultimately your argument, are sound and trustworthy. Citations also help connect your ideas to those of other scholars in ongoing critical conversation and signal that your ideas are credible, based on sound knowledge created by others. Like peer review, source citations are a major convention of the academic discourse community that you're part of as a college student—to be taken seriously as an academic writer and researcher, you must cite your sources.

Different citation styles reflect the different disciplinary needs of researchers. You are probably already familiar with the style of the Modern Language Association (MLA), which you will continue to use in your composition courses at UCI. MLA is the preferred system for literary scholars; it emphasizes authorship and page numbers because researchers who study texts need to know who wrote what and what exactly was expressed. In the context of your own writing in the WR 39 series, your readers—which include your peers as well as your instructor—will need to be able to differentiate your ideas from those of your sources.

Many of the sources you'll find and use in your research will be cited in the style specified by the American Psychological Association (APA), the preferred system for social science researchers. APA style emphasizes publication dates in citations because social scientists want to know what research studies are the most up-to-date.

You may also find sources cited in the Chicago Manual of Style (also referred to simply as Chicago style or CMS), used by historians and other humanities scholars who want to know where information comes from. Chicago style uses footnotes or endnotes, rather than the parenthetical citations preferred by MLA and APA, in order to direct the reader's attention more quickly to the precise origins of specific information.

No matter which particular style you use, your bibliography or works cited page should convey important information to your reader more or less instantaneously; to do so, it must be correctly formatted and contain complete information about the source. When your reader views your works cited page, a quick glance should show the proportion of books to articles, as well as the proportion of scholarly sources to popular ones. Here are a few guidelines that can make citing your sources easier:

- MLA, APA, Chicago, and other citation styles all contain the same types of information, though they organize this information differently. Check—and double-check!—the relevant style guide for precise details on where to put your commas, periods, and so on. A widely used resource for properly using MLA format is Purdue University's Online Writing Lab (OWL): https://owl. english.purdue.edu/owl/section/2/11/

- Citations for electronic sources closely mirror those for print sources—the organizational principles are generally the same within a given style.

- Format your bibliography or works cited page using "hanging indent" (easily done in Microsoft Word by adjusting the left indent arrow in the ruler). Sources should be listed in alphabetical order according to authors' last names.

- When citing articles you found online, don't confuse the name of the database or database provider with the title of the journal or article. Names like "Academic Search Complete" and "Science Direct" indicate databases; cite database names as needed for electronic sources. "Proquest" and "EBSCO" are names of database vendors—that is, companies that provide paid access to specialized types of sources. These names are almost never required for a source citation. (For more information on databases, see the next chapter on finding sources.)

Annotating Sources

An annotation is simply a brief explanatory note commenting on the value of information contained in a source. Academic writers read and write annotations in a variety of contexts. In a published annotated bibliography, annotations appear beneath the citation and briefly summarize important arguments and evidence; the writer of the annotation may also comment on any striking features of style or methodology in the source. Annotated bibliographies also appear in college classes as resources created by the instructor or as assignments to be completed by students in order to demonstrate independent inquiry into particular topics.

However, annotations may also describe the marginal notes you write in your books as you read, which comment on specific passages, ask questions of the text, and make connections to other ideas. "Annotated editions" of literary and historical texts contain copious explanatory notes written by editors to offer context and possible interpretations of specific passages.

There's no particular standard format for annotating sources—the content, style, and length of an annotation depend entirely on the context in which it is written. However, as a general rule when writing annotations, you should always consider the intended audience first and foremost: what information does the reader (yourself or another person) want or need to know about the source?

Integrating Sources

When we integrate a source in our writing, we directly engage other people's ideas in order to develop our own. This process of source integration is arguably the most important and complex aspect of working with sources. The steps outlined below are not complicated in themselves, but performing them successfully requires your careful consideration and judgment from beginning to end.

Step One: Introducing and Framing Your Sources

The first time you use a source in your essay, you must offer your reader some context for understanding the credibility and reliability of the speaker/writer or the information itself. "In just about all cases, you should never stick a quote in your essay without some framing from you, as shown in this sentence." The quotation marks indicate that some specific person said those words, but who? When source introductions are absent, your reader has little idea of how to interpret the relevance of the source to your ideas. "Adding a parenthetical with the author's last name at the end doesn't solve this problem" (Smith). In this second example, who's Smith? Why should the reader care what this person has to say? To avoid confusing your reader, you must introduce your sources whenever you use them with some kind of contextual information: how does the information contained in a source relate to your own ideas and argumentative purposes?

For primary or exhibit sources, begin with a brief explanation of the source's connection to your main ideas. Depending on the source and your particular writing situation, you may describe relevant historical background, summarize meaningful content, or clarify rhetorical purpose. Use your judgment to decide what information will enable your reader to understand why you have chosen to analyze or interpret a specific idea or expression.

For secondary or argument sources, begin with a brief description of the author or publication's credentials, written in your own words—sometimes a name is all you need if it commands broad recognition. Include both first and last names, as well as the author's expertise or significant affiliations. Use your judgment to decide whether you should also include the title of the book, article or journal; sometimes this information is more useful than an individual's name and other times it's unnecessary and distracting. Likewise, use your judgment to decide whether you should emphasize the publication instead of the author; you might choose this approach when introducing an article that appears in a well-known or otherwise significant newspaper, magazine, or website.

Include a parenthetical citation only if the citation style requires additional information beyond what you've already introduced. Remember that MLA parenthetical citations require page numbers at minimum; if the source doesn't have page numbers, you don't need to include a redundant parenthetical citation repeating the author's last name or the name of the website.

After you've introduced a source the first time, you can refer to it again using just the author's last name, either in the body of your sentence or in parenthetical citations. However, you must continue to frame the source so that your reader understands the relevance of the information to your own ideas each time it appears.

Step Two: Summary, Paraphrase or Quotation

Summaries are useful for presenting the main point(s) of a long passage or even an entire source; this type of information often provides a background to your own argument or relevant commentary on your topic. Keep in mind, however, that the best summaries accomplish a specific purpose—they are not merely arbitrary collections of facts or trivia. When you summarize a source, consider what information your reader must know in order to understand the point you are trying to make.

A paraphrase is a more direct way of presenting source material, in which you express another writer's ideas using mostly your own words. Paraphrase is useful for communicating information more clearly and concisely than it appears in the original source, while still expressing the original meaning as closely as possible. When you consider different ways of paraphrasing someone else's idea, experiment with sentence structure as well as word choice.

A quotation in which you reproduce the exact wording of the original source is the most direct way to present source material. Selecting appropriate quotations is actually something of an art and depends on—you guessed it—your argumentative purpose at a particular moment in your essay. Generally, you should only quote when the actual wording of the original idea is important to your discussion; the most effective quotations record an author's ideas or analysis, not their examples or background commentary. We recognize several situations in which a quote is better than a paraphrase:

- When the quote expresses an idea that you cannot clarify or otherwise improve using your own words;

- When the quote contains specific words or phrases that are important to understanding the idea itself;

- When you want to refine or refute the argument made by the author and need to represent their ideas precisely and fairly.

In most writing situations, you want to keep your quotations short and sweet—that is, only quote the words that you plan to analyze directly. Long block quotations are only necessary if you plan to discuss at length the entire quoted passage. When quoting, also remember that the quoted material needs to be grammatically consistent with the words you use to frame the quote; number and tense must agree throughout the entire sentence. To cut down a quote, use an ellipsis to replace the omitted material. You may insert words that don't appear in the original quote with brackets.

Step Three: Analysis and Interpretation

After introducing a source and presenting its relevant information, the final step is to analyze or interpret the information and connect its significance back to your own ideas. How you do so depends on the source information, its value to your project, and the specifics of your argument. Revisit your notes to decide whether the information should be presented as undisputed fact, as evidence to analyze, or as argument to interpret, refine or refute. See Chapter 8 for additional advice on how to engage other people's ideas in your writing.

Patch-writing and Plagiarism

"Patch-writing" is a form of plagiarism in which a writer takes a passage from someone else's work, changes a few words, and then uses this material in an essay as if it were his own writing, usually without quotation marks. Patch-writing may be accompanied by a parenthetical citation, footnotes/endnotes, or even a source introduction, but these don't actually save the writer from having committed plagiarism.

While patch-writing may sometimes result from deliberate cheating, there are also other, more understandable reasons why patch-writing occurs. Sometimes the writer has not achieved full understanding of the material and cannot supply his own words to express the ideas. Other times, the writer's inexperience with college-level academic writing may lead to half-finished paraphrases, the result of misunderstanding how to properly integrate source material. Sometimes, writers who lack confidence may try to disguise what they perceive as flaws in their writing with someone else's more polished writing. In all these contexts, we can regard patch-writing as a regular part of the writing process.

However, patch-writing is never acceptable in final essay drafts; it is always your responsibility as an academic writer to detect and revise all such instances—that is, to ensure that all of your paraphrases chiefly consist of your own words and all of your quotations are purely the words of the original author.

Patch-writing is both serious and common, and you will need to practice vigilance to keep it out of your writing, especially your final drafts. Frequent instances of patch-writing in final drafts can negatively affect your essay's grade and possibly cause it to fail.

Integrating Multimodal Sources

Integrating visual sources relies on the same principles as described above for text-based sources. For images and graphs, first create a caption. Label each as Figure 1, Figure 2, Figure 3, etc., then follow the label with the appropriate MLA citation for the graph or image; if complete information is missing, cite the source where you found it. With source information for each graph or image contained in a caption right next to it, you do not need to repeat this information in your works cited page. However, captions alone are not enough to integrate visual evidence properly.

In the body paragraph adjacent to the graph or image, refer explicitly to the figure and point out what specific information you want the reader to notice. Images and graphs often present a lot of information that can be overwhelming to readers who don't know immediately what to look for. You may also find that some parts of the image or graph are more important to your argument than others. If you're integrating a photograph or political cartoon or some other image, briefly describe the relevant features in your own words; if you're integrating a graph, map or some other infographic, briefly state the relevant information in your own words. The key is to be brief and specific—your goal at this point is to direct your reader's attention, not to needlessly or laboriously translate your visual evidence into words.

Finally, complete your analysis of visual evidence by explaining its significance and relating it directly to your own arguments.

Works Cited and Further Reading

Bizup, Joseph. "BEAM: A Rhetorical Vocabulary for Teaching Research-Based Writing." *Rhetoric Review* 27:1 (2008): 72–86.

Piolat, Annie, Thierry Olive and Ronald Kellogg. "Cognitive Effort During Note Taking." *Applied Cognitive Psychology* 19.3 (2005): 291–312.

Russell, Tony, Allen Brizee, Elizabeth Angeli, et al. "MLA Formatting and Style Guide." *The Purdue OWL*. Purdue University Writing Lab, 10 Oct. 2014. Web. 1 May 2015.

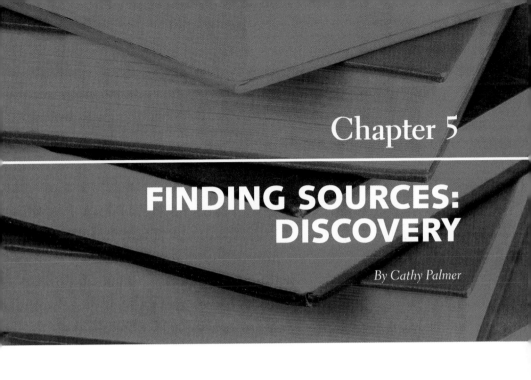

Chapter 5

FINDING SOURCES: DISCOVERY

By Cathy Palmer

*My name is Cathy Palmer. I'm one of the librarians here at UCI and my area of expertise is **information literacy**, which means the ability to think critically about information. You may have noticed that your syllabus and other chapters in this book use that phrase "information literacy." My goal is this chapter is to help you learn about the tools and services that a research library provides, so that you will be more information literate when you complete the Writing 39 series than when you started. The UCI Libraries, librarians, and library staff are your partners during every phase of the research process. Any time you need help, just Ask Us. (www.lib.ask.uci).*

Sources and the Scholarly Conversation

In the previous chapter, you learned that scholars communicate through writing, and they include and refer to sources written by others in the books and articles they produce. They refer back to what is already known about a subject in order to provide a context for the new information they have discovered and wish to share. In this way, scholars engage in a dialogue, or conversation, with each other. As a beginning level researcher, you can "listen in" and learn from this conversation, before adding your own voice to those of the experts you have learned from. Libraries play a vital role in this process because we collect, organize, and preserve the sources produced by scholars.

This chapter will introduce you to tools, techniques, and ways of thinking that will help you locate the sources, or conversations, that scholars have with each other. In simple terms, you need to find, evaluate, and then use things like books and articles to inform yourself and learn about various answers to the research questions you have. As you start to apply the methods of locating scholarly materials, you will begin to see that research is an endeavor that requires both mechanical and intellectual understanding in order to be successful. This chapter will attempt to help you understand the mechanics, so that you can spend your time and energy on the more rewarding task of learning from what you find.

Research Is a Process

Research, like writing, is a process. It is highly unlikely that you will find exactly what you are looking for in your first or second or even tenth or eleventh attempt to locate good sources. What expert researchers know, and what dedicated, intelligent students like you come to understand, is that we learn as we work on our projects, and that our original questions and ideas evolve and change as we consider new ideas introduced by the sources we find. It's very common to begin with one question and realize that, as you learn more, you now have ten questions in addition to your original one.

One way to think about research is as a series of phases. Each phase is an essential step in the journey of discovery that will result in a completed paper or project. Although these phases are often presented sequentially, (i.e., first do this, then do that), the truth is that research is a recursive and iterative process. You may find yourself returning to one phase over and over, while you spend very little time on another. The important thing to remember is that you are learning as you are doing, and you will learn better if you pause to evaluate and reflect while you move through each phase of the research process.

In general, you will cycle through the following phases when you have an assignment or project that requires research:

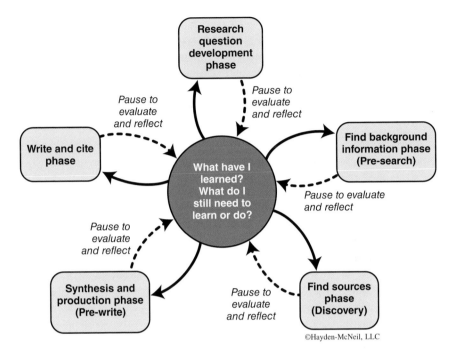

©Hayden-McNeil, LLC

We'll examine what is meant by each of these phases in the pages that follow.

Research Question Development Phase

The best research starts with a good question. Once you have a question or an idea, you can start informing yourself about it. That usually means using pre-search tools like Google and Wikipedia. These tools will provide you with factual information, and help you understand important aspects of the subject. Here are some tips that will help you decide on a subject or topic area that you want to learn more about.

- It interests you! You'll enjoy the research and do a better job.

- It meets the requirements of your assignment.

- It's broad enough to give you several search options.

- It's focused enough that you're not overwhelmed with information.

BEGIN YOUR RESEARCH

Students report that getting started is the hardest part of any research project. This short tutorial will give you some strategies that will help you jump-start your research.

http://www.lib.uci.edu/how/tutorials/BeginResearch/ucionly/info.html

Here's one way to develop a good research question. Start by reflecting on the subject matter of the text you've been assigned to read, or the theme selected by your instructor.

- What important information is the author or instructor trying to convey?

- How does what you're reading align with things you already know or other ideas you might have on the same subject?

- Does the author or instructor mention a fact or cite evidence that makes you curious, or causes you to question your own assumptions about the situation or subject under examination?

You will also participate in class discussions and read blog posts written by your classmates that will expose you to their opinions, questions, and observations.

Make notes on statements by the author, your classmates, and instructor, that interest, infuriate, or intrigue you. These notes will provide the basis for questions you can follow up on in the Pre-Search phase of your research process.

Find Background Information or Pre-Search Phase

Once you have a basic understanding of the text or the research assignment, you can use familiar tools like Google and Wikipedia to familiarize yourself with the subjects that interest, puzzle, and/or challenge you. You can clarify your understanding of the new ideas introduced by the text and check facts. During this phase, you are looking for answers to the following questions:

- Who?

- What?

- When?

- Where?

- Why or How?

You will use the information you find during your Pre-Search Phase to locate sources in the next phase of your information.

Once you have a basic understanding of your topic, you can loop back to the Research Question Development Phase of your project. You'll have lots of opportunities to work on this, but here's a quick exercise that will help you to recognize the attributes of a good research question.

Too Broad, Too Narrow, or Just Right?

Question	Too Broad?	Too Narrow?	Just Right?
What is the cause of climate change?			
What impact does the availability of public transportation have on the use of private automobiles in large urban areas?			
Does the use of solar panels on the top floors of the parking structures at UC Irvine generate enough electricity savings to justify the cost of their installation?			
Is the world safer because of electronic surveillance?			
Which government programs have proven to be most effective in keeping at risk-youth in school and out of prison?			

After you have developed a research question, pause to reflect on the process you used. What worked best for you? How would you evaluate your research question during this early phase?

Find Sources Phase

Once you have a question, and have found enough background information to have a reasonable understanding of what is known about it, it's time to start looking for *sources*. This is where **catalogs** and **databases**, the basic finding tools provided by the Libraries, become your best friends! We'll start with reviewing how to locate books, and then we'll cover how to find scholarly articles.

LIBRARIES' HOMEPAGE

The Libraries' homepage (www.lib.uci.edu) is the perfect place to connect to the tools and services that will take you beyond Google and into the universe of scholarly information.

Find Books

As you know from the chapter on Using Sources, books are an excellent place to inform yourself on the scholarly conversations that address your research question. Libraries use search tools called *catalogs* to let users know what materials the library owns and where to find them.

ANTPAC (antpac.lib.uci.edu) is the name of the UC Irvine Libraries catalog and you can search it by:

- **Title** if you know the name of the book.

- **Author** if you want books written by a particular person.

- **Keyword** if you want to see what's available on a subject.

- **Subject** if you know the exact subject heading for the book.

Whatever search option you use, you need to know the library location (i.e., is it in the Ayala Science Library, the Langson Library, the Grunigen Medical Library?) and the call number for the book in order to find it on the shelf.

Here's where to find that information in a typical ANTPAC search result.

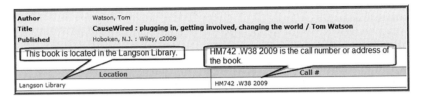

Author	Watson, Tom
Title	CauseWired : plugging in, getting involved, changing the world / Tom Watson
Published	Hoboken, N.J. : Wiley, c2009

This book is located in the Langson Library.

HM742 .W38 2009 is the call number or address of the book.

Location	Call #
Langson Library	HM742 .W38 2009

The screenshot above also includes the information that you will need when you write your bibliography. The five essential pieces of information you need to include in a citation for a book are:

Author: Watson, Tom
Title: CauseWired: plugging in, getting involved, changing the world
Place of publication: Hoboken, N.J.
Publisher: Wiley
Date of publication: 2009

Expert Researcher Tip

Keep track of your sources! Remember to record the following information when you use **books**.

☐ Author or authors' first and last names*
☐ Title of the book*
☐ Place of publication*
☐ Publisher*
☐ Date of publication*

***You MUST include this information in your bibliographic citation.**

It's also helpful if you keep track of the pages where you found ideas that were particularly useful and make notes on what you learned or need to remember.

The Libraries' **Make Citations** lesson explains why and how to document the sources you use.

http://www.lib.uci.edu/how/tutorials/BeginResearch/ucionly/citations.html

In addition to the *bibliographic* information about the items in the Libraries, the ANTPAC catalog record includes *location* information. You'll need to learn how to recognize and use a **call number** to find materials in the library. It seems a little confusing at first, but it's easy once you do a few times. It's also pretty amazing that this string of letters and numbers—HM742 .W38 2009—can help you locate your exact item among all of the 3.5 million books that the Libraries own! The thing to remember is that every book in the library has a call number and that books are arranged alphabetically, first by the letter or letters and then by the numbers. In addition to determining the exact location of the book, call numbers are designed to put materials on the same subject in close proximity to each other. Once you've located the item you are looking for on the shelf, make sure to browse the titles of the books located near it. Chances are you will find other books that are related to your subject.

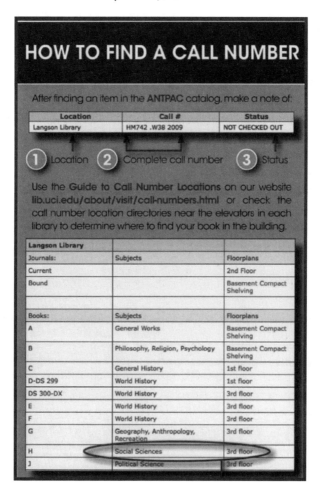

UNDERSTAND CALL NUMBERS

Here's a short lesson on how to use Call Numbers to find your book.

http://www.lib.uci.edu/how/tutorials/BeginResearch/public/books_9.html

The process of finding books is a great example of how research requires both mechanical skills (i.e., you need to know how to use the library catalog, how to interpret the information it provides, and how to use that information to locate your item) and intellectual understanding. The more fun part of research is looking at the materials you find and using them to suggest other ways of extracting information from the finding tool you are using. Once you've done your keyword search, you can scan the titles and subject headings for the materials you find to enhance your search vocabulary. The screenshot below shows what the record for a book looks like when you click on the title and points out places where you can find good search terms to locate related sources.

Search Tip: The example uses a known item to suggest ways to find new key words and link to related sources.

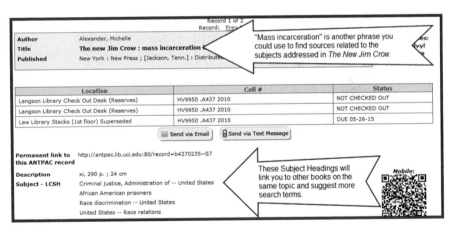

Books are great sources because they are familiar. They provide overviews and background material, and can help you *contextualize* information about a subject. In other words, books can help you gain a broader understanding of what experts know and think about a subject. They can help you understand the historical dimensions of a topic and provide you with different ways of thinking about it. However, books are not the only kind of source that you will use when you conduct research in an academic environment. You will find and read *journal articles* as part of the research process.

HOW TO FIND BOOKS

You can find out more about how to locate books here:

http://www.lib.uci.edu/how/tutorials/BeginResearch/ucionly/books.html

Finding Journal Articles

You are probably less familiar with scholarly journal articles than you are with books. Most of you have probably read newspaper or magazine articles, so you know that articles are shorter than books, that they tend to focus on a single event, person, or particular aspect of a larger subject, and that they appear in publications that come out daily, weekly, or monthly. In many ways that is where the similarity between a magazine article and a journal article ends. Scholarly journal articles are where researchers share the results of their most recent research or their thinking on very specific aspects of their areas of knowledge. Because there are so many journals, and because they cover so many subjects across a wide time frame, libraries have developed search tools, called *databases*, that will lead you to journal articles.

Before you can appreciate the utility of databases, you need a basic understanding of how information appears in journals. Think about a magazine that you read or browse on a regular basis. Let's say you like to read *Sports Illustrated*. No matter how often you buy a copy of *Sports Illustrated* (or read the magazine online at the magazine's website), you wouldn't be interested in it if every issue published the same articles over and over. It's always *Sports Illustrated*, but you know that the content of the September 29, 2014 issue is different than the issue you read on March 31, 2015. If all you want to do is keep up with current sports stories, it's fine to simply browse through the newest issue to see what's there. But what if your information need becomes more sophisticated? What if you decide that you want to review how *Sports Illustrated* has reported on Tiger Woods or Venus Williams or some other athlete's full career and the current issue doesn't have a story on them? How can you find out what's been published in the previous months and years?

Your first thought might be to simply start looking through old issues to see if you could find articles on the athlete you are interested in, but I'm willing to bet that you would quickly become frustrated and bored. This is where databases come to your rescue. Databases are finding tools that help you locate articles on subjects. The good news is that they will tell you when the article was published, what journal or magazine it appeared in, who wrote it, and other information that will help you find the information you want. The bad news is that there is not one big database that will help you look for all of the scholarly journal articles that have ever been written. In order to use databases efficiently, you need to know what subjects they cover. The Libraries subscribe to over 300 databases, so figuring out where to start looking can seem like an overwhelming challenge. Librarians know this and they have created guides that will lead you to the best finding tools to use to locate the information you need. These guides, called Subject and Course Guides, are available from the Libraries' homepage. Find them at libguides.lib.uci.edu.

 WRITING 39C LIBRARY GUIDE

The Writing 39C course has its own library guide. Use it to find databases and other sources of scholarly and popular information.

http://guides.lib.uci.edu/w39c

Find Scholarly Articles with Academic Search Complete

In this section, we'll begin with a few important concepts and tips that can help get you started with the databases available at the library website. All databases will let you search by keywords. You can also search by article title, subject, or author. The important thing to remember is that choosing good keywords takes time and effort. If you try a search and don't find anything, don't find what you expect, or find way too many things, think more carefully about your subject or question.

For students in lower-division writing courses who are just starting to learn how to do academic research, we recommend a database called *Academic Search Complete*, published by the EBSCO company. The following example shows how to use Academic Search Complete to find an article:

1. Write a full sentence or a question that you think describes your information need. For example, "Is there a relationship between unprecedented climate change and the extreme California drought of 2011–15?"

2. Circle the words or terms that are unique or most descriptive of your question. Leave out unimportant words like "is" or "do" or "the." From the question above, you might circle:

"drought"
"climate"
"California"

Notice that these words don't include adjectives like "extreme" or "unprecedented" or words that can be assumed from the question, like "change" after climate.

3. Enter those terms in the database search form. These forms look more complicated than the Google search box, but they search information more efficiently:

Typing these terms gives the following results:

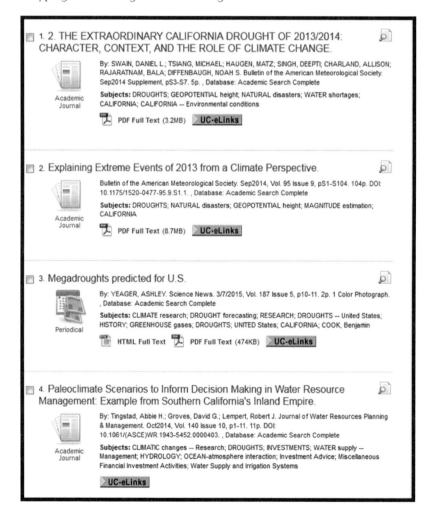

4. Review these results carefully. The title of the article gives you the first clue to its content. Do these results look like they might help to answer the question, "Is there a relationship between unprecedented climate change and the extreme California drought of 2011–15?"

If your results meet your expectations, take some time to review them. How do the experts who are writing these articles present their findings? Can you find new or different words or phrases that you can use to conduct other keyword searches?

If the results aren't what you want, don't assume that your question has not been written about. Think creatively and see if you can generate other words or phrases that describe your topic.

Once you've determined that an article looks like it's about your topic, you can take a closer look. Click on the title. You will see a screen that looks like the one below.

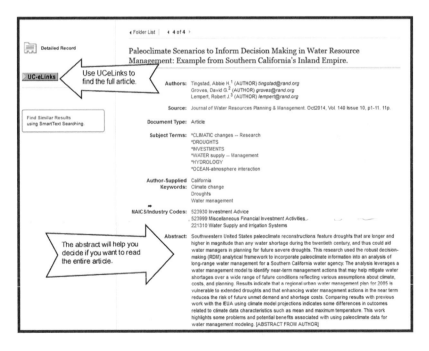

If you are still interested in reading the article after reviewing the *abstract*, use the **UCeLinks** button to find full text of articles that don't appear automatically in the results.

USE UCeLinks

This short video will demonstrate how to use UCeLinks to find full text:

http://www.lib.uci.edu/how/tutorials/UC_eLinks/

Keep track of your sources! Remember to record the following information when you use **journal articles**.

- ☐ Author or authors' first and last names*
- ☐ Article title*
- ☐ Journal title*
- ☐ Volume and issue number*
- ☐ Date of publication*
- ☐ Page numbers*

*You MUST include this information in your bibliographic citation.

It's also helpful if you keep track of the pages where you found ideas that were particularly useful and make notes on what you learned or need to remember.

The Libraries' **Make Citations** lesson explains why and how to document the sources you use.

http://www.lib.uci.edu/how/tutorials/BeginResearch/ucionly/citations.html

 FIND ARTICLES

The Libraries' Begin Research tutorial includes a lesson on how to find articles. You can review it here:

http://www.lib.uci.edu/how/tutorials/BeginResearch/ucionly/articles.html

Expert Researcher Tip

The Libraries provide over 300 **databases** that lead you to scholarly journal articles. Most databases focus on a particular subject area or academic discipline, like psychology, engineering, or art. You can find some of most useful ones by browsing the **Databases To Get You Started** page at:

http://guides.lib.uci.edu/databases

FIND AND CITE IMAGES

The Libraries' guide to Visual Literacy provides tools that will help you find and cite images.

http://guides.lib.uci.edu/visual_literacy

Evaluate Your Sources

Before you use the sources you've found, you need to read them carefully and make sure you understand the information being conveyed. Ask yourself the following questions as you decide which sources to include in your paper.

- Is the information **RELEVANT** to my topic? Does it further my understanding of important issues, or provide me with a new perspective? If so, how?

- Who is the **AUDIENCE** for the information? Is it written for students, experts, people working in the field, the general public?

- What **AUTHORITY** does the author or organization have to provide information on the topic? What education, training, or experience do the authors have that qualifies them to write on this subject?

- What is the **PURPOSE** of the information? Is it to educate, to persuade, to convey factual information, to share opinions, to entertain?

- What **EVIDENCE** does the source include? If the piece is factual, what facts does the author include? Where do the facts come from? If it is an opinion piece, does the author offer sound reasons for his or her opinion?

- How **TIMELY** is the article? When was it written? Depending on the topic and the use you are making of it, some information becomes outdated when new information is available, but other sources that are 50 or 100 years old can be relevant.

- Does the article include **REFERENCES**? Do the authors include citations to the sources they used?

- Is the information **BALANCED**? Do the author's or does the organization acknowledge alternative perspectives or do they include alternative viewpoints?

SOURCE EVALUATION SAMPLE #1

ICAO. *ICAO Environmental Report 2007*: Environmental Unit of the International Civil Aviation Organization, 2007. Web. January 13, 2009.

This report argues for various policies that will help curb greenhouse gases in the future. The report was written because greenhouse gas emissions are growing and must be curbed somehow. It provides statistical evidence and interviews with various experts in this field. It is a report for both the scientific community and those who are interested in this topic. This is one of the best sources in my bibliography. It is very comprehensive and easily readable. It details important trends and problems facing aviation. The part most useful for my topic is Global Emissions. That section provides information regarding aircraft emissions and potential biofuels to replace jet fuel. It discusses the potential rewards and losses to using biofuels, and tries to be as unbiased as possible. Like many other reports, it also gives information regarding the process on making biofuels and the properties of biofuels. This report is definitely credible and citable.

Scholarly or Popular Sources

When you have a writing assignment, your instructor will often specify that you need to use a certain number of "scholarly sources." The Using Sources chapter of this book gives a good overview of the differences between Scholarly and Popular Sources, so you might want to review it at this point. Here are some characteristics that will help you determine if an article is scholarly or popular or somewhere in between.

Scholarly ✓	Newspaper ✓	Popular ★ ?
Scholarly articles provide information and original research that is important to scholars and their disciplines	Newspaper articles provide current coverage of events, reporting of federal, state or local government, and primary sources for historical research	Popular articles provide entertainment, opinion, and summaries of current events
• Structured in a specific manner: abstract, methodology, and conclusion, among other sections • Usually long and can include data and statistics (charts, graphs, or photographs)	• Structured in a specific manner: headline, byline, lead, and story angle • Length will vary but are short compared to scholarly articles	• No specific structure • Tend to be short
Experts in a specific field or discipline	Staff writers	Freelance or staff writers
Technical language using specific terms associated with a discipline for an academic audience	Some newspapers use higher levels of language than others, but they are all aimed at a general audience	Easy-to-read language for a general audience
Scholarly articles cite other experts, have long bibliographies, and/or many footnotes	Usually do not have bibliographies or footnotes but will reference eyewitness accounts, court hearings, and government proceedings	Usually do not have bibliographies or footnotes
• Can be accessed through library databases • Text and data of article only • Name of the journal, issue and volume number, and publication date are generally on the top of each page	• Can be accessed on internet or through library databases • If accessed on internet: text of article, color photos, links to blogs, user surveys, and lots of advertisements • If accessed through library database: text of article, publication date and byline information only	• Usually can only be accessed on internet; library may have access to historical archives to a few titles • If accessed on internet: text of article, color photos, links to blogs, user surveys, and lots of advertisements
• Plain cover with black and white text • Usually no color graphics or advertising	• Mostly black and white text • Mostly black and white photographs, minimal color photographs • Large amount of advertising	• Appealing cover and pictures in color • Large amount of advertising
Psychological Bulletin, Educational Theory, American Sociological Review	Los Angeles Times, New York Times, Wall Street Journal	People, Reader's Digest, Popular Mechanics

The best research projects use a variety of sources, scholarly, newspaper, and popular. Scholarly sources lend credibility and authority to your writing. Newspapers and news websites often provide more up-to-date information because they report on events as they happen. Popular sources should be used carefully, but they can provide human interest and help your readers make an emotional connection to the subjects you are writing about. No matter what kinds of sources you use, it is your job as a writer to make it clear to your readers why you are using them.

MORE ABOUT SCHOLARLY AND POPULAR SOURCES

The Libraries' *Knowledge Cycle* lesson reviews how information moves from current and popular sources into scholarly journal articles.

http://www.lib.uci.edu/how/tutorials/BeginResearch/uconly/info.html

Once you've engaged in the Find Sources Phase of your research project, you'll move on to the Synthesis and Production Phase, and then then finish up with the Write and Cite Phase. We won't spend a lot of time on those phases in this chapter, because they are covered in other places in the guide. Let's just briefly review what happens in the final stages of the research process.

Synthesis and Production Phase

During this phase, you are gathering all of your sources and reflecting on what you have learned. You're organizing your thoughts, and creating outlines of the materials you want to cover and include. You should be doing some pre-writing—jotting down ideas that come to you, or important ideas you want to highlight—without polishing your prose or worrying much about spelling or grammar. The important thing is to put words on a page, so that your thoughts start to take a concrete form.

You may realize that you need more sources during this phase, or that you need to return to the Pre-Search Phase to check your understanding of the factual materials you plan to introduce. It's not unusual to feel a great deal of anxiety when you begin pre-writing, especially if this is your final project. Questions like "Do I have enough information?," "Is this really a good research question?," "Have I wasted too much time on something that isn't important?," "Will people think I'm a complete idiot after they read what I've written?" are common. Don't worry. Just keep writing, even if you really don't want to. Getting words on paper is really important at this point. If you've done a thorough job of investigating your research question in the earlier phases, chances are you will produce a research project that you can be proud of.

Write and Cite

You've formulated a strong research question, you've discovered background information and educated yourself on the subject, you've located a variety of sources (popular, scholary and in-between) you are confident that the evidence you have supports the position you're arguing for, you've done your pre-writing, so you have scads of notes—now you are going to organize all that material, integrate it with your own ideas, and share it with others in writing. Give yourself time to complete this phase. You've done a great deal of hard work and this is your chance to demonstrate what you've learned.

The last task of writing is often creating your bibliography so that you can document and provide credence to the ideas you've relied on to shape your own thinking about your research question. This can be tedious and frustrating, but there are tools to help you. Remember the important pieces of information you need to provide about your sources, regardless of which citation format you use.

TO CITE A BOOK, YOU *MUST* PROVIDE THE FOLLOWING:

☐ Author(s') name(s)

☐ Book title

☐ Publisher

☐ Place of publication

☐ Publication date

TO CITE A JOURNAL ARTICLE, YOU *MUST* PROVIDE THE FOLLOWING:

☐ Author(s') name(s)

☐ Article title

☐ Journal title

☐ Volume and issue number

☐ Publication date

☐ Page numbers

Once the paper is written, you've proofread it yourself, you've had your room-mate proofread it, you've created your Works Cited page in correct MLA format, and you've uploaded your final version to the drop-box for your class, take a minute to reflect on the process. What did you do well? What did you learn? What was most interesting and intellectually challenging about the process? What did you learn that you will use in other classes? What will you do differently the next time? Taking time to pause, reflect, and evaluate after each phase of the research process is an important aspect of moving from a beginning-level researcher to a more proficient one.

Need Help? Ask Us!

Remember that librarians are here to help you during any phase of the research cycle. If you need help, ASK US!

www.ask.lib.uci

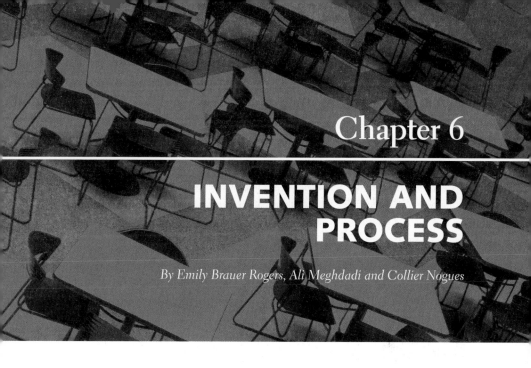

Chapter 6

INVENTION AND PROCESS

By Emily Brauer Rogers, Ali Meghdadi and Collier Nogues

Ali Meghdadi writes: "I've been to school for a lot of my life. I received both my Bachelor of Arts and first Master of Arts in Literature from Loyola Marymount University. Later I completed a Master of Fine Arts in poetry at Otis College of Art and Design, and then another Master of Arts in Comparative Literature at the University of California at Irvine on my way to the PhD I acquired from there in the Department of Comparative Literature. When I'm not strapped to a chair staring at a computer or cloistered behind stacks of books in the library, I escape to climb rocks in Joshua Tree or bomb trails on my mountain bike. I've been known to have some of my best ideas strike while dangling from my fingertips a few hundred feet above the deck or blasting down hillsides trying to outrun mountain lions. On the precipice of death, life is apparently best lived."

Collier Nogues is an award winning poet and former writing teacher at UCI. In the last edition of the AGWR she wrote: "What's most interesting to me about writing is how individual voices come alive on the page—how you can understand someone's values and personality through what they write, and even come to know them in some ways better than you might if you were friends in person. I'm also fascinated by how writing works—how thinking in your head becomes thinking out loud becomes thinking on the page, where it doesn't need you anymore, and can live its own life, interacting with and (if you're really good) influencing other people's ideas."

You can find Emily's bio at the start of the next chapter.

How Does Good Writing Happen?

Academic writers don't always know what we want to say before we start to say it. Instead, we figure out our arguments as we write early drafts, do research, and have conversations with other people. That's because academic writing is about invention and discovery, and adding to an ongoing conversation. You're never writing into a vacuum, or only for your instructor. Your audience is made up of intellectually curious, well-educated, potentially skeptical writers and readers who welcome and value your insights.

So how do conversations, research, drafting, and revising add up to a polished final draft that successfully adds to the conversation? The process varies, though most of the steps are universal (everybody revises!). Most writers end up having a few things that really work for them. For example, I write new material right after I wake up, before I've checked my email or looked at my phone. It's not that I can't write new ideas in the afternoon or evening, but I write more interesting stuff sooner if I do it first thing. That saves me time, which, as you know, is precious when you're trying to balance five classes in ten weeks.

But, of course, what works for me may not work for you. In order to become a strong writer, you have to find your own best process. Here are some great tips from some of my recent WR 39A students:

Here's Alex, on how he gets started:

"I've noticed that I normally get a 'spark' in wanting to write when I am lying down in my bed, nice, warm and cozy. No distractions and maybe a little bit of music on (Pandora) and I'm set to write a paper."

And Marjorie, on how she gets to a full working draft:

"The writing process for me consists of first just brainstorming, writing down any possible ideas I may have, and second is just choosing one of them to elaborate on... I have noticed that it is not until my second draft where I finally bring in evidence to back up my points. This is the process that mentally works for me."

Lilian does it more methodically:

"I usually try to think of questions that I can ask myself, and with these questions in my head, writing will be much easier and I will have more to talk about... I like to be fully prepared before I start writing my first drafts, and finish them carefully... Yet this makes it very hard for me to revise my drafts by myself, because basically I have everything I can have in my first drafts. Unless I get feedback from my instructors or classmates, I won't have many ideas about how to revise my drafts."

Here's Rachel, on using feedback once she has a draft:

"Having a day to mull over the comments I am given then writing the next day has proven helpful in more than one occasion. That said, also some days writing right after I receive comments is even better."

 FINDING YOUR PROCESS

If you're not sure where to start, you can always ask your instructor how she drafts and revises, or ask peers whose writing you admire. Keep trying different strategies until you find the process that works best for you.

The Elements of Every Writer's Process

No matter what your process looks like, it will involve some combination of the following:

- Invention
- Building your argument
- Framing your argument (for a specific audience)
- Polishing your argument
- Getting feedback

This section describes the first two elements in more detail and Chapter 6: *Drafting and Crafting* will highlight the last three elements. You may find some of these more helpful than others, and you might use them at different points.

 GETTING UNSTUCK

If you're stuck anywhere during your writing process, run down this list and pick a suitable strategy to apply. Chances are it will jump-start your thinking and writing, or at least give you an idea of questions you might ask when you seek help from your instructor, friends, or other resources.

Invention

Before you can begin to write, you have to begin to think. Invention is the first stage in most writing tasks: that process of gathering ideas, understanding your task, figuring out what you think and feel. Here are some helpful, productive first steps:

- **Re-read** the prompt. (See the *Unpacking Your Prompt* section.)

- **Make notes** and annotations of your assigned reading or of researched material. (See Chapter 3, *Practicing Critical Reading*, for how to use your assigned reading to raise questions.)

- **Ask questions** of your instructor and of your peers. (See the section *Asking for Feedback* later in this chapter, for more information.)

- **Brainstorm** lists of ideas or research leads.

- **Freewrite** some casual but focused explorations of a particular point.

- **Research** additional evidence or for someone else's points to argue with.

When you're thinking through ideas, this doesn't always come out in an eloquently crafted way. In fact, it rarely does. (And for those who say their writing process works like this, we secretly hate them.) This part of the process needs to be messy while you're getting your thoughts onto the page by any means possible. Don't judge your writing at this point—instead allow yourself freedom; the evaluation of what you write can come later.

The Value of Pre-writing

Why should you pre-write? Isn't it just easier and faster to get to the "real" writing? You need a place to explore and invent, and focusing too early on thesis and paragraph construction can prevent that necessary exploration from ever happening. Without it, papers can lack the depth and insight that is required from college writing. The more you invest in this step, the better the results can be when you start putting the paper together.

Brainstorming

Starting to write is always the most difficult part, and almost impossible if the topic lacks value for the author. There is nothing more crucial than finding a subject that matters to you. The composition process is always more marathon than sprint, so being invested in the topic from the beginning helps when trying to muster the inertia needed to get it going.

Ideally, if you're writing about something that is of consequence to you, then you will have many thoughts on the subject—often even more than you realized until you write them down. Using a brainstorm as an initial invention exercise allows the writer to meander through ideas easily, given that the goal is to merely flood the paper with as many ideas on the subject as you can imagine. When brainstorming try to avoid making connections between ideas right away. Let as varied a range of concepts get out of your mind and onto the paper as possible.

Once you've jotted down as many ideas as you can, then pull back and think about the subject more broadly, not just as constitutive concepts. Is there any one aspect that you seem to have more ideas about already? Do you see some sort of argument unfolding just based on how you have spread your thinking out in front of you? Make connections between the concepts and draw lines that you can follow. This step is called clustering and it's essentially like looking up at the sky at night and drawing your own set of constellations.

Clustering

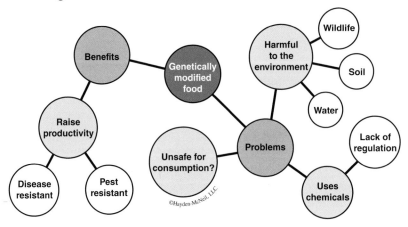

Clustering is a type of free association that often looks like a spider's web. It allows you to start with a topic or main idea and then build additional ideas from this by showing relationships to the other topic bubbles. This might be a particularly good way of looking at papers that talk about cause and effect or process because it allows a writer to start making those connections.

With a mapping of ideas, you can now begin to unpack the relationships between them in sentences—explaining with greater detail what links several ideas and how these linkages represent some aspect of your overall aims. This method can then be repeated multiple times throughout the process of crafting your composition. Especially as you look more deeply into your subject matter, you will develop a broader range of concepts at your disposal, relationships between ideas and thinkers will newly manifest, and your grasp of the nuances of the argument will strengthen.

Images

If you're a visual person, images might serve as a better way to process your ideas. You can make a storyboard that presents a narrative or argument visually. This is often used in film so that the visuals can be organized along with the writing. Similar to a storyboard is a comic strip, which can present a similar argument and can highlight dialogue from the scholars that you're using. There are a multitude of online programs that allow you to easily create storyboards and comic strips.

If you feel that you like the idea of images or illustrating relationships while exploring ideas, but don't want to rely on stick figures, you might use presentation software to organize your thoughts. Tools such as Prezi or PowerPoint can be used to brainstorm your thoughts.

Discussion

For some writers, the best way to think through topics and prompts is to discuss them with others. Consider bouncing ideas off of your friends, colleagues, classmates, or family to get multiple perspectives on the topic and to refine your points. They may question you, ask for clarification, and help develop your stronger ideas. Even if there isn't much response, talking through these ideas can help you to refine your purpose and message.

Using Alternative Genres

Starting a paper can be daunting, especially if we feel unsure about how to express our ideas in an academic genre. However, this should not prevent us from getting started: it can be useful to think about these in genres that you use to write every day such as tweets, blogs, emails, and Facebook posts. So perhaps you decide that you're going to inform your friends about a topic or issue through a series of Facebook posts. Or maybe you want to write an email to a close friend about what bothers you about a particular social problem. This allows you to take ownership, be creative, and avoid being too precious with your writing. While you can use these pieces as a private prewriting exercise, you might even send or post your thoughts and see what type of responses you receive.

Here's one example of a writer brainstorming using an alternative genre about his writing process:

@Emily: Mostly no one gets a perfect essay on his first try. Practice makes perfect. #MultipleDrafts

I learned that having multiple drafts are okay because they keep improving as you keep working on them. It's not a bad thing if you don't get your exact idea or topic right the first time and just to keep trying until it improves. Not everyone gets that one perfect essay on the first try, but it is okay because you can gain knowledge to what works and what doesn't. The process can be time consuming, but it is all worth it in the end when the essay improves enormously.

@Emily: It is important to organize your thoughts when writing an essay. #Brainstorm

On my previous attempts on writing an essay, I always used to skip the step of brainstorming before I actually start writing the essay. I learned that was a huge mistake in my part because that assists you in organizing and coming up with ideas for your essay. If the step is skipped, the essay will lack the right structure and it will be all over the place. It also prevents any repeating of previous thoughts already put in the essay when writing it.

@Emily: Peer reviews are an essential part in writing an essay. #GroupWork

In almost every day in being in the class, we would work in groups to either correct our essays or come up with a good idea. In the past, I never allowed people to read my essays except the teacher or professor who was grading it. Now I learned that other people have great ideas and that they know how to correct the essay just as well as anyone else. Group work benefits everyone in the group by making everyone improve in the way they write and see different types of ways other people write. This is another form of revising. Like Fitzgerald, multiple revision of one's essay can only bring benefits and make it better.

Framing Your Argument

At some point during the early stages of writing, you'll need to consider who or what this writing is for.

If you don't know who's going to be reading this piece, or why, it's hard to make necessary choices about elements like the kind of evidence to convince your reader, the style that's best for an occasion, or the best organization for an argument. Here are some important questions to ask at this stage:

- **Think about who your audience is:**
  Who's actually going to read this? Who would your ideal reader be, and how can you reach them?

- **Think about the genre you're writing in:**
  What are your reader's expectations? What other models of your genre can you find, to see how pros do it? (Now is a good time to review Chapter 2.)

- **Think about intros:**
  What's your reader going to need to know in order to follow your argument?

- **Think about your conclusion:**
  What should your reader understand now that she's read your argument? Why is it important that she understand it?

- **Think about your tone:**
  What kind of relationship are you building with your reader? How do you want her to react to what you're telling her?

Some of these steps are important to think about early on (like figuring out who your audience is, and what they'll be expecting), and some are especially helpful later (like reading carefully for tone, and crafting your intro and conclusion to match the argument you've built).

Know Yourself: General Principles for Developing a Writing Process

One of the most important principles of writing is that what works for someone else might not work for you.

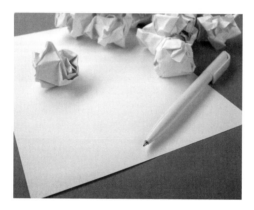

Consider the following questions when determining, for example, if it's really such a good idea to be trying to write your essay at Starbucks when you find yourself doing more people-watching than actual writing:

- How much do you procrastinate? How much extra time do you need to build in to account for that?

- Are you a relatively fast or slow reader? How much time do you need to get a handle on assigned reading? Is this different for different genres (psychology textbook versus literary essay, for example)?

- How do you take notes and annotate class material? Do you print out assigned readings and mark them up with pen and highlighter? Or do you type your notes in a Word file as you read? Or do you take notes by hand with a favorite pencil? If you don't take notes at all, consider starting. (See Chapter 3, *Practicing Critical Reading* for tips on taking notes.)

- Are you going to have to discipline yourself to do a certain task, or will it be easy because you already know you like it? For example, do you enjoy doing research or find it boring?

- Do you find yourself easily distracted? Will you need to isolate yourself in order to hear yourself think, or can you do it at the Starbucks on campus?

- Are you drawn to the idea of planning out your whole argument before you begin to write it in paragraphs? Or does the thought of that much planning make you feel stressed out?

- How organized are you? Do you like color-coding things with tabs and high-lighters? Or do you keep your class papers in a pile next to your bed?

- What kind of time do you have this quarter, and what kind of thinking are you doing? You'll probably manage your writing process for 39B differently if the only other classes you're taking are science labs, than if you're also taking an anthropology class and a political science class that both require multiple papers.

Pro Tip: Use Your Spare Time to Avoid Procrastination

There are probably pockets of time you're not using that you could be. You can break down your writing process so parts of it fit in 15-minute or even 5-minute increments.

You'd be amazed at what you can get done when you're just waiting for someone to show up to lunch:

- Proofread one paragraph.

- Read through for any single element—for example, spelling, MLA format, tone.

- Come up with title options.

- Add a few sources to your Works Cited page.

- Spend a few minutes of research on Antpac, Melvyl, Google Scholar, or even plain Google and text yourself the results.

- Google recent news on your topic.

- Review a source's Works Cited or Bibliography in order to find other promising sources.

- Targeted freewriting—for example, picking one small part of an assigned reading that stands out to you, or focus on one idea in your draft that needs development.

- Write one transition between two paragraphs.

- Brainstorm ways you could make your argument relevant to your reader in the conclusion.

- Look up some words you don't know so you can understand your assigned reading better.

- Google a word you want to use in your essay but whose connotations you're not completely clear on (this is a great thing to do for words you've found in the thesaurus).

- Email your instructor to ask for an office hours appointment.

Know Your Task: General Principles for Knowing What You're Writing

Just as it's true that you can't wear the same outfit for every occasion, you can't use the same process for every writing task, or every genre. Here's a handy list of things to consider for genres you're likely to encounter in your classes at UCI:

- **Timed essays:** the AWPE, the SAT, some in-class essay exams. Planning what you're going to say first works best here. Sketch it out as notes so you don't surprise yourself with a big topic switch in the middle of the third paragraph!

- **Research papers:** for any science, social science, or humanities class. Here, you need to start by asking questions and seeing what other academic writers in your field have to say about your topic.

- **Rhetorical analysis:** If you're being asked to talk about the strategies an author uses to get her message across to a particular audience, you might start by reading or watching the text and taking notes on what stands out to you, or by learning more about the historical context or genre of the film or book you're writing about. You might find one good point to make, and start writing about that, then look for other related examples and discover your thesis in the connections you see.

- **Persuasive argument responding to an open-ended question,** as in the 39A final essay: you're being asked to choose your own narrow topic, and offer original ideas to the class conversation. Here's where a terrible first draft really comes in handy. Get your ideas on the page and worry about sorting them out later.

- **Lab reports:** For these, your instructor may give you a format to use, or may not. Either way, you'll need to include a summary of your hypothesis, your materials, your methods and your results, so to write a strong lab report it's important to keep good notes all the way through the experiment.

- **Source evaluations and annotations:** Keep your purpose in mind here. Evaluations are really for you, so you'll need to include information that will help you keep track of this source and use it well later. Evaluations also are an important prewriting tool: how is the source valuable? Why is the source valuable? How will you use this material in your own essay? Taking notes on the source itself will help. For annotations, you'll be explaining the author, the evidence, the publication and the audience of your source to another reader, so careful, accurate summary is especially important.

There are many different types of documents and genres of writing that you'll write at UCI and beyond. The trick is to know what you're writing, the conventions of the genre, and the expectations of your audience before you begin. (See Chapter 2, *Reading and Writing Genre*, for more tips on this topic.)

Unpacking Your Prompt

No matter what class you're writing for, there's likely to be some kind of prompt you're supposed to respond to. Prompts may be very simple, or may take several pages to explain. Some instructors and some courses will be very clear about exactly what they're looking for. Others will value concision over expanded explanation, and you may have to fill in some blanks yourself. You can always assume that the instructor has thought carefully about how to phrase the prompt so that it allows you to demonstrate the specific skills you're expected to learn in the assignment. And you can always ask your instructor if the prompt is confusing.

Especially for open-ended prompts, finding a way to make the prompt your own will keep your writing interesting for you and your reader. Is there a way you can make the subject of your response something you're already interested in?

Pay Attention to the Prompt's Language

All the language of a prompt is important, but when you're trying to figure out exactly what it's asking of you, it's a good idea to focus on its nouns and verbs. Here's a sample prompt from 39B:

 SAMPLE PROMPT

"Scholar A writes X about our central text, focusing on Jewish/Jewish-American culture. Scholar B, on the other hand, writes Y about our text, focusing on American culture from the '40s to the '70s. Scholar C disagrees with both of the others, focusing on Jewish-American art in particular to frame her argument.

For this exploratory draft, which will serve as a formalized brainstorming session for your first Rhetorical Analysis essay, make an argument that connects the significance of context (cultural, historical, or literary) to the novel. You can use the above sources for inspiration and/or respond to the ideas in those sources as a springboard for your own argument."

Notice the prompt's nouns: this is an *exploratory draft* and a *formalized brainstorming session*, so you know this assignment's job is to help you get started on a bigger project. It's also an *argument*, focused on *the novel* and its *context*. You can conclude that this prompt is asking you explicitly for your original ideas about your class text, and will value your clear expression and support of fresh insight more than perfectly developed, polished sentences.

Next, check the verbs: "*make* an argument that *connects*" those last two important nouns: the novel's *context* and *the novel* itself. So, you'll have to spend significant time on each half—you can't just write about the novel alone. Also note that you "*can use* the above sources." That's a good tip—the sources give you a place to start. The first step of your writing process here? Probably re-reading those source quotes and brainstorming about how you can *connect* their context to the novel.

Understand the Assignment's Genre

Are you in a writing class, doing rhetorical analysis? Or are you in an economics class, writing for an economics TA in a discussion section? Are you writing a midterm in-class exam, or a final take-home exam? A lab report? A book review? There are tons of different genres you may write in for class assignments. A good way to figure out what a given assignment asks of you is to check out models of what you're being asked to write.

Does your instructor have sample essays to share? Or a model text in the genre you're working in? Have you been reading opinion-editorials and now you're assigned to write one? Have you been reading anthropology case studies and now it's your turn? Look carefully at the models you have. Professional writers model their tone, their rhetorical strategies, the ways they use their evidence, and even the way they format their citations on great examples of writing in the same genre.

 COMPARE AND CONTRAST

Compare the genre you're writing in to some that are radically different. That may help you see what kind of structure and tone are appropriate for yours.

Know the Assignment's Page Limits

Usually prompts will include page limits. But that number is almost always shorthand for the complexity of thought required and how much outside information versus your own original ideas you'll need to use. For example:

- Single-paragraph short-answer exam questions are probably asking you to summarize facts you learned in lecture. You might have room for one solid idea, and very little detail in the way of illustration—maybe only one or two examples.

- Six pages due in three weeks will probably ask you for original ideas developed into an argument. That essay will have more moving parts—paragraphs that do different things (give examples, contrast with the paragraph that came before, bring in supportive material to argue with, etc.).

- And then there's the 12-page essay: that one's impossible to do without using some outside research to help frame your ideas.

Too often, page limits produce essays that are padded with B.S. to meet the minimum requirement, or essays that stop when they get to the outer page limit no matter what's happening in the argument. Sound familiar? The more academic writing you do, the better your sense will be at gauging just what a set of page limits mean, in terms of the kinds of thinking you'll need to do and the time it's likely to take you. When an instructor requires a minimum page length, that's because in her experience that's how long it takes to thoroughly respond to the prompt. The maximum is the outer limit—beyond that many words, you're doing too much, or you're rambling.

So don't make it your goal to hit X number of pages with a sentence or two on the next page to satisfy the minimum requirement. Make it your goal to understand the purpose of the assignment and to accomplish that purpose. Ask your instructor for clarification if you need it.

Asking for Feedback

There are plenty of times at various stages in your process when you can seek outside advice and get another pair of eyes on what you're writing. So—who should you ask when you're stuck? This section should help you decide when to contact your instructor or when it might be best to ask your roommate to read your draft.

Getting Feedback from Your Instructor

You can ask your instructor for help or clarification at any stage of the writing process, from unpacking the prompt to brainstorming ideas to revising to polishing. Here are some especially good times to ask:

- when you're in the invention stage and could use some help directing your ideas

- once you have a draft thesis and could use help refining it

- when you've received feedback on a draft, have made some changes, and want feedback on how the revisions are working

- when you've received a grade and would like to talk about how you can improve your work next time

Going to Office Hours

Writing instructors always have office hours, and most can meet at other times too, if you ask. Go to office hours early in the quarter. Writing classes are necessarily tailored to the whole class, not the individual, so the best way to get feedback that's tailored to your own writing is to go see the instructor in office hours.

When you go to office hours:

☐ Come prepared with a list of questions (see the section called *How to Get the Feedback You Need* for examples of good questions to ask).

☐ Bring your current draft, the prompt, and any supporting materials (the class text, notes you've taken, or emailed instructor feedback, for example).

☐ Ask for an appointment if your time is limited. At certain points in the quarter (the end, or when a major essay is due) office hours get crowded.

☐ This is obvious, but show up on time. If you can't make an appointment, email the instructor to let him or her know.

Emailing Your Instructor

If you want to get feedback fast from a professor, it's a good idea to email something limited: a specific question about a single paragraph, for example. Professors are busy, and asking them to read a whole draft and answer general questions, like "Is this what you're looking for?" or "Am I doing this right?" or "What could I improve?" will mean they save your questions for later, when they have a solid block of time. Some professors will even email you back and ask you to be more specific. But if you ask a quick question and paste in a paragraph, they may be able to take five minutes and shoot you an email back sooner. Plus they'll think of you as a considerate, smart student for asking for targeted, specific help. See the section called *How to Get the Feedback You Need* for examples of good questions to ask.

Emailing Your Instructor Like a Pro

When you email a professor, remember you're writing a professional document. Your reader—the instructor who is responsible for your grade—will only have what you put in the email to judge your academic ethos and tone, especially if you haven't yet met your instructor or if you're in a giant class. So here are some guidelines:

- Always check before you email a professor to make sure the information you want isn't available someplace else. Does your class have an online calendar or syllabus? Has the instructor sent out messages via the class listserv? Asking a question whose answer is already out there (especially if you were supposed to read it by now) makes you look like you're not paying attention.

- Once you're sure the information you need can't be found elsewhere on paper or online, consider if a classmate might be a better way to get your answer. For example, if you've missed class, it's unlikely a professor will respond well for a request to review what happened when you were gone. It's your job to keep up, not your instructor's job to give the lecture again. See if a classmate can fill you in!

- When you do send an email, always include a subject in the subject line, and make it clear and brief. For example, if you want clarification about an assignment prompt, you might title your email "Reader Response prompt question." If you know your instructor teaches more than one class, you might include the name of your class or section: "39B Section 25526 Reader Response prompt question," for example.

- Always include a salutation and a valediction; in other words, a "Dear Professor X" at the beginning and a "Thank you, Student Y" at the end. Don't assume your instructor knows who you are just by reading your email address. And make sure you address your professor appropriately. Good options are "Professor," "Dr." if he/she has a doctoral degree, or "Mr. or Ms." if you know your professor doesn't have a doctorate. Don't use Mrs. or Miss in a professional context. And don't use the professor's first name unless you've been explicitly invited to (in which case it's fine)!

- Write your email in standard written English, meaning in full sentences, capitalized and punctuated appropriately (and proofread it).

- Keep your question or message brief. If you have a complicated question, it's probably better to use an email to ask for an office hours appointment so you can discuss your question in detail.

- Be polite, and be conscious of your audience and your writing situation. Your instructor has seen a lot of student emails. It's a good idea to provoke this reaction: "Wow, this is one of the more professional and considerate emails I've gotten from a student lately!" than this one: "Wow, this student doesn't seem to have learned basic email etiquette" or this one: "Wait, who is this and what section are they in?"

Getting Feedback from Friends and Classmates

You have smart friends. If they've been through a writing class, they may be familiar with what you're being asked to do. Also: your friends can be super-helpful one paragraph at a time. If you ask someone to read your whole essay, chances are they're going to say yes, but...maybe they won't have done it two days later when you ask again. But ask for a paragraph, and how can they say no? It takes five minutes.

Getting Feedback from the Writing Center

UCI has a lot of great resources for writing help. The Writing Center features professional tutors and writing specialists, as well as peers who have written essays for the same assignments you're working on. And the research librarians are amazing—if you're stuck, they're great. You can sign up for appointments for any of these, and there are also some walk-in hours and even email feedback. Check out the Writing Center and Library webpages for details.

How to Get the Feedback You Need

No matter where you seek help, learn to ask questions that get you the feedback you need. The better you get at asking specific questions, the better you'll be able to sometimes answer them yourself, because you'll be becoming a better critical reader of your own work.

Examples of good questions to ask, in order of early- to late-stage invention and revision:

"Which of these ideas seems stronger for a potential thesis?"

"Does my thesis clearly signal the organization of my essay?"

"I'm aiming for an authoritative but open-minded tone. Do you think my intro paragraph sets that up?"

"Do I have enough evidence for this point, and if not can you offer suggestions?"

"Am I making the best use of this evidence?"

"Does this transition work well?"

"Is my language confusing in this sentence?"

"Have I formatted this Works Cited entry correctly?"

How to Use the Writing Center

By Sue Cross

The Center for Excellence in Writing and Communication (or Writing Center for short) promotes effective writing and communication as lifelong skills. Not only are these skills necessary for personal and professional survival, they are also powerful ways in which people think through issues, consider multiple points of view, and become more consciously aware of the world around them.

Located in the Ayala Science Library, the Writing Center is the best place to get feedback on your drafts, outside of your class and your teacher's office hours. Here are some of the services you can get at the Writing Center:

Appointments: Set up an appointment with an experienced Writing Specialist if you want to get in-depth feedback for any kind of writing you're working on, or if you just want to toss around some ideas. This is best done well in advance of deadlines to maximize redrafting time and effectiveness. Note: It is also possible to receive a consultation on a walk-in basis, but only if a Writing Specialist is available. Appointments are your best bet.

Online Consultation: When submitting a draft for an online consultation through our website, be sure to email us your prompt along with the paper, and please indicate no more than two specific things you would like us to look for when reading it. The Center's response time will depend upon the volume of papers received.

Peer Tutors: Drop in during the evening at one of four locations to see a peer tutor and get advice about overall writing strategies, general editing, and research strategies. No advance appointment is necessary. However, it is best to come early in the evening in case a number of students are seeking tutoring at the same time and location. For more information about how to schedule appointments, submit a draft online, or view the times and locations of the Peer Tutors, visit http://www.writingcenter.uci.edu.

What Happens After a Consultation?

After a consultation through the Writing Center, you should be able to do the following:

- Identify the rhetorical situation evoked in an assignment prompt. You need to understand what you are being asked to compose, and to whom, before you can effectively communicate. After a consultation, you should be able to identify both the genre and audience called for in a specific prompt, and should be more aware of differences amongst genres and audiences.

- Develop self-guided revision strategies. Revision is more than just correcting mistakes. Most successful writers use it to take a closer look at what they really want to say. After a consultation, you should be able to articulate and execute a plan of action for revision or development of specific writing projects.

- Build flexible writing processes, strategies, and habits. Over time, and with practice and experience, you should be able to transfer strategies and habits for generating, developing, and revising writing from one context to another, even as you recognize that different writing and communicating challenges might require different strategies and ways of thinking. After a consultation, you will be prompted to reflect on what you have learned about your own writing processes, strategies, and habits.

 The Center for Excellence in Writing and Communication supports the educational mission of the university by giving students the tools they need to become better writers. While we will discuss issues we see and ask questions, we have a general rule not to edit or mark up your paper. We highly suggest proofreading your essay prior to visiting us.

Writers in Focus: *Dr. Francisco J. Ayala*

University Professor and Donald Bren Professor of Biological Sciences, Ecology & Evolutionary Biology, School of Biological Sciences
Professor of Philosophy, Philosophy, School of Humanities
Professor of Logic and the Philosophy of Science, Logic & Philosophy of Science, School of Social Sciences
PhD, Columbia University, 1964

For a list of Dr. Ayala's publications, go to
http://www.faculty.uci.edu/profile.cfm?faculty_id=2134

You came to the United States from Spain, something our international students will appreciate. Can you tell us about your first years here?

In 1961, I came to Columbia University as a graduate student in genetics, and for the first semester, I cannot say that I understood any lecture. I could read English when I came, but English had not been my second or my third language. I had learned a little bit of English, mostly to read, because English was becoming more and more important in science, but I grew up in Franco Spain where German and French were exalted, but not English. Be that as it may, I could read but barely communicate in spoken English. So having reached a point some 52 years later at which they're telling me that I'm one of the best writers in English in this subject, makes me feel very good.

How did you do that?

Reading—that's important for learning to write well. I read a lot. I read scientific papers, and those often are fairly clear, though it's amazing how often good scientists do not write well. Then, I read a lot of professional literature—biology, evolution, genetics—in terms of books and essays. But then I read English literature, because I enjoy reading good English.

Has the ability to speak several languages been a benefit for you?

I think so. I have read some recent literature that people who learn two languages as children tend to have higher IQs than those children who learn only one language. So the second language is doing something in the brain. In my case—Spanish is my first language, though I do very well in French; I have written books in French, I have written books in Italian—sometimes I start to express some thought, and the word comes to me in Spanish, or French, or Italian, this subtle way of saying it that comes to me in another language helps me express myself in English. There are many words and ideas that are better expressed in English than in Spanish, or better in Spanish than in English. There's an example that comes to my mind that is in a way trivial. You have harvest? Well, in Spanish, we have two words for harvest: one is *cosecha*, and the other one is *vendimia*. In Spanish *cosecha* is the general word for harvest; but if I tell you, we have just had *vendimia*, you know we have harvested winegrapes. There's another example that comes to mind: In Spanish, the verb "to hope" and "to wait" is the same: *esperar*. Of course, I have used that for literary effect: In Spain, when we are waiting, we are hoping. There's no question that sometimes when I am struggling with something, it comes to me in another language, and that helps me to express it in English.

Chapter 7

DRAFTING AND CRAFTING

By Emily Brauer Rogers and Ali Meghdadi

I'm Emily Brauer Rogers, 39B Course Director and Summer Composition Director. I have an MFA in Dramatic Writing. That doesn't mean that I write overdramatically, but instead that I'm interested in conflict—particularly the way it's structured in playwriting and screenwriting. This love of conflict is also why I enjoy teaching argumentative writing and critical thinking: I can help students explore multiple perspectives on issues. I've worked with many students as they craft their papers for various assignments in the Writing 39 series. This chapter will helpfully give you the tools to use as you begin to draft your essays and fulfill whatever purpose your writing assignment may ask of you.

So You Have a Paper Due...

Where do you start? Do you picture yourself thinking about what you have to write, writing it (perhaps proofreading it), and then turning it in? You might see writing a paper like a race—straight from the beginning to the end. However, thinking about writing as a linear process really isn't the most productive way to draft a paper. Writing is more cyclical or, even better, like a spider's web where you have to move back and forth between the elements to refine your message.

Discovering your own process is crucial. If you haven't read Chapter 6, *Invention and Process*, you should do that now. This chapter builds on the principles of Chapter 6, and provides an overview of the required elements of academic writing. We called this chapter *Drafting and Crafting* because while it's true that writing is an art, writing is also something you design (like drawing up plans for a house) or build (like crafting a piece of furniture). You don't need to follow these steps in the order given here, but if you're going to use this chapter practically, you should probably consider each element as you get ready to tackle it in your paper.

Drafting 101

At some point in the process, you'll have to knuckle down and write. That may mean thinking about how to organize your message into discrete parts, or divide your ideas into paragraphs.

In order to understand how to organize your points, you need to know what your purpose is (discussed in Chapter 6, *Invention and Process*). You have to figure out what you're trying to accomplish, so you can determine the best method to achieve this purpose. For instance, if you want to inform your readers about the results of a lab experiment, a report that clearly states the facts is probably the best method. However, if you want to make a persuasive argument about the solution to the lack of foreign language classes in California high schools, an argumentative essay seems more appropriate.

You have to know if you're trying to express, inform, or persuade. While there can be other purposes, these are three of the more common ones that you'll use in your academic writing. Once you know what purpose you have and what message you want to communicate to your audience, you can select the most appropriate genre for your purpose.

If you haven't read Chapter 2, *Reading and Writing Genre,* you should do that now. A clearer sense of genre will help you make a better plan for your own essay.

Building a Structure

Once you're clear on both your purpose and the genre expectations, you can use this knowledge to determine how to structure your paper. There are many ways to structure papers, but you may use some of these common frameworks to provide scaffolding for your argument:

- **Comparison/Contrast:** compares two or more items in order to analyze and make an argumentative point about the items being compared.

- **Problem/Solution:** defines a problem and suggests a solution or several possible solutions.

- **Cause/Effect:** looks at the determining factors of a particular outcome.

- **Chronological:** considers events in order according to when they happened.

- **Analytical:** breaks down the whole into pieces so that the pieces can reveal a point about the bigger picture.

- **Argumentative:** proves a larger claim with smaller individual claims.

Examine models in your genre and map how they structure their argument. What is the purpose of each paragraph? How does the reader move through the points that the author is making? This can give you a framework that you may be able to follow for your own paper.

Outlining Your Ideas

While you may have dreaded those formal outlines with Roman numerals that you had to do in middle school or high school (I certainly did), outlining can serve a purpose in organizing a draft. However, you have to think about your writing process and whether or not outlining will serve you better before or after a draft.

Outlining Before Your First Draft

If you are the type of writer that needs to have ideas organized beforehand, then outlining prior to a draft is probably for you. It can be a formal outline if you like that sort of thing, but it can also be a sketch outline of topics or claims. It can be a topic sentence outline with full sentences and evidence included under each paragraph. You should take the information that you have from your prewriting and planning and use whatever method you feel might suit you best.

 TRY THIS:

At the top of a piece of paper, write your message and purpose. Then, list individual claims that you want to use to prove your message. These ideas can then be made into complete topic sentences that fulfill your message and purpose.

Outlining After Your Draft

You might be thinking: *why in the world would I need to outline after a draft? I have a completed draft—this is just more work.* If you aren't sure about the organization of a particular paper, outlining after a draft is a great way to check for the soundness of the structure.

 TRY THIS:

Copy and paste your thesis and topic sentences into a separate document. Then read through your shortened argument. By just reading the topic sentences, you should have a clear summary of your argument. You can then decide if you need to move around topic sentences (and paragraphs) for clarity.

Crafting Your Message and Thesis

Just as outlining can be a tool that you use before or after a draft, a thesis can also be developed before or after a draft. Some writers feel that they have to have their message completely mapped out before they can continue with paragraphs, while others find their message and argument as they write. You should start to analyze your writing process and see what the best way for you to write is, and if you feel that you struggle with one technique, you should try the other to see if it makes more sense in terms of your own writing process. Either way, the process is recursive, meaning that you have to keep moving between paragraphs and your thesis to check that they reflect the same point.

If you choose to wait to find your thesis, you still want to make sure that you have a clear purpose for writing. Think about what you want your audience to get from reading your paper. Then as you write, you'll be able to refine your message based on your original purpose.

The following method of developing a thesis is from Sheridan Baker, a professor of English Literature and Language at University of Michigan.

Step One: Identify the Topic

The topic is the broad category that you'll be writing about. This might be defined by your instructor or the prompt, but if you need to, you should narrow to a more specific topic.

- Pursuit of happiness
- Use of satire in *The Daily Show*
- Sex workers in Thailand

Step Two: Propose an Issue/Position

After you have your topic, you want to propose an issue (a question) and then your position (an answer to a question).

- *Is the pursuit of happiness a realistic goal?*
  Happiness isn't a realistic goal.

- *How does satire in* The Daily Show *affect social issues?*
  The Daily Show's use of satire has impacted social issues by calling on the audience to examine their preconceptions.

- *What problems do sex workers in Thailand face?*
  Sex workers in Thailand are at a high risk of HIV and other STDs.

Step Three: Discover the Rationale

The rationale is the reason why the position is accurate. This can often be phrased as a "because" clause.

- Happiness isn't a realistic goal because once it is reached, the goal then changes to another goal, starting the cycle once again.

- Since there are calls to action for the audience, *The Daily Show*'s use of satire affects social issues.

- Sex workers in Thailand are at a high risk of HIV and other STDs because of the government's strict laws on prostitution.

Step Four: Pose a Qualifier

A qualifier gives context and can limit your thesis. It can also relate to any counterarguments you might be making in the paper. One way to phrase the qualifier can be as an "although" clause.

- Although the pursuit of happiness gives Americans goals to strive for, the reality is that they won't reach happiness since the bar for happiness will continuously move.

- While *The Daily Show*'s main purpose is to entertain, since there are calls to action for the audience, *The Daily Show*'s use of satire affects social issues.

- Even though Thailand's economy benefits from sex tourism, sex workers in Thailand are at a high risk of HIV and other STDs because of the government's strict laws on prostitution.

After you have gone through these steps, you want to reverse and test your thesis to see if it is arguable. This also allows you to consider counterarguments.

Sheridan Baker's thesis machine gives you a mechanical way of putting together a thesis. However, you need to polish and refine so the thesis doesn't seem too formulaic. You also want to consider the structure of your paper and revise the thesis so that it indicates the argument in your paper. For instance, if your counterargument will be last in your paper, you may want to move the qualifier to the end of the thesis. If you want to examine an effect and then the causes, you'll need to indicate this in your thesis. These steps give you a starting point for a thesis, but not the end result. Remember, in college, you're expected not to repeat arguments that have been made, but instead to gather and add your own insight to existing ideas. Your thesis should reflect this complexity as well.

Crafting Paragraphs

At some point in your process, you're going to need to think about paragraphs. We all know what a paragraph looks like on the page, but it may be harder to define what a paragraph is. In the simplest terms, a paragraph is a unit of thought, a mini-argument. Each paragraph has its own purpose and argument within the larger framework of an argument.

There is nothing neutral in an expository composition. From the most fundamental purpose of the sentence, i.e. inspiring the reader to read the next sentence, to the nuanced dismantling of counter-arguments, rhetoric is aimed at winning. Either your reader will be convinced that your argument is sound, that your paragraphs are cogent, and that your sentences are worth reading, or not. It your job as the writer to be sure that you do everything possible to compel the reader to not just read, but be persuaded to believe you.

To the end of achieving the rhetorical purpose of convincing one's audience that the message is correct, the argument, as well as its parts serve complementary, although somewhat unique, functions. The introduction of the argument lays out the broad claims that will be proven throughout while explaining its consequence and value. The audience needs to know right away why they should bother with this composition. As the argument unfolds, all perspectives are considered and laid out in the body, which develops through a variety of different rhetorical strategies that will be explained over the next few pages.

Ultimately the end of the argument should lead the reader to a new understanding, where they are persuaded to agree with the author. The final paragraph should not simply repeat the introduction. That would be like going to a movie and the last ten minutes simply repeating the first ten. Just as in films, compositions tell a story and take the audience on a journey. The end must satisfy the agenda laid out in the beginning while delivering the audience to a state of agreement with the author. Initial skepticism is replaced by certainty, different aspects of the argument are aligned, every counter-argument is soundly destroyed, and the composition culminates with the audience convinced of the argument's validity.

Each sentence in a paragraph likewise serves a specific purpose in advancing the argument. The topic sentence clearly lays out the claims that will be explored in the rest of the paragraph. It should be linked to the previous paragraph by some concept that was introduced near the end of the previous paragraph. Following the initial claim in the topic sentence, support from authorities in the field will be needed to underpin that aspect of the argument. Support, however, is not always immediately agreeing with the overall claims of the argument. It is necessary to unfold the argument through the presentation and subsequent destruction of counter-arguments. In any case, the support should then be connected to both the immediate claims in the paragraph it appears, as well as to its broad implications within the argument. No paragraph should ever end with a quote. There must always be some sort of interpretation of the ideas to ensure their effective integration into the argument.

Every single paragraph except for the last one should have a transition, that is, a specific idea that compels the reader to continue with the process of understanding the argument. As such, the notion of one's thesis statement being placed at the end of the first paragraph does not make rational sense. It simply does not follow that the thesis, or the summation of the composition's core claim, can also be a transitional idea the bridges two parts of the argument. The thesis statement considers the implications of the entire work, whereas a transition is merely the connective phrasing between claims within the work. To do so undermines the primary function of each of these particular parts of the composition.

A Paragraph in Action

Here's an example of a paragraph written by 39C student, Devin Yaeger, that has a clear topic sentence, strong support, good analysis, transitions, and a purpose sentence:

During the era of free trade initiatives and economic prosperity, the Dominican Republic paradoxically cut social spending, compounding the humanitarian strife that led impoverished women into sex work. The low level of government welfare spending, both a historical precedent and a product of the 1980s trade-induced austerity measures, is remarkable in Latin America. Whereas other Hispanic nations possess varying degrees of socialist parties and policy, the DR is nearly devoid of left wing political entities due to a long history of the military and social elites suppressing labor movements (Goldfrank 451; Ondetti 49). Gabriel Ondetti, an academic in the field of political science, documents the pitiful amount of social spending the government allocates toward the poor. He deduces that in almost all categories of public welfare spending, from education to healthcare to pension funds, the DR lags behind the rest of Latin America, spending per capita significantly less than even severely impoverished nations such as Honduras and Guatemala (49–51). The lack of social welfare programs deprives Dominicans, including the 40% segment of the population who live below the poverty line, of any social safety net (World Bank). This reality is a significant contributor to women choosing the profession of sex work, a decision of their own free will, as a means to provide healthcare, education, and economic security to their children—the very elements that the government has neglected to provide. As tourism to the Dominican Republic expanded in conjunction with the improved economy, the government made little improvement to these welfare deficits.

Peer Review Questions

As you read the previous paragraph, consider the following:

1. What's the argument of this paragraph?

2. What evidence or support does the writer provide for that argument?

3. Where do you see the writer's own analysis of the evidence? What kinds of conclusions does the writer reach that go beyond merely reporting fact?

Using Sources for Support

Often your support will come in the form of texts that provide credibility. You might not have sufficient credibility to convince your audience directly so you have to appeal to other authorities to give power to your ideas and increase the likelihood that your audience will agree.

In an academic context, authority often comes from formal credentials like a relevant PhD, and from using commonly accepted standards of argumentation and presentation. You'll need to evaluate the credibility of your sources to determine if they're appropriate to use in your paper. You can find more about this in Chapter 4, *Finding and Using Sources*.

When a college writer produces an essay, article, lab report, or any other type of text, that writer enters into an ongoing conversation. Often, that conversation has been going on for a long time before the occasion of the writer's intervention, and it will continue long after. With this in mind, when we write we must take into account both what has been said before and what has not been said. We must exercise what the legal and business fields call "due diligence"—exploring the current state of research and discourse in the discipline, evaluating the accepted knowledge in that field, and making a good faith effort to ensure that what we say will make a significant contribution to the conversation.

Once we have performed this research for our own benefit, we need to demonstrate our competence and knowledge to our readers. It lets them know that they can trust us. If we do a good job of this, our readers will accept our specific claim and begin to consider us as an authority in our own right.

The way in which we deal with sources in our writing varies with context. Most often, the genre of the text you want to create will determine the appropriate ratio between research and original analysis. Sometimes your use of authority will be as a summary of what others have thought, and sometimes it will be an analysis of what they thought in order to arrive at a new conclusion. At all times, you should consider what effect you want to produce in your reader. What are the conventions for research in the genre in which you are writing? Will including another source dilute or bolster your own analysis?

Additionally, you must evaluate the credibility of your sources. The venue or medium of your source will affect its believability in the eyes of your readers. For an academic audience, an anthropological journal carries more weight than a documentary on the History Channel, which in turn has far more credibility than the *National Enquirer*. So you must spend a good deal of time evaluating the credibility of your source. Wikipedia may be a good place to go to get an informal point of view, but its lack of rigorous oversight keeps it from being a credible academic source.

When marshalling sources to your cause, keep in mind that knowledge and information are power. By effectively citing sources and treating them in an ethically responsible manner, you will better persuade and/or inform your reader. By accruing a credible *ethos*, you establish a relationship of power with respect to your reader. You have the power to sway your reader this way or that. To misuse sources—to unethically appropriate their data without credit, quote them out of context, or to misrepresent their conclusions—constitutes an abuse of that power.

Integrating Sources into Your Paragraph

Authority and credibility (**academic ethos**) come in large part from the writer's ability to demonstrate his or her knowledge of and fluency with the conversation or discourse within a given subject or discipline. You achieve this in writing by distinguishing your sources from your own original material, and this is done with citation. Since composition classes are offered by the School of Humanities, we use the Humanities-preferred method of documenting and formatting—MLA. Other disciplines have their own style and formatting guides. When you begin writing in a particular academic discipline, always find out which formatting style is preferred.

Four Ways to Integrate a Quote

1. Signal phrase set off by a comma.

   According to Michael Levin, professor of philosophy at CUNY, "There are situations in which torture is not merely permissible but morally mandatory" (298).

2. Signal verb with a "that" clause.

   Michael Levin, professor of philosophy at CUNY, argues that sometimes "torture is not merely permissible but morally mandatory" (298).

3. Signal clause or full sentence set off by a colon.

   Michael Levin, a professor of philosophy at CUNY, argues for state-sanctioned violence against certain criminals: "There are situations in which torture is not merely permissible but morally mandatory" (298).

4. Quotation is integrated into the grammar of the sentence.

   According to Michael Levin, sometimes "torture is not merely permissible but morally mandatory" (298).

The Three-Step Method for Integration

Step 1: Introduction

Start by introducing the source with a phrase or sentence that lets the reader know that you are about to quote, summarize, or paraphrase. If you are quoting passages from an assigned text in class, then you probably don't have to establish credibility before you use the source, but you do still need to introduce it.

If you're working with outside sources and the author's qualifications are not generally known to your audience, establish credibility when quoting from or even paraphrasing the author for the first time, using an introductory phrase that indicates what makes her a significant and reliable source. If you're quoting from a source that is already credible and doesn't need credibility established (because it is a news report, it has no author, or for some other reason the author himself is not important), then don't waste words.

For example, if you are using a quote from the *L.A. Times* to help establish background and context, you don't need to introduce it with something like this: "Joe Potato, who graduated from UCLA *cum laude* and was a star football player in high school, is now a reporter for the *L.A. Times*. He argues that..." In a case like this, you don't need any of that information to establish credibility with an academic audience. Just tell your readers that your information was reported in the *L.A. Times*.

Perhaps the trickiest part of integrating quotations is making the quotation match the grammar of its surroundings. All pronouns used should be clear, the verb tenses should match, and the sentence in general should make sense grammatically. Here's a quotation that goes awry:

CONFUSING INTEGRATION

Hardin argues that "since we all share life on this planet, they argue, no single person or institution has the right to destroy, waste, or use more than a fair share of its resources" (452).

This is not only a grammatically incorrect run-on and a mixed construction, but it is confusing to the reader. Who are the "they" referred to in the quotation? To solve this problem, use the introduction to the quotation to clarify who "they" refers to, and use less of the quote:

BETTER INTEGRATION

According to Hardin, environmentalists believe that since everyone "share[s] life on this planet...no single person or institution has the right to destroy, waste, or use more than a fair share of its resources" (452).

When editing, make sure you have not overused signal verbs such as "states" and "argues." Think about what the verbs mean; for example, don't use "says" unless the author was actually speaking, and use a more specific verb like "writes" instead. Vary the mix and choose your verbs for their precise meaning. Signal verbs are not exactly interchangeable: your choice depends on the context of the quotation and the point you are making in quoting it. Signal verbs such as "states" or "reports," for example, let the reader know that what will follow is a fairly neutral statement of facts or data. Signal verbs such as "argues" or "claims," however, suggest a more debatable point, while "concedes" or "acknowledges," strike a more conciliatory note.

You need to be aware of the verb's connotation in order to use it correctly. If you're unsure, the best way to find out quickly is to enter it into your word-processing software's thesaurus function, or to look it up in an online thesaurus. If you aren't entirely certain how to use a particular verb, don't use it, and pick one that you do know, instead.

Step 2: Evidence and Citation

Include an MLA style "in-text citation" in parentheses after a quotation, para-phrase, or summary. The purpose of the parenthetical citation is to show the readers which entry in your Works Cited you're including material from, in case they want to look at your sources. By using citations, you're letting other scholars follow your research tracks—that's why you need to include the citation after paraphrase and summary as well as direct quotation—you are showing your reader that the ideas included here are not your own.

If you're only quoting from assigned texts in your essay, ask your instructor whether she wants you to use parenthetical citations and a Works Cited. The answer will probably vary depending on the assignment.

What goes in the parenthetical? Whether you're quoting from assigned texts or using outside authorities, there is one simple rule to follow about what goes into the parenthetical. If you have included the author's name in your introductory remarks, then include only the page number in the parentheses. If the author's name is not included in the introductory clause, it must be included in the final parentheses. If there is no author name for your source, then include the first few words of the title from the bibliographic entry in the Works Cited and the page number.

Variations on page numbers. If the source uses paragraph numbers instead of page numbers, then include the paragraph number in the parentheses: (par. 4). If there are no page numbers or paragraphs (as will be the case with many inter-net sources), then no page number is necessary. However, always make sure that you have given your readers tracks to follow so that they can turn to your Works Cited and figure out what you've quoted from.

Block quotations. Finally, if you are using a quotation longer than four lines of text (or more than 40 words), follow the format for a block quotation. However, please be aware that in shorter essays, a block quotation is probably too long to include. You should consider paraphrasing or summarizing some of it, and quoting only the words and phrases that are necessary to your argument in their original form.

Step 3: Commentary

Provide your reader with commentary of your own that refers to, explains, and clarifies your use of the source. In other words, after providing the quotation, paraphrase, or summary from the source, take some time to make the significance of the material clear. Don't just repeat what the quoted material already states—enhance it, add your own ideas to it. Consider the following two examples of commentary:

 COMMENTARY 1

However, along the same line of thought it could be said that the current ability grouping practice allows high-track students to benefit at the expense of low-track students. Maureen Hallinan, Professor of Sociology in the Center for Research on Educational Opportunities at the University of Notre Dame, notes that there are also concerns about teachers having to "teach to the middle" and to cut material from the curriculum in order to instruct a diverse classroom. The policy quells these fears by stating that detracked classrooms will not revert their curriculum standards, but rather make the best curriculum, i.e., the high-track curriculum, the default curriculum for all classrooms. The idea is that detracking should maintain appropriately high standards for all students in heterogeneous classrooms.

 COMMENTARY 2

Murakami's departure from Japanese characteristics is one aspect that helps give rise to this technique. As Lougham explains, "Murakami's works are almost completely emptied of Japanese signs," and it is possible to see how this is carried out in "The Second Bakery Attack." Murakami's only reference to Japan is when he reveals Tokyo as the name of the city in which the couple lives in. To further support this idea, Murakami also never reveals the names of his two main characters; therefore, it is not possible to presume if the couple is Japanese or not. As the article "Haruki Murakami" further elaborates, "the protagonists are generally stripped of Japanese traditions." Thus, by refraining from identifying his writing with a specific culture or location, Murakami's writing does not become directed towards any specific audience, but rather it can be read and understood by many.

Both of these examples choose different elements to emphasize and interpret. If you're having trouble writing your commentary, think about why you chose that quote in the first place. What is it that you want your reader to understand about the quote? Why did you choose to include it? What's important to your argument? If you can't answer these questions, maybe you don't need the quotation.

Crafting Analysis

Analysis is one of the most important modes of composition for college. The word "analysis" generally means dividing something into components, carefully scrutinizing each one, and then seeing how the parts relate to the whole. In an analysis, you break the object of analysis into parts, you closely look at each part (you define, you describe, you summarize) and then you synthesize this information to say something about how the parts work together to produce the whole. In other words, analysis is about describing the relationship between the parts of something and the whole.

Analysis isn't easy, and it takes practice to do it well. The good news is that you've been practicing for a good portion of your life. If you've ever predicted the ending to a movie or a television show, you've practiced critical analysis. What you are picking up on is not so much the content of the story (what the story is about), but its formal aspects (how the story is presented). By the time you are experienced enough to be able to figure out how a story line will end, your analysis tends to be so quick that you are not aware of it as a process at all.

Before you think you will leave all analysis behind when you get out of college, there are whole professions dedicated to nothing but analysis. Systems analysts determine the computer systems and software for a business's particular needs. A business analyst figures out what a client needs, and how best to meet those needs. An industry analyst sifts through data and predicts market trends. And of course, a psychoanalyst investigates the underlying, unconscious causes for human behavior and formulates treatment and therapy based on those causes.

Planning Your Analysis

Academic analysis is a more deliberate version of the same analytical process you use every day. Like all the modes of development discussed in this chapter, it's a way to develop your topic in order to make a critically informed argument about it. Academic analysis can take many different forms. The process you use to craft your analysis will depend, in large part, on your focus and purpose. No matter what the object of your analysis, there are certain steps you must take before you even begin.

 The Four Steps to Analysis

1. Understand the "big picture."

2. Break down and select parts of the text you want to examine.

3. Describe your selections carefully.

4. Describe how those parts interrelate, the "big picture," and your argument.

Analysis in the 39 Series

In WR 39B, you'll write texts in several genres that employ analysis, and also compose a Rhetorical Analysis of a text and its context. In WR 39C, you will not only be asked to analyze texts, but also to become an expert on the history of a particular problem and then write about this historical context; instead of breaking a text into pieces, you will select moments from history to research, dissect, and discuss, and show how those moments contribute to the current problem in an academic argument. You will demonstrate not only the insights or results of your analysis, but also how you got there. In other words, you have to show your work. You'll find more examples of analysis in the course-specific chapters.

Questions to Ask When Performing Analysis

1. What is the text's primary message? Is there a scene, sentence, or passage that sums up that primary or controlling idea? How do titles or headings hint at or sum up the message?

2. What seem to be the text's primary and secondary purposes? Persuasive? Expressive? Stylistic? Informative?

3. Who is the target audience of the text? What textual evidence and other clues suggest that this is the primary target audience? Are there any secondary or additional audiences to consider?

4. Has an editor provided introductory notes to the text, and if so, what further information do the notes offer about the text's thesis, audience, and purpose? What research could I do to better understand the author's rhetorical situation?

Crafting a Summary Paragraph

Summary is a widely used rhetorical tool that isn't limited to book reports and essay exams. Everywhere around us, we can find summary being used to communicate ideas: movie commercials and theater trailers often tease audiences with just enough plot and character information to inspire interest, while the reviewers who critique these films provide synopses that help to illustrate the films' strengths and weaknesses. Academic articles are often preceded by abstracts, outlining the whole argument in a few sentences.

However, effective summaries aren't just a random collection of high points. A good summary can (and often does) serve a greater purpose than simply providing a quick overview of the text. The best summaries arrange information around a specific rhetorical goal, often dictated by the purpose, genre, and audience of the particular text.

Knowing the Purpose of Your Summary

Summaries usually focus on the most important elements of a text, but what's important is often dependent on what the summary is trying to accomplish. "Previously on…"-style synopses for TV shows don't revisit every character and plot point in the show's history; they usually include only the information and events that are vital to understanding the episode you're about to watch.

Often the genre of the text will dictate the information that can or should be included in the summary. A film review may give a plot synopsis in order to analyze its good and bad aspects, but will almost never give away its ending, since the purpose of a film review is to help readers decide if they want to see the movie. Academic articles often contain another form of summary called an abstract, a brief paragraph containing the writer's primary argument, along with a brief description of its main supporting points. After reading such an article, you may be required to write an annotation in your Working Bibliography, very briefly summarizing the article's purpose, audience, and usefulness in the field.

All of these forms of summary change the information they include based on audience. Movie previews for an action film might spend less time outlining the plot and more time on the shootouts, car chases, and explosions. The audience of a romantic comedy, on the other hand, might be drawn to time spent on the characters and the conflict that keeps them apart.

Summarizing in the Writing 39 Series

Each class in the Writing 39 series will require you to practice using some form of summary in order to develop your ideas. In 39A and 39B, you will need to write focused, brief summaries of elements in a text as a way to introduce evidence in your essays. You'll also summarize the arguments of others in your essays to support your own claim, or as grounds to refute another writer's claim.

When composing a summary for your own work, keep in mind not only what your readers *want* to know, but also what they might *need* to know. If your reader is unfamiliar with the text you're analyzing, your summary may need to be more comprehensive. Or your instructor may direct you to assume the reader is familiar with the text, so you need only to summarize in order to situate the reader in your argument, to support and develop your point. In the following example, the student's purpose was to provide an example within her glossary definition of the term **imagery** for the audience of her fellow 39B students.

The student uses a text from the class, so she knows her readers are familiar with it. Her summary is light-handed because of this: she's using quotation in her summary just to orient the reader in the text so she can make her real point about one type of imagery. This is a common purpose of summary: using it as a setup for your own analysis.

SAMPLE SUMMARY

An example of *auditory* imagery can be seen in *Sandman: The Dream Hunters* when "the fox strained to hear another word, but there was nothing." She wants to hear a more human sound, but "all she could hear was the whisper of the wind as it stirred the fallen leaves, the sighing of the trees as they breathed and swayed in the wind, and the distinct *ting ting* of the wind chimes in the little temple." The peace of the sounds the fox hears after eavesdropping on the conversation of the creatures she comes across signifies the finality of the monk's fate. Instead of hearing what she wants to hear, the fox hears only the peace of the countryside, which serves to worsen, rather than alleviate, her anxiety. The auditory imagery makes the moment more vivid.

Questions to Ask When Writing Summaries

1. Why am I summarizing?

2. Which details should I select for inclusion?

3. Is the summary accurate? Comprehensive enough for my purpose?

Crafting Examples

The concept of "learning by example" isn't new to you. Such learning begins when we are children and continues throughout our lives. We make use of examples every day—in conversations, in emails, in class—and our understanding is enhanced by the practical use of examples. Say, for instance, you wish to rent a room in a hotel; you might go to the website and view a *sample* room so as to get a better idea of the amenities. Similarly, when it comes to your writing, appropriate examples can help your audience understand your message or concept. Your choice of example should reflect your awareness of your audience and purpose.

Knowing the Purpose of Your Examples

Aristotle defined rhetoric as the ability, in each particular case, to see the available means of persuasion. Successful rhetoric, then, will require you to choose and use the right example at the right time. Examples can take many forms, but whatever form they take, their success or failure as support depends upon their suitability to a given rhetorical situation. In your classes at UCI, you will encounter a wide range of rhetorical situations; in each instance it will be up to you, as rhetor, to determine which examples will resonate most effectively with your context, purpose, and audience.

When choosing examples for a given argument you must always ask yourself *why* you feel that example will be beneficial to your argument and *how* it will enhance your audience's understanding. If the idea you are discussing is complex, perhaps a simple, expository example would be most beneficial. For example, "America is like a salad bowl: individual ethnic groups come together in one place, yet maintain their cultural uniqueness."

On the other hand, perhaps you wish to complicate your audience's understanding of an idea or challenge biases; an example may do that as well. For instance:

- While we tend to think of pre-1960s Hollywood films as very conservative in their portrayals of women, before the censorship guidelines of the Hays Code were put into effect in 1934, women were frequently portrayed on camera, in films such as *The Divorcee* and *Blonde Venus*, as assertive, street-smart and sexually uninhibited individuals.

Examples in the 39 Series

An example can be anything that increases understanding of an idea. In academic arguments, supporting evidence can come in the form of images, graphics, quotations, summaries, or paraphrases from the text you are analyzing. This means that assertions in academic writing need to be *supported*, *illustrated*, and *developed* through the use and subsequent analysis of specific examples.

In 39A, you are asked to read and analyze a wide variety of texts; your writing will require you to support your claims with examples from those texts. Likewise, in 39B, you'll be analyzing texts from many different media, genres, and historical periods, looking particularly at the variety of rhetorical strategies rhetors use to achieve their desired purposes with a variety of audiences. Again, you will need to wisely choose examples from the texts themselves to develop your ideas: a quotation from a novel or short story, a certain aspect of a scene in a film, or a particular element of a print image. In 39C, you may be asked to write a formal advocacy essay; in this case, your examples are more likely to be comparative: in order to argue that one given policy will work, you might offer an example of a similar policy that has worked.

Like choosing which elements to focus on for a summary, choosing which examples will best illustrate an idea is a complex and important decision—one you can only get better at making with time and practice.

When choosing examples for a given argument you must always ask yourself *why* you feel that example will be beneficial to your argument and *how* it will enhance your audience's understanding.

Consider the following example, from a Rhetorical Analysis essay on the great Hindu poem, *The Bhagavad Gita*:

SAMPLE EXAMPLE

The omission of conjunctions provides Krishna with authority and control of his message. Through this technique, the translator is capable of reformulating the appeal of Krishna's message through the direct style of Krishna's voice.

To support her point, the student must choose the best possible example, one that not only supports her point, but the point of the poem as well. The lines are simple, but the student's point is both illustrated and supported by it:

Knowing the Self, sustaining
the self by the Self, Arjuna,
kill the difficult-to-conquer
enemy called desire.

Questions to Ask When Using Examples

1. What kinds of examples would be appropriate for my point?

2. How many examples should I use? Do I show a variety of examples that may support my point?

3. Am I choosing the best possible examples from the text?

4. Do I adequately set up and analyze the example in light of my point?

Crafting Introductions

Introductions serve several purposes in your paper. First, they are there to entice the reader into actually reading the entire paper. So, in your introduction, you want to find a way to hook the reader into your topic as well as show them why it is important for them to learn more about this topic. Your introduction also serves as a way to provide context for the reader to understand your argument. This is where you provide enough information for them to understand the issue that you're writing about and the reason for writing about it. Several strategies can help you introduce your topic and hook your reader into your paper:

Anecdote

An anecdote is a quick story (whether it is fact or fiction depends on your genre) to describe the context and issue to the reader. Because it heavily relies on description, it allows the reader to relate and even empathize with the situation at hand.

> "AHHHHHHHH!" Everyone zoomed past me riding X-2. The trembling noise of metal clashing against metal vibrates through my body, shaking every part of me. Suddenly, I thought to myself, is this true happiness? Is our pursuit of happiness the little things that make us scream and laugh and not the full journey?

Statistic

A statistic can be an effective way to illustrate the importance of the issue you're writing about. This quickly allows the reader to understand the reason why you're writing and can draw them in if this is a surprising or shocking statistic.

> For over a century, child prostitution in Thailand has become an overwhelming problem plaguing the country due to poverty and lack of education. According to Lisa Taylor from the Coordinator of the Regional Counter-Trafficking Foundation, Thailand has been ranked within the Tier 2 by the U.S. Department of State in the 2011 Trafficking in Persons Report, which indicates that the country has a significant child prostitution problem. It is estimated that over 800,000 children are currently working in the lucrative sex industry that generates roughly 37% of Thailand's GDP generating $22 million of the country's GDP. However, some citizens still live in extreme poverty while others reap the luxurious benefits of the thriving business of prostitution.

Example

While you usually want to save your best example for the body of your paper, you can start with your second best example to explore it and indicate how it illustrates the message that you'll be arguing.

> The doorbell of a dim erotic massage parlor breaks the silence on a frigid night in San Francisco, California. The customer is greeted at the door by an elderly woman and escorted inside as the massage parlor manager searches for any sign that he could be part of law enforcement. In another room is the slight pitter patter of a dozen oriental masseuses positioning themselves and getting ready to be selected. They wait nervously, keeping their eyes on the ground, and hopelessly awaiting their fate. With over ninety sex-for-sale massage parlors stretching across San Francisco, according to myredbook.com, this customer is sure to be the first of many during the night (May).

Strategies to Avoid

There are several strategies that you may have used in the past that aren't good ways to begin a paper. First, you may have been told to start broadly and move to a specific topic. While this can work, you don't want to start too broadly such as "Throughout history." You need to be in the same ballpark as the topic that you're discussing. Similarly, you don't want to use quotes that you find on a quotation website that are vaguely related. If you want to use a quote, it should be from a source close to your topic. And in some cases, a definition of a term or issue is necessary in the introduction, but you don't want to find a dictionary definition online and quote that—

instead it is better to build your own definition with research and analysis.

Once you've hooked your reader, you have to move towards your message and/or thesis. But what's supposed to be in between the hook and thesis? Again, go back to your purpose—you need to give enough information so the reader understands where you're coming from and where you're going in order to then understand the message.

 ## SETTING THE SCENE

Consider how movies introduce you to their stories—through movie trailers. How do movie trailers quickly bring you into the world they're creating? They set tone and mood through music and sound. They quickly flash through the main points and present the dilemma that the characters are going to face. For this exercise, describe what a movie trailer for your introduction would look like. What music would you use to set the mood? What images would you show and why? How would you present the dilemma of the paper? What would entice your reader to read the whole paper? Once you've thought about these issues cinematically, think about how you can then transfer this to your writing. For instance, can you describe an important location in full detail? Or can you show particular characters/scholars facing off against each other? How do you show each position? See if you can translate this to an introductory paragraph.

Crafting Conclusions

Conclusions also serve a particular purpose and that purpose isn't just to repeat your thesis or what you've already written in the paper. You may have heard the advice "Restate your thesis," but you don't want to repeat yourself. Here are better questions to ask when considering how to conclude your essay:

1. What are the larger implications of this argument? Remind the reader how this argument is connected to a larger conversation in the academy or in the world.

2. Is it important to get your readers to care about this argument? Perhaps you could do that by asking your readers a probing question, or by giving them a lasting image.

3. Does this argument demand a call to action? If so, make it clear what that action is, and how your reader can get involved.

You'll have to analyze your writing genre and see how other writers conclude their arguments (with a question, an image, a quote, a warning, a universal statement or a summary of results).

In general, if you can show the reader why this topic and issue matters, then you can successfully conclude your paper.

Revising Your Draft

Once you have a fairly solid draft, it's time to start moving to revision. Revision requires you to shift from being a writer into being an editor. You have to actually re-see the paper from a different viewpoint. In order to do this, you need to look at your paper as a whole as well as in smaller parts.

Global Revision

Global revision requires you to look at the big picture elements of your paper, which normally include argument and organization. You want to check your thesis and topic sentences when you're looking at your argument and make sure that they fit together. You want to check your evidence to see that it supports the claims that you're making. Check out Chapter 7, *I Came Here for an Argument*, for more specifics about making your argument sound.

You also want to make sure that your organization is appropriate for the genre. This might also be a place to use a reverse outline so you can look at paragraph order.

Paragraph Revision

Once you've revised the larger issues of your paper, you want to look at how each paragraph works on its own.

Paragraph Revision Checklist

☐ Do all of the ideas work together within the paragraph? Which ones may need to be revised to make their purpose and message clearer?

☐ Does the evidence support my claims?

☐ Are any ideas separate and need to be cut or moved to another paragraph?

☐ Have you made your sentences work together through transitions?

Proofreading

This might be the aspect of revision that you're most familiar with. However, proofreading is looking at the small stuff—grammar and mechanics. While it is very important, you don't want to do this until you've fixed the larger issues in the paper. As you proofread, make sure you also look at the citations and properly format your paper accordingly.

A few proofreading tips:

● **Read the paper aloud.** Hearing the paper allows you to see what you stumble on and what flows well. You can make adjustments when the words and sentences don't flow smoothly.

● **Read the paper backwards**—no, not word by word, but sentence by sentence. Read the last sentence and then move to the next sentence. This allows you to stop reading for meaning and focus instead on grammar and mechanics.

● **Use a grammar checker.** You can can find a grammar checker in most word-processing programs (and an even more robust one on Turnitin. com). However, you should understand that while grammar checkers can be helpful, there are also limitations to any computer program.

Three Big Tips

☐ The more time you give yourself between drafts, the more you can see easily when you come back.

☐ Leave yourself next steps before you quit writing, so that when you next sit down to work, you won't waste time remembering what you were doing or what you meant to say.

☐ Remember that you are always writing to one person at a time. Reading is fairly private: there's a real person at the other end of the page, and your end goal is to communicate your ideas in a way that person can understand.

Crafting a Title

Once you've finished drafting and have a polished final draft, you want to put a title on the paper. The title should draw the reader into your paper and needs to be specific to the argument you're making to the reader in the paper. Academics often begin their titles with a creative or catchy phrase, followed by a colon and a clear statement regarding the paper's argument. For instance:

The Day the Music Died:
How California Reduced Arts Education in Elementary Schools

The first part references a popular song and the second part introduces the reader to the issue and argument being addressed in the paper.

 EXAMPLES OF TITLES

This Is Not a Love Story:
How *(500) Days of Summer* Breaks Conventions to Attract a Younger Audience of Men and Women

Never Too Late to Educate:
A Proposal for Addressing Thailand's Dependency on Prostitution

The Long Struggle Continues:
The Androcentric Ideology that Influences Scientific Research

Remember that different genres have different expectations for what's appropriate for a title. Look at different examples of the genre you're writing to see what your options are.

Now What?

After moving through the required elements of the paper, you're probably ready to turn it in. Of course, it might be that you need more outside feedback from your instructor, peers, or the Writing Center to help refine and revise your paper. It really depends on the complexity of the task and your familiarity with the genre. Keep in mind that even professional writers edit and revise their work obsessively. If you've written more than three drafts of your essay and you're still finding things to improve, then you're in good company. Think of this essay as just one step in a longer journey. What you didn't master this time can be on your agenda for the next assignment.

Writers in Focus: *Dr. Elizabeth Loftus*

Distinguished Professor
Psychology & Social Behavior
Criminology, Law & Society
Cognitive Science
School of Law
PhD Stanford University

For a list of Dr. Loftus' publications, go to:
http://socialecology.uci.edu/faculty/eloftus/

You've become somewhat a household name. Were you always a good writer?

In high school, I was very good at mathematics, possibly because it was one of the few things that I could talk with my father about. English and writing was, I felt, one of my weakest subjects. I could barely get a good grade on an essay. I remember that once I got an A on one and only one essay. It was about my mother's death, and I decided that the only reason I got an A was he felt sorry for me because I was writing about this sad subject.

My younger brother used to help me with my essays. I had absolutely no confidence in my essays. Even after I got married—I got married to somebody'd who'd gone to an Ivy League school and he was really polished at expressing himself—I would give him my papers and give him a pencil and say, "Would you read this?" I still had no confidence in my ability to write. Then, I'm not quite sure what happened, but I've now authored or co-authored 22 books and more than 500 scientific articles, and it is one of the most important things I do in my field, both as an academic, university researcher, and also in publishing and in communicating my science to a larger audience.

Was there a period where you were conscious of your confidence changing?

No! It still stuns me! I wrote an autobiographical chapter for a book called *A History of Psychology: An Autobiography*, and the editor said, "This is amazingly well written." I said, "Really?" So, even still I'm a little surprised when I get feedback about my writing.

Your work studying the fallibility of memory crosses over into the legal field, so you've also done a lot of expert testimony—which involves conveying your work to those who are not experts in this field. Is there anything particularly difficult about that, or particularly gratifying about that?

One thing that's particularly difficult—sometimes when I have to convey something to a group of twelve jurors who don't necessarily have a lot of college education, who almost certainly don't have statistics under their belt, what it means to say that the correlation between how confident a witness is and how likely they are to be accurate, that it's relatively weak, that it's on the order of .25. How am I going to explain this to people when they haven't had statistics and they don't have a feel for correlations. That is something that I'm still struggling with.

The one thing that I have that I'm really lucky about is this involvement in the legal system, because I then get involved with these lives and these really powerful stories of individuals. As a consultant, as an expert witness, I get to read police reports and look at surveillance tapes. I'm usually starting my writing with some human story, and I know that makes it more interesting to people.

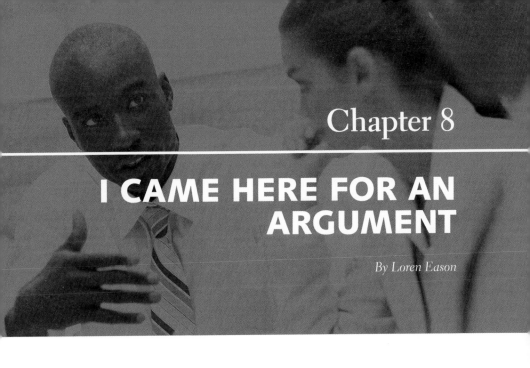

Chapter 8

I CAME HERE FOR AN ARGUMENT

By Loren Eason

I'm Loren Eason, a lecturer in UCI's Composition Program, and I study and write about the rhetoric of video games and how they relate to other media. (I get to study video games? How cool is that?) Because my work bridges two very different areas of study, I often find myself explaining work written for one specific group of readers to another group of readers with different interests, knowledge, and ways of seeing things. I'm writing this chapter on argument for you in the hope that it will help you, too, to understand how you can understand other people's arguments and their own purposes for writing them, explain those arguments to others, and use them to support your own claims and purposes.

We've All Been Here Before

Bad news. Your professor has assigned an argumentative paper and you've been working for days (well, minutes a day, in between all the rest of your classes and necessary college activities), trying to put together your paper, going over your notes, asking questions about the prompt and summarizing all of the things you remember from the class discussion and any outside reading that you were forced at gunpoint to collect. It's getting down to the wire and you are still not at all sure how to put it all together and make it work. Despite your efforts, all you have are a few rambling paragraphs of truth-y facts and a vague idea of what you want to say. You know you are supposed to have a claim of some sort in your paper, but you aren't even sure what that really means. Something is still missing...

...That Something Is an Argument

Not all writing that we do is argumentative. We also write to communicate a way of doing things, to describe surroundings or everyday happenings or to make observations, to tell a story or to otherwise divert and entertain a reader. Yet even if a particular genre of writing is not primarily organized around the staging of an argument we will oftentimes find that sections are given over to argumentation. Even popular entertainment genres rely on argumentation in order to make their point. Take, for example, *South Park*'s classic, second season episode, "Gnomes." The episode itself revolves around the boys having to research current events and to present their results in class the next day. (Sound familiar?[1])

The episode's most enduring legacy, however, is not the plot or the various arguments it presents for and against Harbuck's Coffee, but rather the appearance of what would become a classic Internet meme, the Underpants Gnomes. These gnomes keep stealing all the underpants in South Park as part of a secret business plan, which looks like:

Screencapture from "Gnomes" (Wikimedia)

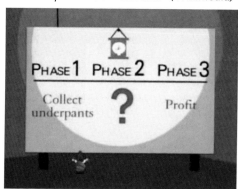

The punchline here, of course, is that the gnomes have no real idea of how collecting all these underpants will yield a profit because they have not formulated a plan of how they will use those underpants.

If you've been following along and actively reading here (as you should have been if you've read Kat and Leah's chapter on critical reading), you should be able to guess what is coming next. Here's the turn...

---

1 Of course they fail to complete the assignment and end up using a presentation written for them by someone else and end up suffering horribly, as all plagiarists do. Let this be a lesson to you all.

Having a Plan

Too often the novice college writer finds him or herself following a plan that looks remarkably like the Underpants Gnomes' business plan. The professor assigns a research paper or an argumentative essay and the diligent student formulates a cunning plan that looks something like this:

Phase 1	Phase 2	Phase 3
Do research; read book	?????	Paper

Without an argument—something that connects your own thoughts or the thoughts of your sources together—you have no way to profit from having done all that collecting of sources. All you have is a big pile of evidence in the middle of your room.

Jackie's chapter on using research should give you some idea of what is going on in Phase 2 so that you have *something* other than a question mark at this point, but putting everything together in a way that makes sense—"*Logos*" from the rhetoric chapter—requires more than just a pile of relevant evidence. You need to understand how to put that evidence together in a convincing manner to show your readers not just all of the pieces of your evidence, but how they fit together, what they build, and why this new information you have built is important.

Writing Tip

Remember the rhetorical triangle from Chapter One—a triangle is delta, and a delta means change. An argument is a way of presenting new information (or old information in a new way or new combination) to an audience in order to build a bridge from their old way of seeing things to the new way that you are showing them.

The Steps of Argument

You might have noticed in the Gnomes picture that the plan has three steps to it. Part of the reason for this is the longstanding tradition of classical argumentation that came into use in the West largely through the influence of Aristotle. Classical arguments are formal arrangements of terms that combine together like a geometric proof to lead the audience from a first step that they agree with through a series of reasoned steps to a new conclusion. The classic example of this is:

Statement 1	Statement 2	Conclusion
All men are mortal	Socrates is a man	Socrates is mortal

There can be more steps in the process and the conclusions can build on each other, but this is the basic idea. As it developed, lots of rules grew up around it as well that you see referred to in guides to argument that use Latin terms like *post hoc ergo prompter hoc* to describe errors in the logic that work like bugs in computer code to break the sequence and keep the argument from reaching its intended conclusion.

While it is good to know the classical method of argumentation, and reading works like Aristotle's can help you to become much more systematic in your approach to thinking through a problem or analyzing what you are reading, it's also fairly complex in structure and requires a degree of formality that you don't often find outside of academic sources. Most everyday forms of communication approach argument more casually, operating on informal rules, loose definitions, and commonly accepted notions of how the world works.

Arguments: Claims Based on Data, Supported by Evidence

Stephen Toulmin, a mid-20th-century British philosopher, came up with a flexible system for thinking about all sorts of arguments without having to get into a lot of technical jargon and details that's rigorous enough to get you through most sorts of college writing that require argumentation. In Toulmin's influential 1958 book, *The Uses of Argument*, he argues that we can outline most arguments as having a Claim based on specific Data or Grounds, supported by further Evidence or other Backing:

> It's better to have a fire axe in a zombie apocalypse than to have a shotgun because the axe is more versatile. It never needs reloading and doesn't make noise.

Hovering in the background of these arguments are many unspoken or unwritten assumptions that the people involved tend to take for granted. Toulmin calls these assumptions Warrants. (The warrants here are that zombies exist, are dangerous to humans, and are attracted to noise.)

Of course, few arguments worth the energy required to debate come without at least one other side that needs to be considered, and for this reason Toulmin also includes two other useful and important categories in his system: Qualifiers and Rebuttals (or Reservations, depending on how you decide it is most useful to frame your argument). We can define these elements this way:

Toulmin's System to Outline Arguments

☐ **Claim (C)**: The conclusion to which the writer wants to lead the readers: the thesis or main point in an argumentative paper. [*For a paper, this is your thesis and not another author's thesis. Their claims become either Backing or Reservations, depending on whether they support or undermine your claim, respectively.*]

☐ **Backing (B) or Evidence (E)**: The examples, statistics, analogies, or findings that the writer uses to convince the readers that they should agree with the claim. [*Bringing in other voices or your own experience.*]

☐ **Grounds (G) or Data (D):** The beginning foundation for the proposition. What the reader must know in order to understand why the claim is being made. [*This is shared between you and your reader. If they don't see and understand these grounds they will not understand what you are claiming. Why are you making your claim?*]

☐ **Warrant (W)**: The more general reasons or assumptions that are associated with the Claim and Data. The premise. [*Tricky, because your audience may not agree with them or you and your audience may not see them because they assume them automatically.*]

☐ **Qualifier (Q)**: Used by the writer to narrow down the claim in order to specify the case in which the claim is most probable or applicable, or to highlight an uncertainty in your own case. [*Are there cases in which your evidence does not apply? Is there disagreement over data? Do we need to keep options open?*]

☐ **Rebuttal or Reservations (R)**: Counterarguments or counterexamples that the writer puts forward on his or her own of necessity or in order to build his or her own ethos as a trustworthy person.

Please note, here, that when we are dealing with evidence in the Grounds, Backing, or Rebuttal, this evidence should always be *Sufficient, Typical, Accurate, and/or Relevant—S.T.A.R.* If the evidence you want to use is too limited in scope or number, too unusual, inaccurate, or too tangential to your claim it will not further your argument and should not be included. If the example or evidence is so cool that you feel your life is diminished by not including it, then either put it in a separate file to use in another work, change your claim so that the example is relevant to the claim, or put it in a footnote or endnote where it doesn't disrupt the central argument but still shows the world just how mindblowingly cool you are.

When it is all put together in one place, Toulmin's system looks like this:

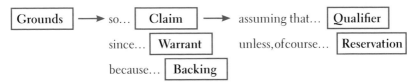

Don't worry if all of this sounds a bit abstract. It's easy to get hung up on the names of the different parts of an argument, or to get distracted trying to figure out how to break down a writer's argument into the different parts above. Truth is, though, that the names are far less important than understanding what we are trying to do with an argument. The most important things to take away from Toulmin's explanation is that we need to base our claim on clear grounds and back it with solid evidence, and that we need to consider and include the exceptions our audience will raise and the situations in which our arguments do and do not apply. Like this…

Argument in Action

Let's go back to the thesis statement about weapons in the zombie apocalypse:

It's better to have a fire axe in a zombie apocalypse than to have a shotgun because the axe is more versatile. It never needs reloading and doesn't make noise.

In it I'm making a claim about fire axes. My claim is that if you are caught in a zombie apocalypse and have to choose between a shotgun and a fire axe, the fire axe is a better choice. I then offer three pieces of backing for that claim.

Oh, crap…that thesis *looks* a lot like a five-paragraph essay thesis. What I need to do here is think about how all of this information goes together and why I might need all those pieces to convince my readers.

First off, while it might look like my thesis has three points, when you look at the structure, you'll notice that the claim is that the axe is a more versatile tool. That's not *actually* three pieces of backing—it's a claim and two pieces of backing for a separate, but related, comparative claim. If I wanted to turn this into an actual piece of writing, one written for a real audience that I can't converse with, I'd need to make the pieces of my argument a lot more clear.

What I am really doing here is imagining a conversation and thinking about all the points that could be made and selecting the most important ones. Why did I choose to emphasize that the axe is quiet and that it doesn't need reloading? What is it about the world of the zombie apocalypse that makes these things matter? That is to say, what are the Grounds on which these facts become important?

> **Grounds:** In a zombie apocalypse world, both stealth and scarcity matter. You can't just go out and buy the stuff you need, you have to scrounge for supplies. Moreover, because zombies are everywhere and they are attracted to noise, you have to sneak around when you are looking for those supplies.

Now that we have those two defining points, we can begin to think about a better structure for this argument. We know that we are arguing about shotgun versus fire axe, so what are the strengths of the shotgun? What makes all your friends go "oooh!" when they think about fighting zombies with one? It's a powerful weapon that does a lot of damage and requires less skill than many other weapons.

So what is a shotgun good for in a zombie apocalypse? You can use it to kill zombies. You can use it to hunt game for food. Drawback? In both cases you make a lot of noise while doing it, and noise attracts zombies. And a shotgun needs shotgun shells to work. Using the shotgun means that you will also need to scrounge more for supplies to replace the ammunition that you use, which means you will need to go to places where zombies gather to get those supplies.

Why is a fire axe a useful tool in the zombie apocalypse? You can use it to defend yourself from zombies AND you can use it to get into places that have been boarded up while you are looking for supplies. More importantly, the axe doesn't use up any supplies in the course of making it work. Drawbacks? One drawback is that it makes noise when you are breaking in. Sure, but you'd need to make that noise anyway if you had to find more ammunition, so you are no worse off than you would be if you had a shotgun. The other big drawback is that the axe can only be used against a zombie if it is close enough to reach you, and that one is not so easy to explain away.

Knowing these things, then, why is it that so many of your friends would pass up the axe for the shotgun? Maybe because they have played a lot of video games or watched a lot of films, and shotguns are more exciting and dramatic than people sneaking around and trying to be quiet.

Putting It All in the Right Order

Now that we've finally got the whole shape of the argument out, we can better see what's going on here and start to put this all together in a way that makes sense both for us and for readers who can't see all the things that are going on in our heads. An outline might look something like this:

1) What most people think a zombie apocalypse is like. [Rebuttal]

  a) Zombies chasing people

  b) People shooting zombies with shotguns

2) What a real zombie apocalypse would look like [Grounds]

  a) People sneaking around trying to avoid zombies

  b) People having to scrounge for dwindling supplies

3) An axe is better in a real zombie apocalypse because…[Claim]

  a) Can be used for more than just shooting things [Claim/Backing]

    i) Chopping things for fires [Evidence]

    ii) Opening doors and containers [Evidence]

  b) Doesn't need ammunition and supplies [Backing]

  c) Quieter than a shotgun [Backing]

4) But an axe is not perfect [Qualifier]

  a) Requires close range to use [Reservation]

    i) True. This is a danger.

    ii) Shotgun may be more effective early on when supplies are more plentiful.

    iii) But the longer things go on, the harder it will become to find supplies and ammunition. [Rebuttal]

    iv) Attracting fewer zombies means having to fight fewer zombies, so the battles should be smaller. [Rebuttal]

This is the outline of a paper with an argument. But what's important here is not that I know all the terms for the parts of an argument, but that I have thought through the details of what my audience believes and why (i.e. shotguns!!!) and have shown them why they need to reconsider, given them an alternative, and shown them when and why that alternative is preferable to their previous thought on the matter. And where I saw potential objections to my argument, I demonstrated to my audience that I had considered alternatives and was being reasonable.

Writing Tip: Audience Expectations

If you know that your audience expects a particular topic or genre to be addressed in a particular way, you should take that into consideration in your formal organization. I started the essay outline above with a rebuttal in order to set the grounds of my argument early on.

If you know for a fact that your audience is going to view your claim with suspicion, you need to work hard to build some common ground before you tackle their opposition and present your own side of the issue.

An argument always needs a claim and backing. An argument with a **complex thesis** (the gold standard of a solid academic paper) will need more than just a claim and backing—it will require some sort of extra consideration of alternative approaches or interpretations along with some demonstration that the writer has weighed these carefully before making his or her claim. Doing this allows us to show our readers why they should consider changing their minds (if we know that we are taking on a common belief) or it helps us to build our *ethos* as a careful and rational thinker (by showing that we have thought of alternatives that our readers may not have noticed or stopped to consider). All of these are good things.

Reading for Argument vs. Reading for Content

In order to argue effectively, a writer must be able both to read and understand other writers' arguments and to produce his or her own arguments. Claims are built out of Grounds and Warrants, and both of those things must be shared between the writer and the reader, so they must be established and agreed upon before the argument begins for the argument to make any sense. This is the argument's history. Whatever Backing, Grounds, or Warrants you use— whether in support of your own argument or as Qualifiers or Reservations to be accounted for in the building of a consensus—you have to understand how they are being used in your sources' arguments before you can use them convincingly in your own. This means reading not just for facts and information that can be used as Backing or overcome as Rebuttals, but understanding how the author of a particular source is using that fact or bit of data his or herself: reading for argument as well as for content.

When reading for content, we tend to scan the page looking for definitive claims, facts, and concrete details that support those claims, and especially for the conclusions drawn from these claims. Most qualitative tests that you are given are designed to check reading comprehension and not critical thinking. If you can identify and remember concrete facts and the conclusions that are drawn from them, you will usually do well on multiple choice and short answer exams. But this method of skimming can create misunderstandings and lead you to misinterpret the writer's purpose when you mistake the role these concrete facts play in a writer's overall argument. What appears to be a definitive statement of facts may actually be a writer's presentation of someone else's backing for a claim that the writer of the current piece of writing is preparing to refute. Mistaking Reservations or Qualifications for Backing can lead you to claim that the writer believes the opposite of what he or she actually argues. Doing this can wreck whatever trust you have established with your reader.

When reading for argument, on the other hand, we scan the page looking for clues that track who is making which claims as well as the writer's attitude towards the claims that are being made. While writers sometimes state these attitudes explicitly within the text as a formal evaluation of another person's claims or evidence, quite often writers use much more subtle clues to indicate their attitudes toward the claim (for example, by using phrases like "While writers sometimes state…, quite often writers…"—I used a Qualifier there). The evidence used in these claims is important, but no less important than the words that the writer uses to link together his or her phrases. We call the practice of using these linking words "signposting" because the words act the same way that signs do to show the reader where the writer's argument turns or takes a detour so that the reader does not get lost in all the details.

Some Common Signposts and Transitions

☐ **Backing** (cause and effect): accordingly, consequently…

☐ **Backing** (related point): furthermore, in addition, likewise…

☐ **Qualifier** (concession): although, even though, in spite of, despite…

☐ **Reservation** (comparatives): conversely, in contrast to, on the other hand…

☐ **Reservation** (evaluative): alternately, rather than, in lieu of…

EXERCISE: MAPPING AN ARGUMENT

Try mapping out an author's argument using Toulmin's system: Identify which sentences function as Claim, Grounds, Backing, etc. Then go through and look at what, if any, linking words and signposting the author used to signal to the reader what part of the argument the sentence functions as.

Building Your Own Arguments: The Rhetorical Situation

Writing instructors talk a lot about how writing a paper is like joining a conversation that started before you got there, and this sense of joining a conversation already in progress holds just as strongly when we are talking about arguments, and especially when we are talking about academic arguments and research papers. As writers, we are never starting from scratch; we are always building onto or branching off of other people's words and arguments. In a way, then, the rhetorical triangle diagrams that we use to think about our relationship to our audience are misleading and incomplete because we ourselves are already a part of other writers' triangles.

Say, for example, that instead of the essay about choosing a weapon for the zombie apocalypse, I am writing a paper about how many modern zombie films play on our fear of losing control of our lives, and to talk about this I am bringing in Naomi Klein as an outside source, using her book *The Shock Doctrine: The Rise of Disaster Capitalism*. Rather than thinking about my paper simply in terms of a single rhetorical triangle,[2] it might make sense for me to begin thinking about myself as the middle point in two (or more) triangles: one triangle to describe my relationship as a reader to the other writers whose voices I will feature in my paper and the second triangle for myself as a writer in charge of providing my own readers with enough context to understand my argument.

The reason that I want to think about this in terms of two triangles rather than one is because my own purpose in writing what I am writing is not necessarily the same purpose that Naomi Klein had when she wrote her book and my own audience may differ significantly from Klein's audience.

I have to help my audience understand both what Klein meant in her own context and how it fits with the new context I am creating in my paper. This might look something like this:

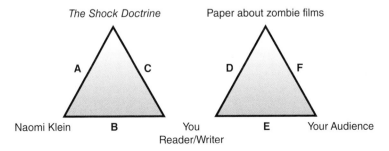

---

2 See Chapter 1, *Why Rhetoric?*, for an overview of the Rhetorical Triangle.

Using two triangles rather than just one allows me to begin to think about how I relate to my sources as a reader and take those things into account when I then begin to add my own voice to the conversation as a writer. My first job will be to lay out how my sources fit with my own argument and purposes (the first triangle).

My Sample Critical Questions about This Source

A. What is Klein trying to tell her audience about how powerful people manipulate us into giving up our own power out of fear? (Logos)

B. Do I believe that Klein is presenting her evidence fairly and accurately? Why or why not? (Ethos)

C. What does Klein do in her book that resonates with my own values and sentiments? (Pathos)

Once I have a good sense of this I can begin to make a much clearer argument in which my own voice in the paper is distinct from the other voices found in my source material (the second triangle).

My Sample Critical Questions for My Own Paper

D. How much of what Klein writes in *The Shock Doctrine* do my readers need to know before they will be able to follow my argument about the appeal of the zombie film?

E. How can I best present Klein's work to my audience in order to show my readers that they can trust my judgment?

F. What part of what Klein writes will resonate most strongly with my own readers while also serving my own purpose in writing?

The other writers who are present in our sources provide us with the material out of which we build our own arguments, but it is up to us to explain how these sources connect to each other and what new tools or perspectives these connections give us to help equip us to live better, and better informed, lives.

When I put this all together, then, what I need to do is decide how I am using Klein in my own paper. If I agree with the parts of her writing that I am quoting or paraphrasing in my own paper, am I using it as backing for my own claim or as a rebuttal for someone else's competing claim? If what she claims contradicts what I claim, am I trying to rebut her argument or am I showing how her claim does not apply in the particular case I want to discuss [Qualifier]? In all of these cases I will need to explain to my reader, accurately and fairly, what she writes and what her original context and intent for writing it was, but once I do this, the way that I unpack it for my own audience depends on how she functions in my own argument and on the signposts and connecting words I choose when I transition from summarizing her writing to furthering my own claim.

- **Backing:** "Klein's discussion of how disaster capitalism stirs up fear and mistrust in order to sell us a sense of security helps to explain why most zombie films include scenes where…"

- **Qualifier:** "Although Klein's 'Disaster Capitalism Complex' gives us a powerful tool for understanding modern, contagion-style zombie films, it does not work as well to explain earlier films where…"

With skill and practice a writer should, in this way, be able to guide the reader through both examples and counterexamples without the reader becoming confused as to who wrote what or which side of the argument the writer is on. The transitions help the reader to keep it all straight.

Exercise—Building an Argument Using Toulmin

Whenever a film, TV show episode, or other piece of audiovisual media recorded in one language gets purchased for use in a market with a sizeable population that does not speak one or more of the languages spoken in the recording, the producers have to decide how to make the material accessible to that population. The main two ways in which they accomplish this task are either to subtitle the work in the other language or to re-record and replace (or "dub") the original spoken dialogue with new dialogue spoken in the target language.

Many people have a strong preference for one or the other of these methods of translation and in some fan subcultures (e.g., Anime) the debates in favor of one side or the other can become quite heated.

Your mission: Construct an argument made out of all of the parts that Toulmin lists in support of each of the two following Claims: [C] Dubbing is better than Subtitles; [C] Subtitles are better than Dubbing.

1. Start by considering when and why we use dubbing/subtitles on video.

2. Consider how each of these translation features work (reading vs. hearing) and for what groups of people these methods either work or do not work.

3. Think about the genres of video for which one or the other of these methods might be preferable based on the purpose or content being shown.

4. Think about Toulmin's model and work to put the parts of your argument together in the appropriate sections (Claims, Backing, Qualifiers, etc.)

Once you have the argument mapped out using Toulmin's model, try writing topic sentences for each step of the argument that include transitional phrases that identify what role the sentence is fulfilling in the argument.

Works Cited and Further Reading

Alexander, Jonathan and Margaret M. Barber. *Argument Now: A Brief Rhetoric.* New York: Pearson Longman, 2005. Print.

Aristotle. *Rhetoric.* Trans. W. Rhys Roberts. Aristotle's Rhetoric: A Hypertextual Resource. Lee Honeycutt and Alpine Lakes Design. <rhetoric.eserver.org/aristotle/>. Web.

Toulmin, Stephen. "From *The Uses of Argument.*" *Teaching Argument in the Composition Course.* Ed. Timothy Barnett. Boston: Bedford St. Martin's, 2002. Print.

Young, Richard E., Alton L. Becker, Kenneth L. Pike, and Carl R. Rogers. "From Rhetoric: Discovery and Change with Communication: Its Blocking and Its Facilitation." *Teaching Argument in the Composition Course.* Ed. Timothy Barnett. Boston: Bedford St. Martin's, 2002. Print.

Writers in Focus: *Dr. Michael R. Rose*

Professor & Director of NERE, Ecology & Evolutionary
Biology, School of Biological Sciences
PhD, University of Sussex, 1979, Biology

For a list of Dr. Rose's publications, go to:
http://www.faculty.uci.edu/profile.cfm?faculty_id=5261

Your book, *The Long Tomorrow*, came out in 2005. How many drafts did you say it took you to complete the book?

More than twenty drafts.

Twenty? Let's talk more about that.

I enjoy writing. When I was an undergraduate at Queen's University in Canada, I wrote for two different student newspapers. I've always written different kinds of material for different kinds of audiences. After publishing four or five technical books, I decided to write a popular book, i.e., a book that I could give to my parents to read. So, I had to convert decades worth of data and math and very abstruse scientific theorizing into a book that a normal person might conceivably read. And that took years of writing and rewriting to accomplish.

Why years?

Everyday language, the way most people use it, is informal, emotion laden, full of contractions, conventional sentiments—and from the standpoint of someone on the Sheldon Cooper end of the spectrum, it's... insane. In good scientific work, you're trying to be quantitative, precise, exact, definitive, in my case massive—meaning, in my lab, we collect ridiculously insane amounts of data. So how to convey what I was doing to a general audience? That was the problem. The reason why I thought that was an important problem to solve was because up until the time I worked on this book, mostly what I worked on was aging. It turns out that a lot of people care about aging.

But also, what had happened to me starting almost 30 years ago, was that my work had become known to the general public. I was really the first person to blow apart the normal limits of life span in an animal. That was the fruit fly that I've spent my career working on—laboratory fruit fly *Drosophila*. I have been interviewed by journalists ever since 1984, over and over and over again, with spectacularly little in the way of general edification or clarification occurring, which is to say I was talking to people with journalism and humanities backgrounds—or sometimes, worst of all, with biology backgrounds—who would then convert what I said into their version of prose adequate to the task.

Which was often not adequate?

Which was almost uniformly not adequate. I decided I would attempt to remedy the situation. Now, having decided on making that attempt in about 2002, I acquired an agent in New York City, and the agent in turn elicited a book auction (which led to a publisher's contract, which, as I later discovered is often the case, was followed by the collapse of that contract and a new editor)—and all through this three-year process of attempting to publish a more appropriate vehicle of communication of my thoughts, I just kept writing and rewriting the book.

The Long Tomorrow is now available through the Oxford University Press: http://global.oup.com/academic/product/the-long-tomorrow-9780195179392?q=The%20Long%20Tomorrow&lang=en&cc=us

Chapter 9

WR 39A: INTRODUCTION TO WRITING AND RHETORIC

By Bobbie Allen

Hello, writers. I'm Bobbie Jo Allen, the Course Director for WR 39A. You could say that writing is what I do for a living: I not only teach writing, but I freelance write, I co-author a fairly popular blog, and I write poetry. In spite of all that written work, I find writing challenging and regularly struggle with it. That could be why I like teaching it, and why I have such an interest in designing the best possible course for you: It's such a struggle, I'd like to make it easier for others. Still, "easier" is a bit of a trick word when it comes to writing; what I might mean instead is "easier to find rewarding." And it's true that if you find it rewarding, you're more likely to get better at it.

Before you get too far in this chapter, a word of warning: this part of the guide won't provide examples of the kind of writing you'll be doing in your WR 39A class, nor will it provide detailed lists of rules and tips. Instead, this chapter introduces you to the course by answering four (seemingly simple) questions:

- What is WR 39A?

- How is my progress evaluated?

- What can I expect to learn from this class?

- Why am I doing all this?

The answers to these four (seemingly simple) questions aim to get you in the right frame of mind for this course—or, to be more precise, to get ready to have your mind changed about writing.

What Is WR 39A?

Each of the courses in the Writing 39 series focuses on a specific set of skills to prepare you for academic writing. WR 39A: Introduction to Writing and Rhetoric assumes you have a certain amount of catching up to do.

This "catching up" can be in a wide array of areas. You may have only learned to write one type of essay, usually of the five-paragraph variety. You may still be struggling with academic English. You may have not yet learned the connection between analytical reading and your own writing. You may not be unable to identify and adapt to different writing situations yet. It may be any combination of these things, or all of the above.

So, your 39A instructor recognizes there's a big job to do in ten short weeks, and has designed the class so you unlearn bad habits, and replace them with good ones.

Where 39A Begins

39A starts from scratch. Your instructor begins with a basic set of reading and writing skills and gradually builds them up until, at the very end of the class, you're ready to take on a complex essay. Each 39A instructor designs and builds their own course, but each class has this gradually building layers of difficulty in common, plus a few other things:

- Your instructor will choose outstanding examples to use as a model for your writing. You and your instructor, as two different readers, will identify the qualities of that text that make it convincing, entertaining, important, and interesting.

- You will imitate those qualities in your own writing, doing what writers have been doing since pen was put to paper—imitating good techniques.

The reason for this is pretty simple. If it works for other writers, it will work for you.

To Survive, You Must Adapt

But first you have to figure out what "it" is. A lot of time is spent in 39A teaching you various tricks of the writing trade. The idea is to learn to adapt your writing to exactly suit the many different situations you face as an academic writer, to be able to shift gears quickly and with confidence. This means you'll need to learn to identify the qualities of style a writer uses, and use them yourself. You'll need to become hyper-aware of not just what a text says or means, but how it says or means it. Your instructor will use a variety of tricks to help you to do so.

- You may be recording your own voice and listening to the playback.

- You might be asked to read your writing and/or the writing of others out loud.

- You may be given assignments designed to exaggerate certain qualities of voice or purposes, like a persuasive argument, a scientific paper, or a poem.

This is because, in your life as a writer, you'll constantly be forced to identify the writing situation and adapt your style to suit it.

Learning to Read like a Writer

Because of this need for adaptability, 39A emphasizes rhetorical awareness. What does this mean, you ask? It means that your 39A instructor is going to teach you to figure out the ways different writers appeal to the reader, based on the purpose they are trying to achieve.

 For additional tips on reading carefully, make sure you read Chapter 3, *Practicing Critical Reading.*

All writers choose from an enormous—nearly limitless—range of options to achieve their purpose. The first step to having a choice is becoming aware of what the choices are. The readings for your class have been chosen for the variety of styles they represent, yet they all address the same question. Our job, as your writing instructor, is to teach you to do the same. You'll need to identify genre, style, the writer's purpose, and audience—and the complex way these things effect each other. It's a chaotic world where rules don't always apply and at the same time precision is key. So, we read the writing of those who have gone before and pulled it off.

You're here not to become an expert in a particular text, though, but to discover the connection between the *style* of the text and the way it conveys meaning. Let me give you an example. This is a limerick:

> The limerick packs laughs anatomical
> In space that is quite economical.
>> But the good ones I've seen
>> So seldom are clean
> And the clean ones so seldom are comical.[1]

It has a very rigid form, with no room for variation or improvisation. To get technical: it's five lines, anapestic, aabba, with eight syllables in the first, second and fifth lines, five syllables in the third and fourth.

The form itself, without any specifics plugged in, is funny, and you can sing it out: *da dah dah du dah dah du du*, etc. Form, in this case, is *imposing* purpose (humor). Imagine what may happen if you tried to write a serious limerick, about, say, death. What would you have to do to make that work? Word choice, punctuation, rhythm—all the rules would have to be bent or broken, even tossed out the window. This is the relationship you need to imagine between you as a writer and the form you write in, no matter what it is; poetry, fiction, personal essay, analytical essay or academic writing, whatever—you are dancing with the rules of style.

Your Instructors Are Writers, Too

Your WR 39A instructor recognizes the difficulty of this challenge; this is because your instructor is a writer, too. In fact, this chapter is dotted with examples of 39A instructors' actual writing. Each of us (myself included, the designer of 39A) have gone through the same struggles you are going through.

We write in many different genres. Some of us are poets, some of us are academics, novelists, social critics, science fiction writers, or reviewers. The examples you'll find in this chapter exemplify that range of styles, even and perhaps especially within a genre. All of us have learned to brainstorm, draft, revise, revise again, pound our heads on the desk, revise again, and turn it in (to a professor, or an editor, or a website reader) for judgment. You may, as a result, get

---

1 Feinberg, Leonard. *The Secret of Humor.* Rodopi, 1978. 102.

sympathy, but don't expect leniency. Writing is hard, and nobody knows that better than your instructor.

- You will not be expected to nail it your first time out, though; 39A is also designed to teach you to learn to improve your writing through revising it. Your instructor will take you through the entire writing process, from your initial ideas all the way through to the final polish.

- The writing process itself is messy and often frustrating. And it's much more complicated than the way you may have learned it: a thesis sentence, and outline, write it, and run a spell check before you turn it in.

- Real writers spend hours in the very first stages of writing following a lot of ideas to dead ends. They revise their work as those initial ideas gain strength; a more focused purpose, a clearer sense of style. Most writers throw out much of what they start with in favor of a better plan, and continue to revise right up to the moment.

What you just read, for instance, was something like the second draft of what I wanted to convey at this point in the chapter. Here's the final version:

- You won't be expected to be perfect on your first attempt, however. The greatest emphasis in 39A is on teaching you *revision*. Revision doesn't mean a quick read-through and a spell check. It means to *re-see*: You'll be taught to learn to think through your writing, and to make your essay more complex, interesting, and precise with each new draft.

- The writing process itself is messy and frustrating. You may feel like you can sit down and come up with a "thesis sentence" and an outline, then just write. Usually, the thesis doesn't come until deep in the revision process, at which point you often have to throw everything out and start again.

- This is why writers spend a lot of their time tracking down bad leads and heading down dead ends. It's a necessary part of the process. Then, when they find the good idea, and have a focused purpose, the real work of writing begins: writing with awareness of purpose, and focusing all the energy of the essay on that purpose.

When I revised this section, I sought to clarify my purpose by connecting ideas more carefully. I also kept my original intent of a casual, yet authoritative voice, but cut some colloquial language. And I included more examples of what I was talking about, so you, the reader, could connect it to your experience. I had to think long and hard while I was revising, and I sought the advice of the editor, Tira Palmquist. Because *you* will be learning this difficult and time-consuming process for the first time, you should prepare yourself for a lot of mental labor.

To help you learn, and accommodate the individual pace of your improvement, 39A uses a unique method called portfolio. Which leads us to the next question:

How Is My Progress Evaluated?

Your instructor will evaluate your progress as a writer by using a portfolio evaluation. A portfolio, simply put, is a collection of work offered for evaluation. You may be asked at some point in your future to produce a portfolio of some sort in order to apply for a job or promotion. A designer may be asked to select and arrange examples of his work. A photographer might produce a portfolio of images that represent the best examples of a photographic style. In 39A, you will not receive a grade until the very end of class, and your portfolio will represent how well you learned the skill of revision.

There are many ways to do a portfolio for a writing class or task. 39A uses a *comprehensive portfolio* method, with a single, cumulative grade. There are a number of important ramifications to this that you need to make yourself aware of right now:

- You can revise all your work up to the day the final portfolio is due. (You will have deadlines for drafts, essays and other assignments—so don't be fooled into thinking that you can put off doing any work until the day you turn in the portfolio.)

- You need to save all your work for this class, including all *significantly revised* drafts, notes, annotations, classwork, or other supplemental assignments.

- You need to keep your work organized from the start, and follow your instructor's guidelines for presenting your work carefully.

- There are no restrictions on how often you revise your work, which means you are completely responsible for your portfolio, and for how much work you put into the class.

- Because there is a direct relationship between reading and writing in this class, you must find your own connections. Stay engaged with the readings, and demonstrate your understanding in your writing.

- The syllabus is your contract with your instructor regarding class policies and expectations. You'll be held accountable for all that's in it, so read it and make sure you understand.

- Ask questions and participate in your own learning—either in class, or in office hours. Questions are expected. If you don't ask, your instructor assumes you understand.

- Save everything, and then save it again.

Portfolio works well for a beginning writing class because you're learning new skills. You will be asked to significantly rethink and revise all your writing, trying again and again until you and your instructor either feel satisfied, or you run out of time (whichever comes first). Because the first essay won't be "averaged" with the score of the last, you won't be penalized for a skill you have not yet learned. Once you have learned it, you can go back and include it in your earlier work, getting more practice, and demonstrating the strength of your awareness.

Your portfolio itself will take the form your instructor has chosen. Some prefer notebooks, some binders, some like online or electronic versions. Whatever form required, take care to stay organized. If a draft with your instructor's comments is lost, it's gone forever. So keep it together.

When it's all gathered and complete, you'll have a comprehensive record of what you achieved in Writing 39A. Which brings us to…

What Can I Expect to Learn from This Class?

If you put in the effort, you'll learn to be a better writer in this class. But this can really be split up into a few writerly skills:

- Learning to be a better reader

- Revising more productively

- Learning to provide feedback to other writers (including yourself)

- Finding a process—to identify what needs work in your writing, as well as what you've done well.

Learning to Read like a Writer

You can expect a lot of difficult reading. It's part of the philosophy of the course design that difficult reading that challenges your intellect will also teach you to push your own writing to new limits. Your instructor has chosen her own way of helping you deal with the difficulty, so in addition to the essay assignments she has designed, you'll have work to do in order to get the most out of the readings *as a writer*. So the approach to these difficult texts is what you might call more *writerly* than *readerly*.

Each of these readings will focus on a question your instructor will ask you on the first day of class—a class problem, if you will. The question will have many possible answers, and provoke many possible approaches. It will be your choice, in the end, how you answer the question.

Revising More Productively

You will also be writing a series of essays that culminate in a "final answer." Each of these essays, including the final result, will go through at least three revisions, although you are encouraged, and are indeed being taught, to do, basically, as many as it takes. You will have the entire quarter to complete all your revisions.

You will not get a grade until the end, based on your entire body of work. But you will get a lot of feedback, and in a variety of forms. Your instructor may email you, write on your draft, provide electronic feedback in some form (such as annotations), conference with you one-on-one, group conference, or chat. You will get similar forms of feedback from your peers.

You can expect, then, to visit your instructor in office hours for personal attention on your draft. You should take advantage of this, and bring your best work with you, along with questions you may have. Your instructor will be extremely generous with her time, so don't miss it.

Learning to Provide Feedback to Others

You'll also learn to provide feedback to others, both on their ideas and on their writing. While this can be very useful to the writer, the real purpose is to get you more comfortable with critical feedback on writing, so you can lift these skills off of someone else, and apply them to yourself.

When you get feedback, you're expected to take it, think about it, and then make your own choices on how to apply it. Even feedback from your instructor should be carefully considered in light of your own writing—the choices you're making, what might have been misunderstood, and why.

Finding a Process

In other words, the reader of your work is responsible for providing a direct and honest response. As the writer, you are responsible only to consider it. Whether or not, or *how*, you take the advice is up to you. Of course, if both a peer and your instructor are saying something should be cut, they're probably right.

You can expect lots of drafting as a result, lots of dead ends and frustrating hours. This is writing. Save everything you do, collect it at the end of class, and present it to your instructor.

For additional tips on finding your own process, read Chapter 6, *Invention and Process*.

You will get an opportunity to explain yourself, however. When you have collected your work at the end of the quarter, the last thing you'll write for your instructor is a cover letter. In that letter, you will introduce your instructor to the work inside, analyze your overall performance and what you learned, and direct attention to specific areas of the portfolio as the best examples of your work in the class.

All of this sounds like a lot of work. Which may make you wonder...

Why Am I Doing All This?

Ah, good question. The main goal for 39A is to teach you to write. In some ways, this is a lot like teaching you to think. As you can imagine, that's not easy.

But in other ways, it's a simple series of steps: Analyze the problem, identify your purpose, gage the audience, tailor your style to the purpose, account for the situation and the audience, and write.

That boils down to two things: awareness and *control*.

You have to be *aware* of what's going on all around the writing situation: What are the conventions and expectations of the assignment? But you also have to be *aware* of your own writing, what works and what doesn't, what needs to be cut and what needs to be expanded. That's where *control* comes in: The more control you have over your writing, the more efficient you can be at achieving your purpose.

Neither one of those things will do you any good, though, unless you know what choices you have, the repertoire of styles (and, by extension, voices) you can choose to write *in* so that you can achieve your purpose.

In 39A, you'll be spending a lot of time on "style." You'll be looking at a series of texts that deal with the class question in different genres and styles. Your job is to, yes, understand what these texts mean, but your real job in 39A is to become more aware of *how* the writer conveys meaning: Not just what a writer says, but how she says it, and *why* she says it that way.

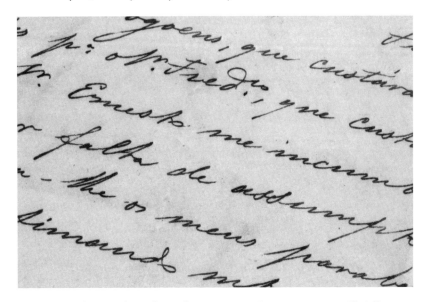

In other words, in order to learn *how* to write, it's necessary to artificially separate *content* from *style*, *voice*, and *tone*.

"But I know what those three things are," you may be saying, "I learned that in high school." Let's just assume that you might know what they are, but not how to use them. So I must request that you ask:

What's the difference among style, voice, and tone?

Glad you asked. It may sometimes feel like your instructor is using these terms interchangeably when it comes to looking at examples in your reading. That's because they are closely related terms.

"Voice" is something individual to the writer, as specific as a thumbprint—no two voices are alike. Your voice involves how you choose to implement your individual vocabulary, attitude, experience, and perspective.

"Tone" is a bit more general. It's the way the writer positions him or herself, attitude-wise, in relation to the subject she's writing about. Tone is attitude.

"Style" is even more general and involves a complex set of relationships. Style is in part influenced by the genre the writer is working with: An academic essay is going to be different than a travel essay, although both may be on the same subject. Style also involves the writer's relationship with the audience, and the devices used to achieve a specific purpose.

Understand, in order to begin implementing these tools, you have to first be able to detect them in your reading. The reason why you haven't is two-fold. You've been given a massive amount of perhaps good intentioned, but arbitrary rules about what *not* to do in your writing. These rules are completely detached from style, and won't help you find it.

The result is that you don't hear style, tone, and voice when you read. Because you don't hear it when you read, you can't try it out in your own writing. In essence, your reading has been like trying to understand a song by just reading the lyrics without the musicians or the inflections of the singer. You have to learn to *hear* what a text sounds like in order to unravel how the writer achieves that effect.

This explains why it sometimes may seem as if your instructor can hear things you can't; you may experience the phenomenon of, "I didn't understand that until I heard you read it out loud in class." When you read silently, to yourself, you're tone deaf.

To give you a sense of the ability to hear a writer's style, it may be useful to look at a set of examples that represent the range of styles available to you as a writer. It seems fair that the examples be taken from the teachers of 39A, their work as writers. We spend the quarter breaking down your writing, after all.

You should know that your teachers were both excited but also reluctant to provide me, the writer and editor of this chapter, with examples of their work. This might indicate to you how universal anxiety is when it comes to writing. Let's begin with a poet.

The Details of Language

No other genre of writing demands more attention to detail and sound than poetry. As a writer, it has much to teach you about the reverberations that a single word choice can carry throughout your writing. It can also teach you the value of detail. This is from Collier Nogues' poem, "In My Father's Airstream Trailer"; pay careful attention to that title, and the way each item in her list evokes not only the scene, but what it is she wants her readers to understand about what she learned there:

The metal walls are hot,
the dog bed dented and smelling like dogs with women's names.

Over ice cream my grandfather and the Old World cousin enumerate
memorial services, then our clan's signature renewable resources:
goat milk, cabrito, the circle of corn growing over the septic tank.

I have a tourist's love of family, of being near the more articulately faithful.

My mother was grammarian, librarian, detention master, expert teacher of
    remedial fiction.

My living uncles are all pastors.[2]

This poem uses specific detail, but in this case seems designed to disturb you. It uses first person, but the sound of the speaker's voice is entirely different: this voice is more deliberate and the use of first person is more slippery and intimate. There are playful tricks with sound, with "c" and "s." The way the words are arranged on the page changes your perception of their importance. This is the effect of genre on style: A poem describing a scene in a trailer is going to be very different from an essay describing a ritual in a temple in India. That may seem obvious to you. But can you hear the difference? And can you identify the differences as deliberate choices on the part of the writer?

Description and Point of View

Poems provide you with a concentrated way to learn about syntax and sound. Fiction writing is the place to go to learn about description and point of view. It's important in good fiction that the voice be consistent and believable. Fiction is a mystical place where you're asked as a reader to crawl inside someone's head and see the story from a particular perspective, like a camera lens. If that perspective is focused on a single point of view, the use of detail is intense. The writer is taking on a *persona*, choosing what, exactly, the character notices and arranging that detail in such a way that it illuminates the character herself—often giving away things about the speaker the character him or herself doesn't even know.

---

2 Collier Nogues. *On the Other Side of Blue.* New York: Four Way Books, 2011.

Anita Fischer's short story "Hana," follows the eyes of a character as they wander across a page of the Koran, lingering over Arabic letters. As the details pile up, they result in a thought, the inner workings of her character, which Fischer conveys with italics.

> I went to my Koran, wrapped in a clean white cloth on the shelf above our sleeping cot, opened it and took out the pages of the poems I'd inscribed so long ago, as my mother had recited them to me. Unfolding them now next to the words of the Koran, I saw that the letters looked the same. *Aleph. Lam.* The soft circle of *meem*, like a mung seed dropping down its stem. The curved cup of noon with its floating tea leaf. The curled *qaf*, like a sleeping baby with both mother's eyes watching over. All the letters flowing one into the next like Farah's fine embroidery, creating sounds, lines of meaning. *Maybe this is the whole problem*, I thought to myself, *the same letters arranged differently are not the words of Allah. They are dangerous and bad. Their beauty misleads, a woman especially, to think about love.*[3]

Fischer's speaker seems to be turning the sound of the letters' names over in her mouth like chocolate. Her savoring of the sound also gives away the writer's affection for her character. This is a very important lesson you can take from fiction writing: A deep respect for the subject you write about can come through to the reader through the point of view you choose.

Things can get more complicated to write when the point of view switches around. You know these distinctions as choices of "person": first (Fischer's choice above, "I"), second ("you"), third ("s/he"). Which choice you make has enormous repercussions for the reader.

This excerpt from 39A teacher Kat Eason may give you a sense of those repercussions, from a short story titled "Ten":

> It is sunset, and the angel stands in the threshold. Black wings spread like panic across the walls, the ceiling, until it fills your house with twilight.
>
> Smoke-skinned, supple as ink. It touches the lintel. Tastes the ruby drop on its fingertip.
>
> And looks at you. At your sister. At your father, who knots his fingers and asks, "Is it done? Is it finished?"
>
> There is blood on the lintel, and it is sunset, and the angel's eyes are pitiless as the noonday sun.

---

3 Anita Fischer, Honorable Mention in *Zeotrope*, All-Fiction Short Story Contest, Joyce Carol Oates, judge.

> You have time for a Yes, papa before your breath shrivels in your throat. Your
> sister screams and begs
>
> I did it, I
>
> but the angel knows only the terms of its covenant: only a lamb's blood can buy
> its mercy, and you are the firstborn. Crisp and crackle, skin and fat and bones,
> only bones, grease and char and ash.
>
> And when the angel leaves, you follow. Dust in the wake of the storm.[4]

Eason is carefully placing her words on the page, taking a lesson from poetic lines. The passage describes the Angel of Death coming for the Firstborn (an episode from the Old Testament). She is using both first and second person, and a third-person point of view that can switch between them, quotes the father speaking, silently quotes the child, but connects that child with the reader in the form of "you." The combined effect is efficiently creepy.

As you gain more experience as a writer and reader, you can identify the effects of these choices and perhaps use them less deliberately. But for now, if you don't start experimenting, you won't ever get comfortable with them.

Character and Voice

Somewhere in between the tonal demands of poetry and the "in character" demands of fiction lies dramatic writing, the work of the playwright. Because plays are designed to be read out loud and seen, no other genre can teach you more about creating an authentic voice than drama. Because characters interact with each other, you can get a very good idea of the way to write emotional expression and how to make distinctions as you write in your own attitude toward your subject. It's an effective way to learn how to *develop* tone within the same essay: You need not stick to the same voice throughout, and indeed you should vary your tone as you write.

This is from Tira Palmquist's play, *Age of Bees*. Because it's in the form of a script, I'm leaving it in its original format. Even this can teach you something interesting about authorial control:

> She goes back to reading, and he goes back to gingerly working out his
> ankle.
>
> JONATHAN
> I haven't seen anyone else. You sure there's some gang of girls up there?

---

4 Kat Eason, "Ten." *Postcards from Hell: The First Thirteen*, Jeff Cook, ed.

MEL

Yup.

JONATHAN

Nobody's come down here.

MEL

Nobody's supposed to. The girls stay pretty close to the house.

JONATHAN

You're here.

MEL

I can take care of myself.

JONATHAN

Yes, you can. (Beat.) Is that my book?

MEL

<u>My</u> book.

JONATHAN

Right. What do you think?

MEL

Good. It's kinda … sad, though, in a way.

JONATHAN

What do you mean?

MEL

Well, here we are: we've kept bees for— thousands and thousands of years.

JONATHAN

Well, it's hard to say that we <u>kept</u> them—

MEL

OK, but … even thousands of years ago, they found them, and took them in, the bees.

> She leafs to the section of the book about the Egyptians, and shows it to him.

MEL (cont'd)

Here. The Egyptians. Did you read this?

JONATHAN

(Looking at the page. Lying.) Not really.[5]

---

5 Tira Palmquist, *Age of Bees*, premiered MadLab Theater, Columbus, OH, November 2012.

There are all kinds of tricks a new writer can use here. Because Palmquist has clear ideas about who her characters *are* and how they should speak to each other, she incorporates emphases on certain sounds in their voices. She uses punctuation to do this—italics (in the form of underlining), ellipses, dashes. She also uses parenthetical stage direction, like "(Beat.)," but also direct interpretation, like "Lying." This means that when you read Jonathan saying, "Not really," it needs to sound like a lie. It's Palmquist controlling all these voices, like a puppetmaster. And the linguistic strings she chooses to pull are designed to have a specific effect on her audience.

While plays can teach you to convey authenticity in the sound of your writing, the easiest voice to write in is your own. This is the "personal essay," the first-person speaker telling a true story. But that's a tricky business. The playwright may be able to get away with writing exactly as a person would speak: "yup," for example, is not an actual word, but is sometimes the way "yes" comes out of a speaker's mouth. For most writing situations, naturalness is more a matter of simplicity and clarity.

Using the Paragraph

This excerpt is from Peg Hesketh's short essay, "Something about Backdrafts." It's important to know this is the very beginning of the essay. The personal essay (in this case, a memoir) can teach you to recognize that when it comes to descriptive details and your purpose, less is more—as long as those details are very carefully chosen and well placed. Consider how Hesketh uses paragraphing here:

> My aunt told me many years later that the fire had been started by children flinging sparklers at the sky.
>
> I don't even know if my aunt's explanation is true.
>
> All I know is that I woke up screaming, the curtains in our one-bedroom duplex a roaring orange lion's head, and my father bounding up the stairs to scoop me into his big bear arms to shield me from the flames that licked angry red splotches on his bare shoulders as my mother fought through the glowing ashes swarming like butterflies in the middle of the room with flames roaring all around us because the bedroom door was stuck. There is something about backdrafts, heat expansion, doors swinging in instead of out.[6]

---

6 Peggy Hesketh, "Something about Backdrafts," *The Independent*, forthcoming.

This isn't "spoken" language, but at the same time, it's not hard to read out loud. The descriptive details are intense and frightening. But Hesketh is also teaching us something about the manipulation of detail. She is an adult, looking back, but also keeping the emotional truth of the memory, which is from a child's point of view. Long and short sentences change the pace. It's jammed with symbolic choices that indirectly convey her purpose ("lion's head," "bear arms," "butterflies"). These animal choices will connect with another detail, a stuffed monkey named "Zippy," that will help her develop her idea. All of this is in perfectly straightforward language. In some cases, paring down your writing means getting out of the way of your purpose so it can shine.

Informing While You Analyze, Analyzing While You Inform

Poetry, fiction, and the personal essay often have strongly emotional purposes. The language they use is designed to make you *feel*. Most of the writing you'll do in college is designed to make the reader *think*, but it's a mistake to think that you can't be analytical and expressive, informative and emotional at the same time. Indeed, the best experiences you have as a reader are when you think and feel at the same time. Often this happens when the writer's purpose is very specific.

I'll use my own work as an example. In this case, it's a travel essay about my visit to a Siva temple in India. Because it's a travel essay, my purpose is to convey the emotional effect of my visit, but also to inform the reader about the things I saw.

> Siva is worshipped here as sky or ether or Emptiness. In the inner sanctum,
> there is literally an empty space for *darśan* with Siva the Unmanifest. There is
> Nothing to see.
>
> But the visual journey to see the *akasha* lingam prepares you for this. The black
> granite of Tamil Nadu that forms the floor, walls, columns and ceiling of the
> inner sanctum absorbs the light from the butter lamps completely, giving you
> the feeling that the walls were falling away from you into emptiness, a black
> hole. Yet the sense is not exactly of boundless space; you can't see the bound-
> aries, but you *sense* they are there by the weight of the air. As the chanting
> of mantras began, the air itself underwent a metamorphosis, from absence to
> substance to metaphor to Siva. Ghee lamps running up the columns and over
> the top of the arch in front of us lit a black curtain. The priest at once pulled
> back the curtain (of your ignorance) so we could see the space where Siva *is*.[7]

You, the UCI student, are not my audience; certain ideas are familiar to my
readers already. Because I know this, I don't have to stop and define terms (such
as the Sanskrit words *akasha* or *darshan*). While I'm describing, I'm also informing. This does not stop me from pulling some tricks from my poetry bag,
or from shifting points of view, or using first person. I am also performing a
certain amount of analysis of the situation, interpreting the visual setup of the
altar in relation to its role in Siva worship and theology—religious theory. My
interpretation requires proof—here, in the form of visual detail. But it can still
be disputed.

Control of an Academic Voice

This brings us to academic writing. Academic writing is extremely useful when
learning about audience, because all forms of academic writing have a very
particular audience: specialists in a field, certainly—often a small group of readers, indeed. For most of your time here, you'll be writing academic essays for a
reader of one: your professor.

This is an excellent example of where that may take you, style-wise. It's an excerpt from Loren Eason's doctoral dissertation about video games:

> The key difference here between this impulse within the context of a novel or
> memoir and the similar moment within a film or video game has mostly to do
> with the flow of time and attention for the audience. Within the context of
> reading a text the reader can, and often does, go back and reread a particularly

---

7 Bobbie Jo Allen, "This Is India!" *Namarupa: Categories of Indian Thought*, forthcoming.

striking or lyrical passage about the beauty of battle and can pause to deliberate over whether the effect is intrinsic to the scene being described or to the
writer's skill with words. Within the context of a film or video game the moment
can be punctuated by the creator, but the audience cannot go back and review
the moment in the same way because these media tend to retain for the creator
a much greater control over the flow of time and the pacing or rhythm of the
work than does a novel or even a poem. Cinema carries the audience along with
its flow, lingering over details that the director wants the audience to notice or
passing quickly on to other things if the director wants to force the audience
forward and not let it linger over the details. Writing can achieve a similar effect, but only through reticence. Within the context of the video game the
forward progress, absent any designer imposed time limit, and lingering over
details is in the control of the player, somewhat like reading, but because so
many events are scripted and triggered this control is never absolute.[8]

There are a number of indications that this is an academic voice. First, there's
a kind of intellectual swagger in this voice, a confidence in his claims. It's pure
analysis, building point by point, developing a claim. You can learn from academic writing the way to present a "thesis" and elaborate on an idea in a complex way that is still interesting and compelling. Eason is arguing that video
gaming represents a shift in control—something of a common thread in what
we've been talking about here. Interestingly, control of his argument is firmly in
his hands as a writer. Academic writing is often very methodical in its elabora-
tion of an argument, and is the most direct in its claims of all the genres.

What Was That Last Question Again?

Your last question turned out to be the hardest to answer. In short, you can
expect to learn *adaptability* and *control* over your writing, but you should look
at the choices you make as a writer as a spectrum, a range of styles that are the
result of the dynamic play among the writing situation, the reader, your own
thinking about the problem, what you hope to achieve.

Good luck in that endeavor, new writer.

---

8 Loren Eason, *Figments Under Fire: Identity and the Transmedial Rhetoric of Combat in
Film and Military Shooter Games.* Diss., University of California, Irvine, 2012.

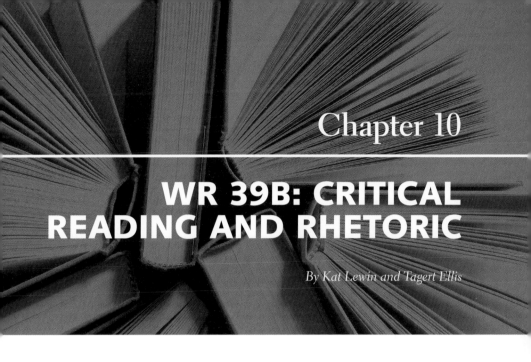

Chapter 10

WR 39B: CRITICAL READING AND RHETORIC

By Kat Lewin and Tagert Ellis

Hey y'all—I'm Kat Lewin! I earned my MFA in Fiction at UCI, and have been teaching Composition here since 2011. Along the way, I accidentally fell in love with rhetoric for the exact same reason I love fiction: it's a way to see the world in terms of choices and the effects of those choices. When I write fiction, I let my characters make a choice (steal that hot air balloon!) and spend the rest of the story exploring the effects of that choice (ugh, your hot air balloon drifted into another volcano?!). Rhetoric works the same way, but with less Grand Theft Zeppelin. As an academic writer, you make choices—like including a credible quote or using a semi-colon or choosing diction that evokes a particular tone—in order to create certain effects on your reader. And then through the process of revision, you can keep tweaking your choices until you've finally nailed the effect you want.

I'm Tagert Ellis. Just like Kat, I earned my MFA in Fiction at UCI, and have been teaching Composition here since 2011. When I'm not teaching, you can find me writing fiction, composing hypertext, playing video games, composing music, laying out websites, photoshopping graphics, closing business deals...oh, have I mentioned that I also make longform video mashups? Some people might say I'm unfocused. I like to say that I'm versatile. While I only get paid for some of these tasks (injustice!), the cool thing about rhetoric is that knowing a few simple principles can make you into a jack of all trades. You'll start to see life as it is: a series of rhetorical situations to which you need to find the best possible approach.

When we say "we" in this chapter, we're not referring to the Robotic Rhetorical Hivemind (RRH)—we are just two humans who love teaching rhetoric because we believe that mastering rhetoric gives people the power to change their own lives for the better. And trust us: there's no better training ground than 39B.

Writing 39B: What Is It?

In Chapter 1, you learned that rhetoric is the art of effectively communicating by accounting for the rhetorical situation of a text: its ethos, audience, genre and cultural and historical context. In Writing 39B, you'll gain hands-on experience in critically reading texts in order to understand their rhetorical appeals, and cultivating your own skills as a **rhetor**: someone capable of successfully communicating in a variety of contexts by analyzing rhetorical situations and using that analysis to make focused, effective decisions in order to best communicate your message.

The work in Writing 39B is likely different from—perhaps wildly different from!—work you have done in previous English or Writing courses. Writing 39B demands that you shift from an imitator to an innovator. In this course, you will take ownership of your writing by defining the rhetorical situations of your writing tasks and using your understanding of those rhetorical situations to make meaningful decisions about *how* you write.

While the number of assignments in Writing 39B is finite, the **rhetorical know-how** you will cultivate in order to understand and master those assignments will give you the ability to better address *any* future communications—formal or informal, academic or personal—as a skilled and confident rhetor.

Writing 39B will equip you with the tools you need to:

- Recognize rhetoric at work in the world around you—it's everywhere, once you see it!

- Actively read and understand different types of texts, with an eye to the rhetorical appeals these texts use to communicate their messages

- Analyze the rhetorical situations of any text in order to help you gain fuller understanding of the text itself and how that text creates meaning

- Take control of your own identity as a rhetor, and particularly master the academic ethos that you will rely upon to enhance your credibility in every step of your university career

- Compose sustained, persuasive argumentative essays shaped by strong reason and expert appeal to the specific audience you aim to persuade

- Master revision so you can become your own best editor, reduce your reliance on instructor feedback, and figure out how to make better choices as a writer, based on the rhetorical situations of your writing tasks

How to Use This Chapter

Over the course of your writing life, and over the course of 39B, you will learn small skills, practice using them, and then when you've started to achieve mastery, be asked to use those skills in new, more complicated ways. We have written this 39B chapter with that idea in mind. Throughout this chapter, you will find we keep coming back to some of the same ideas—but those ideas grow more complicated as the chapter progresses, just as your own work and thinking will complicate as you proceed through the course.

We have organized this chapter in a modular way, to help you build and combine small skills. Imagine the sections in this chapter as small plates—tapas. Get a bunch of them together, and they're a fantastic meal—but they're awesome on their own too. You can dive in and out of sections of this chapter as you please, depending on what you're wondering about at a given moment in time. So, please: be inquisitive, jump around, and make the most out of this chapter, compadre. Olé.

Argumentative Writing: Joining the Conversation

A good portion of the writing in 39B will focus on helping you develop your skills in one specific rhetorical situation: writing analytical, argumentative essays within an academic context, and developing the academic ethos to make those arguments credible.

Argumentative writing, in 39B and beyond, can be seen as an entry into an ongoing conversation. Let's say you're making an argument about why you think it is important to wear pants. Debates have been raging in the outside world for centuries, eons even, about whether pants are a good idea or not. People have written books, made cave paintings, and written lots of angry forum posts about the utility and social necessity of pants. Sometimes they got into fistfights. Imagine this ongoing conversation as a rowdy but refined cocktail party. You wouldn't just barge into the room uninvited and start shouting at everybody about your opinions (or maybe you would, in which case: reconsider the decisions you've made about your life). Most likely, you'd make sure you were invited to the party (by having a personality, or ethos, that convinces people you're going to add to the intellectual atmosphere). Then, you'd find the people talking about pants, and you'd listen carefully to what they say. Only then would you add your own opinion—and you'd communicate it in a way that was relevant to what had been said before.

Argumentative writing is no different. In order to establish yourself as a credible rhetor, you must listen to what has been said about your topic before, acknowledging and understanding it even if you don't plan to directly respond to it. Then you must make sure that your opinion is backed up by evidence—and that it's intellectually interesting and unique (since, you know, you want these people to think you're interesting, so you get invited to the next pants-or-no-pants party).

To insert yourself meaningfully into a conversation, you need to appeal to your audience by understanding that audience's expectations and meeting or exceeding those expectations—and in the case of academic arguments, that means you need to know how to effectively respond to other people's ideas, make sure you have something worthwhile to say, and develop your own credible voice. 39B will help you learn all of these skills.

The 39B Assignment Sequence

Writing 39B's assignment sequence is meant to help you think deeply about rhetoric, craft essays that reflect that deep thought, and hone awareness of your own position as a rhetor in every one of your communications—formal and informal both.

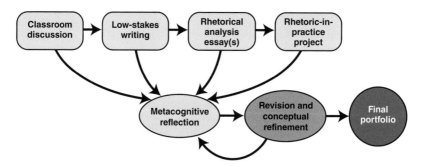

The formal work of 39B begins and ends with the Final Portfolio. Every assignment in the course is designed to lead to this portfolio, which serves as a platform for you to make a meta-argument that you've grown into a sophisticated rhetorical thinker.

This sophisticated thinking begins with **classroom discussion**, which provides the foundation for everything that follows. In-class discussions, pre-writing, and group work start you thinking about the texts you're examining as a class and about your own development as a writer and rhetorical thinker.

Low-stakes writing assignments and online discussion posts will allow you to strike out on your own and focus on building individual skills that you will combine for the major assignments, as well as provide you with spaces for meta-cognitive reflection—thinking about your own thinking.

These discussion posts and low-stakes writing assignments will prepare you for a **Rhetorical Analysis Essay** (or essays): sustained and formal argument about the rhetoric in a particular text. This assignment requires you to collect evidence from a text, build an original argument about the text's rhetoric, and sustain that argument over many paragraphs, assembling a compelling, persuasive essay.

The quarter's final major standalone assignment is the RIP, or **Rhetoric-In-Practice project**. For the RIP, you will produce a text that seeks to achieve a certain purpose while targeting a certain audience. You will write an accompanying RIP Essay that explains, in detail, the rhetorical situation of that text: the rhetorical decisions you've made and how those decisions help you communicate your message effectively.

All major assignments, in addition to other artifacts of your choice, will be assembled into your **Final Portfolio**. You will curate a document that makes a big-picture argument about your growth and mastery as a writer over the course of the quarter. You will compose a rhetorically sophisticated Portfolio Introduction to introduce this portfolio and annotate the work within it, as a way to direct the audience's attention as they read the document and give evidence of your ability to reflect meaningfully and productively on your own writing process and growing rhetorical awareness. The majority of your success in this course will be evaluated based on the success of your Final Portfolio and the revisions it contains.

Why a Portfolio?

Writing 39B runs on the portfolio system. What does this mean? On a basic level, it means that while you will receive constant feedback on your writing and revisions, you won't receive a grade on the majority of your writing until late in the quarter.

Instead of grading your drafts, your instructor will give you targeted feedback throughout the quarter about how your draft can be improved and strengthened—and your instructor will ask *you* to show the initiative to give yourself feedback. You'll use feedback from your instructor, your peers, and yourself to dramatically and fearlessly revise your work: rethinking your positions, rewriting your arguments, and pushing yourself closer and closer toward mastery. By the end of the quarter, you'll have drafted each essay multiple times. You will include the most polished, truly *final* drafts in your portfolio, and only then will your essays receive a grade—one that reflects your effort and abilities as a result of the full quarter's learning.

Looking Towards the Portfolio: The Rubric

Your performance in 39B is predicated upon your instructor's evaluation, at the very end of the quarter, of your accumulated effort and success in the course, as represented by your Final Portfolio and a handful of other important qualities. The Portfolio Rubric that your instructor will use to determine your grade doesn't only judge the portfolio, but also, to some extent, asks how you've been performing all quarter as a writer and as an engaged scholar. Some of the qualities that the rubric asks about include ownership, awareness, initiative, and the ability to meet benchmarks. You should get a copy of the newest Portfolio Rubric from your instructor at the beginning of the quarter. If they don't give it to you, ask them for it—it's a fantastic way to show initiative!

This portfolio process demands a lot of you as a student. It is not enough to write a paper, squeeze your eyes shut, submit it, and pray for leniency. You must look at your work with eyes wide open and be willing to accept constructive criticism. What's more, you must be proactive about seeking this criticism, visiting your instructor during conferences and during regular office hours to ask about your work and how it can be improved. If you don't do this, you're not going to get arrested or anything, but you are going to miss out entirely on the benefits of the portfolio model and sacrifice opportunities to grow as a writer.

It's important to remember that **needing to revise (or even completely rewrite) your essay does NOT mean that you've fundamentally failed**. Do not let it get you down. First off, revision is the hallmark of a brave, confident, intelligent student. It takes bravery and confidence to make major changes to a draft, and intelligence to know where and how those changes should occur. Besides, *every* draft of an essay—even if completely different from the final draft—represents exploratory work that increases your familiarity with the text, deepens your understanding of how its rhetorical gears interlock, and offers valuable practice with fundamental compositional skills. The students who do the best in 39B are willing to revise early, revise heavily, and revise often, frequently visiting their instructors in office hours and the tutors in the Writing Center to solicit feedback that they can use to direct their next revision.

Not every revision will make it into the portfolio—lumping all of your major work in the course together thoughtlessly is not a rhetorically effective means of persuading your audience of your success in the course. Rather, the work you select should be assembled carefully: *curated*. Each page should add to your argument that you've become an effective rhetor, a sensitive communicator. You will write an introductory letter explaining what you hope to demonstrate in the portfolio and how your work reflects your progress in the course.

We will discuss this curation in more detail later in this chapter. In fact, **it might be a good idea to skip ahead to the Portfolio section of this chapter** and get acquainted with what will be expected of you, so that you can keep the portfolio in mind as you approach every assignment in this course.

Throughout this chapter, also keep an eye out for Looking Towards The Portfolio sidebars, which have been designed to help you keep your finger on the pulse of the portfolio and its requirements throughout the quarter, and to help you understand how each assignment builds towards the portfolio.

 METACOGNITION

"Metacognition" is a word that we use to refer to the process of thinking about your own thinking. The root *meta* means "above" and "cognition" is another word for thinking. So "metacognition" refers to thinking that's raised up a level—thinking that's reflexive. This type of *thinking about thinking* is very important in 39B, and you'll be provided with lots of opportunities to practice it.

The Rhetoric of the WR 39B Classroom: Building Skills and Ethos

One of the most important things to remember in Writing 39B is that *you are a rhetor all the time*. Everything you do in the course, from writing assignments to emailing your instructor, represents a form of communication that you have the opportunity to rhetorically shape as you see fit. So, before we even get into the assignments, it might be helpful to think about how *you*, the human behind all of this work, can present yourself successfully to your instructor and your peers. This is a life lesson, dude.

We'd like to encourage you, in this section, to think about how your the success of your written work begins with your in-class engagement—and not just whether you're doing the work (or even paying attention!), but whether you're demonstrating a conceptual understanding of the principles the class asks you to grasp.

Let's get real deep for a second and consider your face as a text. Ha ha, yes, but really—your facial expression (and even your posture) can communicate any number of things to people around you: it can tell them whether you're happy, sad, bored, or engaged. It can tell them if you're angry or dejected. If you come into class in a bad mood, disaffected and sullen, your instructor might just think you don't really care about the material. Maybe that's not what you intended to communicate, but it was what you communicated nonetheless. **You are always a rhetor, and your choices determine your ethos.**

Think of *ethos* as broken into two parts: clout (AKA credibility) and persona. The first part of ethos, clout, involves to what degree (and in which situations) people feel like they can trust you based on your past actions or your qualifications.

In the absence of clout, every one of us has the ability to leverage persona. Persona is the face that we're putting on, the mask that we're wearing. Persona is a performance. You can leverage persona in many ways. No one wakes up one day as a perfect college student—it's a role you imagine yourself into until you master it. In other words, you fake it until you make it. When you send an email to your professor, for instance, you realize that a professional email includes a salutation (Dear Professor...), some social niceties ("I hope this letter finds you well. I have a question...") and a valediction (Sincerely, Derek). Maybe these aren't tools you would use in a casual email to a friend (or a text message to your sister, or a vlog for the senior citizens' home), but they're expected in formal written communication, so you put on a mask for a second and inhabit that role. This persona lets you build clout, and shapes the way others perceive you.

On the other hand, failures of rhetoric can have catastrophic social consequences. Using bad pickup lines can scare off potential love interests, because those canned one-liners don't account for that person's humanity and intelligence. Cursing and using slang in a job application, similarly, represents a failure of ethos. You won't get the job because you didn't understand the rhetorical situation. **Understanding the rhetorical situation of the classroom environment and of academic professionalism means you've taken the first step to proving that you're able to perceive and utilize rhetoric**—one of the major goals of this course.

Ethos and the Final Portfolio

While the Final Portfolio is primarily a venue for you to show off your written work in the course, it's important not to forget all the things that lead up to (and help you craft) that written work. **The Portfolio is an opportunity to assess not only the quality and clarity of your writing, but also your ability to cultivate successful processes for writing and revision.** To create a successful portfolio, you will need to persuasively articulate the skills you have demonstrated in this course: initiative (did you take charge of your own learning or were you merely a passive recipient of knowledge and feedback?), ownership and awareness (did you understand the feedback given to you, incorporate it well, and take responsibility for your own performance?), and how often (and effectively) you sought help and asked targeted questions. So, when you sit down to curate (and write the Introduction for) your Final Portfolio, your written work should not be your only concern.

Think of the Final Portfolio as a meta-argument—a way to persuade your instructor that you've been successful in the course. Your written work is strong evidence you can analyze to make this argument, but your drafts alone do not tell the full story of your growth as a writer in this course. You have plenty of other evidence you can bring in as well. Did you have a perfect attendance record? Did you attend office hours every week? Did you participate frequently and thoughtfully in classroom discussions? Did you otherwise make an effort to go beyond the minimum expectations in contributing to the intellectual culture of the classroom?

Right now, as you read this (and as it is early yet in the quarter), **think about the types of claims you want to be able to make about your own engagement, initiative, and ownership once you finally sit down to curate your Final Portfolio.**

 OFFICE HOURS, CONFERENCES, AND THE WRITING CENTER

You have lots of resources available to help you develop your writing. Among these are your instructor's office hours, the Writing Center on campus (as well as their Peer Tutors division), and regularly scheduled conferences with your instructor. Seeking help in this way is something you should do regularly. The most important reason is that it will help improve your writing. But, as a corollary benefit, imagine your instructor's reaction when a well-mannered, confident student strides through their door, wanting to improve their work without being asked. What a fine ethos you've developed! What a demonstration of the engagement that the Portfolio Rubric specifically calls for!

Using Low-Stakes Writing to Build Rhetorical Know-How

Before you dive into writing a full-fledged essay, you'll hone your skills using low-stakes writing assignments, prewrites, freewrites, and other preparatory work. The key to succeeding in any given task in 39B is to remember that, from participating in classroom discussion to writing weekly discussion posts, **every assignment has its own rhetorical situation**, and the key to your success as a rhetor is understanding that rhetorical situation and using it to craft an effective response.

Before you begin an assignment, fill in the "fishbowl" of its rhetorical situation by asking yourself: What is your **purpose**? What **ethos** are you being asked to adopt? Who is the **audience** and what are their expectations of you? What is the **genre** of the assignment and which conventions of that genre will the audience expect you to follow? What is the **context** of the assignment and which conversations will your work be adding to?

Let's take, as an example, a discussion assignment, where you and your classmates write responses to a central prompt and discuss these responses.

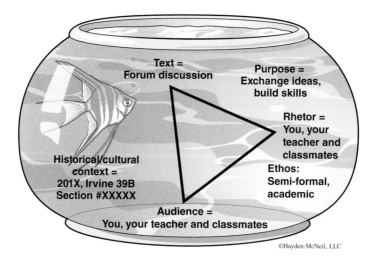

©Hayden-McNeil, LLC

In this particular rhetorical situation, the genre of a forum post demands that you and your classmates (and your instructor) switch from rhetor to audience and back again—participating in a collaborative, reciprocal exchange of ideas which may serve as part of the context for your class's future discussions on the same topic.

Considering the rhetorical situations of assignments will not only improve your know-how as a rhetorical analyst, but will also help you make more effective choices as a rhetor. Just as in-class discussion is meant to help you develop ideas and contribute to the intellectual culture of the class without a fear of feeling judged or called out, so too do these low-stakes writing assignments represent a sort of rhetorical charm school—a place to practice thinking rhetorically about *how* to communicate in a given situation, and then honing the composition skills to do so successfully.

The Difference Between Literary Analysis and Rhetorical Analysis

In many high school English classes, essays require students to perform literary analysis. That process often involves looking at *what* happens in a book (identifying themes, character arcs, and literary devices) and using that information to argue about *what* the author's message is—or, simply, *what it all means*. Details from the text are used to support an argument about the author's message. A diagram of literary analysis might look something like this:

Literary analysis

```
┌──────────┐        ┌──────────┐
│  What    │───────▶│  What    │
│ happens  │        │ it means │
└──────────┘        └──────────┘
```

The thinking and writing that you'll do in 39B represents a pretty big shift in focus. Think of it this way: rhetoric is the art of effective communication. Or, to unpack that: **rhetoric is a series of decisions that are made in order to help a text most effectively communicate its message(s)**. Rhetorical analysis begins when we ask *how* a text communicates.

Rhetorical analysis

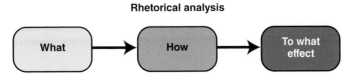

We're still interested in what is being depicted and, in turn, we're interested in what message the rhetor is trying to get across, or what purpose they're trying to achieve. But as rhetorical analysts, **we're most interested in asking *how* that communication is crafted and what effect these decisions have on the way** the message is communicated?

Let's consider, for example, HOW one could communicate the message: "I'm angry." Telling someone that you're angry by saying "I'm angry at you" gets the message across simply and directly. Changing your **ethos** by intensifying your word choice to create a sterner tone ("I'm absolutely furious with you") will change the message, as the recipient now knows that you're not just angry, you're *very* angry. On the other hand, changing the **genre** to a text conversation and using emoji might tell the recipient that you're not very serious about your anger, since you felt that cartoon emoticons could reasonably express it (and you ended the chain of emoji with a rainbow and a bicycle). Changing the **context** of the communication makes a difference too: imagine telling a friend "I'm angry at you" in line at Subway, versus saying it to them as you drive them to a funeral. Changing the rhetorical situation of a message makes all the difference, and learning to spot and articulate a message's rhetorical situation is the first step to rhetorical sensitivity—and to performing rhetorical analysis.

Reading for Rhetoric in a Text

Full-tilt rhetorical analysis of a text is not something you'll arrive at on day one of the course. It takes sustained attention and lots of figuring out. It's very likely that you haven't been asked to read texts this way in an academic setting before. So don't feel bad if it takes some getting used to!

The first step in being able to analyze rhetoric is recognizing rhetoric at work in a text and reading attentively to determine the function of that rhetoric. Chapter 3 has a lot of great tips for how to do this—read that chapter, and read it closely. Once you've done that, read on to get our recommendations on how to effectively read for (and subsequently research) each aspect of the rhetorical situation in a text in ways that will specifically help you build a sustained argument in 39B.

Sample Arguments

Targeted rhetorical reading not only helps you understand a text better, but also prepares you to develop an interesting, complicated argument based on rhetorical analysis. Throughout this chapter, we have included thesis statements from real 39B students who have chosen to make arguments about these aspects of rhetoric. From these examples, you can see how rhetorical reading transitions into strong rhetorical argument.

Reading and Researching for Message

In order to read rhetorically, you must ask: *to what effect* does this text seem to have been written? We need to know *to what effect* a text has been written before we can begin to understand *how* that effect was created, and *how* is the heart of rhetoric!

Good news: there isn't just one "correct" message, which means you're not going to get an F for "choosing the wrong message." Most texts have dozens, hundreds or thousands of messages—some big, some small, some explored throughout the text, and some only emphasized in sections of the text.

Bad news: *thousands* of messages? Stressful. We know.

So how do you find the message you want to write about? There's no single way to go about this monumental task, but here are some ideas to get you started:

- **Ask yourself: What is the text trying to argue here? What does the text seem to believe?** That's really all a message is. You might find on the first try that you come up with a message that's a bit vague or generic, something like "don't judge a book by its cover," or "if you're mean to people, bad things will happen to you." That's a totally fine place to start. Your ideas will get deeper as you continue exploring them through the drafting process.

- **Why do you think that the text has this opinion? Which particular scenes or events made you believe that this message is in the text?** Yes, of *course* you'll have to reread at least parts of the text. Making good margin notes on your first read will save you lots of time when you reread.

- **Does all this evidence 100% agree with your message?** Probably not! You could just ignore all the evidence that disagrees with or complicates the message you want to argue. But ignoring parts of the text just because they're inconvenient is like running a lab experiment and throwing away or falsifying data just because it disagrees with your conclusion. It's lazy and slightly unethical. Plus, if people realize you're doing it (and they will), your ethos goes down the drain.

- **Does the text seem to explain why its message is true?** One good way to start complicating a thesis is to think about adding a "because." *The text argues that you shouldn't judge a book by its cover because doing so will cause you to miss out on important opportunities.* Not perfect but much better, right?

As you think about the text's message, try to figure out which parts of the rhetorical situation help the rhetor effectively communicate that message. Look out for the decisions made about HOW that message is communicated in the text!

Reading and Researching for Medium and Form

Medium and form can seem very simple on the surface, and, in some ways, they are: medium is simply a text's means of transmission, and form involves the structure and style of the text.

When it comes to medium and form, your job as a rhetorical reader is to figure out how your text's meaning is tied to (or inextricable from) the means of transmission and the structure of the text. This task will often involve understanding how to properly *read* the medium and form you're dealing with. Some forms and media share reading techniques. Reading petroglyphs, for example, has striking similarities to reading a graphic novel. Reading a poem shares some of the qualities of reading a rap song. But you must also understand the characteristics unique to each form and medium. While both petroglyphs and graphic novels require you to understand the spatial relation of images on a two-dimensional plane, graphic novels place more emphasis on the sequence of the images presented, and use that sequencing to determine spatial and temporal relationships.

 RESEARCHING MEDIUM

In your research, look for scholars who specialize in a given medium or form, and learn their techniques for effectively reading these texts. For instance, Scott McCloud, a comic theorist, has written a book called *Understanding Comics* that has emerged as the contemporary bible for theorists and analysts (such as yourself!) who seek to understand the ways that visual/spatial/graphical meaning (pictures) and lexical/verbal meaning (words) interact in a comic or graphic novel.

Reading and Researching for Genre

Your instructor may provide readings to help you discuss the genre (and generic conventions) of the texts you're reading, but you may also need to do some of this research yourself. Genre is, after all, just a set of conventions shared among multiple texts. Not every text in a given genre will share every convention of that genre. Not every rap song will feature curse words and misogyny, and not every novel will feature traditional chapter divisions.

First, you'll need to figure out which genre(s) you think your text falls into. Let's say you know that you're reading a horror novel. Well, excellent! You now have two genres: *horror* and *novel*. Are there any others that you think may apply?

Does the text follow conventions intended for romance novels? Does the text follow the conventions of satire? Here's where research can come in handy. You can look for academic scholarship on your given genre—perhaps scholars have traced the lineage of your genre over time or suggested texts that they consider to be prime examples of that genre. Finally, less formalized sources, such as the website TVTropes, can help you identify genre conventions and linked texts (particularly conventions regarding theme and subject matter)—although sources like this (publicly editable as they are) are not sufficiently credible to be used as sources for your essays.

Sample Argument: Genre

In Sherman Alexie's short story "What You Pawn I Will Redeem," Alexie blurs the line between social classes by not only having Jackson conform to the picaresque genre convention of the protagonist's low social status, but also by having Jackson diverge from it. Illustrating Jackson as a respected member of society despite his low economic bracket allows Alexie to offer a social commentary on judgmental attitudes within civil stratification.

If you've identified the conventions of your texts, and figured out which conventions are followed and/or subverted, you are then prepared to begin to ask: *to what effect?*

Reading and Researching for Genre: Guiding Questions

☐ What are the conventions of each of the genres I've identified in this text?

☐ Which of these conventions are present in the text?

☐ Are there conventions of the genre that the text does not use?

☐ Does the text defy (or "subvert") any of its genre conventions?

Reading and Researching for Rhetor

When we talk about rhetor, it's not enough to know *who* the rhetor is—as you read, consider the rhetor's persona and credibility, and how those factors are communicated through the text.

Here are some questions you should ask about the rhetor(s) of a text:

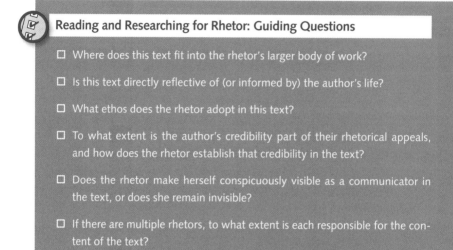

Reading and Researching for Rhetor: Guiding Questions

☐ Where does this text fit into the rhetor's larger body of work?

☐ Is this text directly reflective of (or informed by) the author's life?

☐ What ethos does the rhetor adopt in this text?

☐ To what extent is the author's credibility part of their rhetorical appeals, and how does the rhetor establish that credibility in the text?

☐ Does the rhetor make herself conspicuously visible as a communicator in the text, or does she remain invisible?

☐ If there are multiple rhetors, to what extent is each responsible for the content of the text?

Reading and Researching for Audience

Some texts answer this question for us. If we pick up *A College Student's Guide to Surviving Dining Hall Food*, we know its intended audience right off the bat. Other texts may seem to appeal to one audience but actually be targeting multiple audiences. Consider a television commercial for a children's toy. The **primary audience** of the text is children, and the commercial uses one set of appeals to target that audience (bright colors! sound effects!). However, the commercial must also appeal to the **secondary audience**—parents who have the money to actually purchase the toy—and might target that audience through very different appeals (emphasizing the toy's educational qualities or reasonable price).

When we ask about the audience for a given text, we're actually asking a very complicated question. After all, which audience do we mean? Do we mean the **intended audience** (the people that the rhetor *wanted* to experience the text)? Do we mean the **actual audience** (the people who actually ended up experiencing the text)? Was the audience captive (think political propaganda) or self-selected (think a book at a bookstore)? What about audiences in unintended (or unanticipated) times and places? For instance, was it Shakespeare's intention to force high-schoolers across America to read his work 500 years after his death?

In 39B, when we discuss audience, we're interested in all of these things. Answering each of these questions, and understanding the answers to them, can expand our rhetorical understanding of a text. Typically, though, most of the work we do in 39B tends to focus on *intended* audience. In other words, what audience was the rhetor aiming for, and what choices did the rhetor make in order to appeal to that audience?

The following questions can help you locate the audience of a given text:

Reading and Researching for Audience: Guiding Questions

☐ Who is the intended audience for the text?

☐ How was the audience attracted to the text?

☐ What do the audience's shared concerns, interests, and assumptions seem to be?

☐ How can your questions about the text lead to a more nuanced understanding of audience?

Think about how readers were brought to the text. For example, if you're writing about a story published in a particular magazine: who are the actual readers for that magazine? If you're writing about a specific book, how are readers likely to have learned about the book? (Perhaps it was reviewed in newspapers with certain types of readerships? Or the book appeals to fans of the genre, or of the rhetor's past work?) Research can help you determine who the initial audience was for a text.

Sample Argument: Audience

D. B. Weiss' elicitation of ideals which constitute realities accentuates the allurement of video games in his novel *Lucky Wander Boy*. To a subculture of gamers who identify with the enticement of arcades and a culture that prizes practicality over irrational interests, Weiss published his novel centered on the perfected reality Classic video games embodied as to uphold the apotheosis video games represent. Weiss manifests the perpetual endeavor for quintessence so as to address its unobtainability and the essence of human consciousness.

- **What do the audience's shared concerns, interests and assumptions seem to be?**

Consider the issues that the text seems to think are important, or which concerns and interests might have drawn the audience to the text in the first place. **Often, shared interests and concerns are in some ways dictated by historical or cultural context.** As you figure out the focuses of the text, do research to consider what the initial audience of the text might have known or believed about those issues. Understanding the context of the text can help you develop a meaningful understanding of what cultural conversations the text's audience may have been listening to or participating in. Once you better understand the audience's backgrounds and shared assumptions, you can analyze how the text attempts to appeal to that audience.

Sample Argument: Audience and Context

Although *Pale Fire* portrays Gradus as an incompetent killer throughout the commentary, it is through the multitude of effects Gradus's presence has on Kinbote that the paranoia and anxiety become real. The novel's initial audience, Americans in the late 1950s, is called to experience the feelings of paranoia and anxiety caused by the Cold War and thus to reassess the social environment that they lived in.

That said, **do not base your ideas of an audience's shared concerns or interests on broad stereotypes.** If you say "Western novels appeal to men because men like violence," you're saying that all men like violence. Is that true? Well gosh, of course not. It's actually kind of offensive, when you think about it. It's good to practice spotting overly general claims about audience now, when you're just in the reading and thinking stage, because when you're writing analytically, making overly large, untrue claims about people or society seriously hurts your ethos—it makes you look untrustworthy, or like a shallow thinker. If you take care not to rely on these huge assumptions when you're reading, then you won't be tempted to lean on them in your writing!

- **How can your questions about the text lead to a more nuanced understanding of audience?**

When beginning to attempt to define audience, it is important to remember one thing: **You may not be the intended audience for the text.**

If you don't enjoy a text, or don't understand it, don't assume it's automatically meant for "the audience of everyone who is not me." In other words, what's important is not to use yourself as the master barometer for audience.

Instead of thinking in binaries (ME and NOT ME), think on a spectrum. If a text seems too difficult, don't think: "The audience has to be smart." Ask: "How much more educated than me would the audience need to be to understand this?" or "What specific body of knowledge would they need?" If a text includes lots of biblical allusions, don't just think: "The audience is religious." Ask: "How familiar with the Bible would the audience need to be to understand these references? Does the audience need to be Christian?"

In short, make sure that you're not seeing audience in terms of simple binaries.

Reading and Researching for Context

Historical and cultural context involves the world into which the text was released—the specific historiocultural moment in which the text emerged. Just as no text exists in a vacuum, no rhetor creates their text in a vacuum. Their understanding of the world around them, their concerns (possibly as expressed in their text), their understanding and depiction of social dynamics in their work— all of these things stem from the historical/cultural context in which the text was produced and transmitted.

Basic questions to ask as you read, then, include:

Reading and Researching for Context: Guiding Questions

☐ Where was the rhetor living when they wrote this text? Where was the text released or transmitted?

☐ At what time was the rhetor creating this text? At what time was the text released or transmitted?

☐ Of what culture(s) or discourse communities was the rhetor a part when he/she released or transmitted this text?

☐ What were the dominant social dynamics/hierarchies at the time of the text's release?

☐ What were the dominant societal concerns and debates at the time of the text's release—specifically those that might relate to the content of the text?

For example, let's say you're reading a speech from the 1960s about the need for equality among ethnic groups in America. Without understanding the speech in the context of the ongoing Civil Rights movement, and the debates and societal upheavals that were occurring at the time, you won't have a full understanding of how the text is situating itself in regards to that aspect of its historical/cultural context.

Sample Argument: Context

In *Lucky Wander Boy*, Weiss argues that The American Dream is dead for contemporary immigrants, by conveying the daily struggles of Anya and the Mexican Day Laborers. All of these characters resemble the archetypal, contemporary immigrant: one that comes from a poor background, works at a menial, minimum wage job, and struggles simply to survive. Weiss utilizes their stories as a representation of the broader immigration situation, one that is starkly different than the romanticized version many still believe.

Asking these questions of any text can be difficult if we haven't lived in the time period during which the text was created and transmitted (which we most likely have not, being mere mortals with finite life spans). Funnily enough, though, it can almost be more difficult to ask questions about contemporary texts, since we're living in the context that surrounds the text, and we take it for granted. Helpful questions to ask in either case include:

- How would the meaning of this text change if it were released fifty years later? What if it were released fifty years earlier? What if it were released into a very different culture, a very different economy, or into a society with a very different set of social codes?

Remember also that texts are not produced instantaneously. Writers may spend a decade or longer writing their novel and waiting to get it published—so a novel released in the year 1990 likely reflects the ideas of a writer who has many years of social, cultural, and historical movements resonating in her head as she writes it! And, of course, events that occurred many years before the release of a text can be part of that text's context if those events would have still been resonating in the world into which the text came. Decades after a war, combatant countries may still be recovering from social, political, and economic devastation. And large cultural conversations (like those about race, politics, and social equality) span decades or centuries, gaining complexity and new voices as time passes.

Sample Argument: Context and Genre

Throughout his work, deWitt utilizes the picaresque convention of satire to portray a majority of his male characters similarly with regard to several particular aspects, thereby mocking the societal masculine "standard," while also developing the complexity and dynamism of these same characters in other aspects in order to demonstrate that masculinity is not limited to any specific definition. The obsession with complying with this nonexistent standard ultimately serves as deWitt's primary social critique of the fact that society uses past standards of masculinity to set an unreasonable expectation for men in the present.

Crafting a Rhetorical Argument: Deep Water

Writing an argument isn't the hard part; thinking of an argument is the hard part.

Two of the most common complaints we hear our students express, when it comes time to write a rhetorical analysis essay: "I want a thesis that's easy to argue" and "I suck at analysis."

Here's the thing: if you choose an easy-to-argue thesis—an argument that's so obvious and easy to defend that no one would ever argue that you're wrong—then of course you're having a hard time writing analysis. You've given yourself nothing *to* analyze.

Consider the relationship between argument and analysis.

What Is an Argument?

As you remember from Chapter 8, an argument is more or less the use of evidence and data in order to persuade someone of an opinion. You state the central message you will argue (in the case of a rhetorical analysis essay, that message is your thesis), then you present evidence (in the case of an RA, evidence from the text you're writing about and from secondary sources) that you think supports that opinion. And then—the most important step—you *explain **how** the evidence you presented supports your central claim.*

Pro Tip: Pre-write

You know that terrible sinking feeling you get when you arrive at the end of an essay draft and realize your thesis has totally changed? Or, worse, your instructor highlights a sentence in your conclusion and writes: "This should be your thesis!"? Pre-writing lets you work through your logic and all of your just-okay ideas BEFORE you spend hours writing them with an academic ethos.

Flip to Chapter 6 right now. Use the pre-writing techniques it contains. Save yourself hours of heartache.

What Is Analysis?

The single most misunderstood part of argumentative writing, for starters.

In the context of an argumentative essay, *analysis* of evidence means nothing more than explaining why you think the evidence you presented backs up your argument. If you've written a thesis and have chosen evidence that you think supports that thesis, then you must already have some ideas about why you chose the evidence you chose and how it backs up your argument. Writing analysis just means explaining those ideas clearly and logically, so your reader can understand your thought process behind choosing the evidence you chose.

So if you're walking around worried that you don't know how to write analysis, or your analysis is repetitive, or your analysis is too simple and obvious, or you never know what to analyze—consider: What if there's nothing wrong with your analytical skills? What if the problem is with your *argument*?

Rhetorical Situation: Writing an Academic Rhetorical Analysis Essay

A rhetorical analysis essay is a sustained, argumentative analysis of a text, analyzing the rhetorical decisions that the text made and *HOW* those rhetorical decisions help the text communicate.

Even as you analyze the rhetoric of one text (the core text you are making an argument about in your essay), you are *making rhetorical choices* as the rhetor of another text (the essay itself). As with all writing tasks, familiarizing yourself with the rhetorical situation you're entering will set you up for success as a writer.

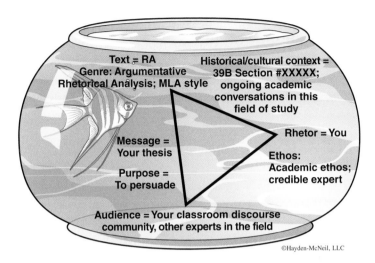

Text = RA
Genre: Argumentative
Rhetorical Analysis; MLA style

Historical/cultural context =
39B Section #XXXXX;
ongoing academic
conversations in this
field of study

Rhetor = You

Message =
Your thesis

Ethos:
Academic ethos;
credible expert

Purpose =
To persuade

Audience = Your classroom discourse
community, other experts in the field

©Hayden-McNeil, LLC

The **purpose** of an argumentative essay (like a rhetorical analysis essay) as a text is to persuade. Persuade the reader of what? In an argumentative essay, your **message** is your thesis: an insightful, sophisticated, argumentative opinion about the text's use of rhetoric. The **rhetor** is you, of course, but a specific version of you—you adopting an **academic ethos**, establishing your *credibility* (through logic and research) and a particular *persona* (of a formal, articulate, academic expert in your subject).

You'll communicate your message to an **audience** consisting of your instructor and classroom discourse community, while also keeping in mind the potential audience of other academics in the field, who might read your essay in order to learn something cool and insightful about the text. To successfully appeal to these audiences, you must consider **context**: both the context of your particular classroom discourse community, and the broader academic context of your paper—keeping track of and meaningfully acknowledging ongoing academic and cultural conversation about the text and subjects that you have chosen to write about.

Finally, the **genre** of the essay is an argumentative rhetorical analysis—specifically, one that follows MLA format. The advice in Chapter 7, and suggestions later in this section, will help you understand some of the genre conventions of a rhetorical analysis. Being able to understand and follow these genre conventions ultimately helps your piece achieve rhetorical sophistication and success, by communicating to your audience that you understand what is expected of you when you set out to communicate an idea through formal academic writing!

Developing Rhetorical Arguments

There is no one way to write a successful rhetorical analysis. If you have been reading your text closely, asking questions, and thinking about *how* the text communicates meaning and achieves it purpose(s), then you are well on your way to developing a successful, effective argument. The following are examples of a few focuses that might help you develop your own rhetorical analysis argument:

Context Argument

A context argument can define a very specific aspect of the novel's historical/cultural context and focus on examining **how the novel responds to, critiques, or otherwise joins an ongoing conversation about culture and society.** Remember that your ultimate goal is to argue about HOW the text uses its rhetorical situation to help communicate its message. Context should help us understand the text—not the other way around. We're not analyzing the world here; we're making an argument about the text.

Audience Argument

Defining a specific intended audience for the text and then analyzing how the text specifically appeals to that audience is one excellent way to frame an audience argument. Alternately, an audience argument might not define a particular audience for the text. Instead, you might argue *how* the text seems intent on eliciting a certain type of response, and what type of response that is, then consider how the text's appeal to audience might support or complicate its other rhetorical decisions!

Genre Argument

A genre argument will typically focus on one or more conventions of the text's genre(s), seeking to identify those conventions and examine how the text's adoption (or rejection) of those conventions helps the text achieve its rhetorical purpose or communicate its message.

Arguments about Multiple Aspects of the Rhetorical Situation

As you develop your rhetorical analysis argument, remember that the elements of a text's rhetorical situations all work together to help that text achieve its effect. For example, as you learned in Chapter 2, genre and audience often work together—a particular genre might appeal to a particular audience, and, in turn, an audience's expectations of a text might be defined by their understanding of the conventions of that text's genre.

Your rhetorical analysis argument may well require that you focus on multiple parts of the rhetorical situation and explain how they work together.

Refining Your Argument: Think *Narrow and Deep,* Not *Broad and Shallow*

All of your thinking has likely given you *many* ideas. The biggest challenge before your write is choosing *one* argument that you can sustain and develop meaningfully over the course of an essay. Make sure you have an idea of HOW the different parts of your argument work together, or else you might end up with an essay filled with small, disconnected arguments about different parts of the rhetorical situation. This scattered handful of arguments may fulfill the page requirement, but it will not create a coherent, successful essay.

Academic writing rewards specificity and depth. If you choose a very, very broad topic ("I'm going to look at every use of every convention of the Western genre in every single scene of the book!") it can be hard to narrow down which evidence will be most helpful to you. If your topic is smaller, you will be able to analyze it more deeply.

Case Study: Birth of an Epic Thesis

Every thesis has to start somewhere! Follow a former 39B student's process, as she came up with what was ultimately an exceptional thesis for a rhetorical analysis essay:

Defining an area of interest: The student chose twenty pieces of evidence from the novel and came to the conclusion:

"Through this process, I learned that corruption is high in a lot of the characters, regardless of age or gender. I think that if I go back and reread some parts of the book that I mentioned in my brainstorm, I would be able to get a clearer picture."

Pre-Writing: The student used pre-writing techniques to narrow her idea further:

"Both the boy at the duel and the intermission girl are examples of corruption in children."

(continued)

Pre-First-Draft Hypothesis: The student chose parts of the rhetorical situation but hadn't yet figured out how they communicated message:

"In Patrick deWitt's novel, corruption is very prominent among the characters; however, it is also apparent in the young children of the novel as well, such as the boy at the duel and the girl in the intermission. DeWitt uses historical context and genre to convey to his readers this message of corruption in children. The message of corruption in children in The Sisters Brothers *gives the readers insight into this societal problem."*

Final Thesis Statement: After several revisions, the student finished refining her complex, rhetorical thesis statement:

"DeWitt exaggerates society's culture of apathy toward what children are allowed exposure to and uses the picaresque genre's convention of a corrupt world to underscore the message of depravity found in children who are negatively influenced by the horrors that they see in their world. Through this message, deWitt gives the reader insight into this societal problem and lends support to the growing culture of recognition that is needed in the world today."

Organizing Your Argument

In the "Drafting and Crafting" chapter, you learned techniques for organizing your paragraphs and the larger shape of your essay. But don't wait until it's time to write your draft to start organizing your essay: as you develop and refine your larger argument, imagine how that argument will be organized in the final essay. Planning the organization of your essay can show you which parts of your argument need further development which will, in turn, give you ideas about how to best divide your ideas into paragraphs and order those paragraphs. Continuing this cycle of organization and argument will allow you to develop and re-conceptualize your argument until it is as sophisticated and logical as you can make it.

The "I Came Here for an Argument" chapter taught you that arguments are made up of *claims* that are supported by specific *grounds* and *evidence*. Using the concepts from that chapter to separate your thesis statement into its claims will allow you to easily see which ideas you'll need to organize in your own essay.

How NOT to Organize an Argument: The Five-Paragraph Essay

A five-paragraph essay is not necessarily five paragraphs long. When we say "five-paragraph essay," here's what we mean: An essay with an intro, a conclusion, and a number of small separate arguments, each made in a single paragraph, that do not tie together to make one larger, more complicated argument.

There are many ways to develop a sustained, complex argument. There is one way *not* to develop your argument: the good ol' five-paragraph essay. **Writing a five-paragraph essay is not a rhetorically effective choice for an argumentative academic assignment** because the format is incapable of establishing the kind of deep, sustained argument required to succeed in the task.

You can typically tell a five-paragraph essay by the thesis—they often include a list of three things. Here's an example from a former 39B student:

In *The Hawkline Monster*, by having a mysterious setting, supernatural occurrences, and female characters in distress, Brautigan creates a true gothic text.

In order to persuade the reader of his argument this writer needs to persuade his reader of the following claims:

Claim 1: *The Hawkline Monster* successfully follows the genre conventions of a gothic fiction novel

Claim 2: Mysterious settings are a convention of a gothic fiction novel

Claim 3: *The Hawkline Monster* follows the gothic fiction convention of mystery

Claim 4: Supernatural occurrences are a convention of a gothic fiction novel

Claim 5: *The Hawkline Monster* follows the gothic fiction convention of supernatural occurrences

Claim 6: Female characters in distress are a convention of a gothic fiction novel

Claim 7: *The Hawkline Monster* follows the gothic fiction convention of female characters in distress

All of the claims are about the same level of complexity, and they interact with each other very little. In this student's essay, each of his body paragraphs used the same organization strategy: defining a convention of gothic literature, then listing examples to show that the novel uses that convention. No individual body paragraph is necessary in order to help the reader understand any of the other body paragraphs.

The logic of a five-paragraph essay is flat: the writer makes a point, then moves on to the next point, then moves on to the next point. While a five-paragraph essay might achieve the appropriate *length*, its format will not achieve superior *depth* in the subject.

Thesis → Claims → Organization

A sustained, sophisticated argument about a text's rhetorical situation will contain a number of claims—ranging from relatively straightforward to very complex—and, unlike the claims in a five-paragraph essay, the claims in a sophisticated rhetorical analysis will build on one another.

For example, check out this thesis statement from a truly magnificent rhetorical analysis essay by a former 39B student writing about the novel *The Sisters Brothers*, which was published in 2011:

> In *The Sisters Brothers*, Patrick deWitt exaggerates society's culture of apathy toward what children are allowed exposure to and uses the picaresque genre's convention of a corrupt world to underscore the message of depravity found in children who are negatively influenced by the horrors that they see in their world. Through this message, deWitt gives the reader insight into this societal problem and lends support to the growing culture of recognition that is needed in the world today.

When we write a thesis statement, we are making a contract with the reader, promising that by the end of the paper we will have persuaded them of our argument. In order to make good on the promise in her thesis, this essay writer needs to convince the audience of the following claims:

Claim 1: The novel exaggerates society's culture of apathy toward children's media exposure

Claim 2: There actually is a culture of apathy toward children's media exposure in the historical/cultural context of the novel (North America, early 21st century)

Claim 3: The picaresque genre features the convention of "a cruel world"

Claim 4: The novel follows the picaresque genre convention of "a cruel world"

Claim 5: The novel sends the message that children who are negatively influenced by horror that they see in the world end up depraved

Claim 6: The particular way that the novel follows the picaresque genre convention of a cruel world helps it send the message that viewing violence leads to depravity in children

Claim 7: The novel's message that viewing violence leads to depravity in children ultimately supports a growing culture of recognition regarding what types of media children are allowed to be exposed to

Claim 8: There actually is a growing culture of recognition regarding what types of media children are allowed to be exposed to in the novel's cultural context (North America, early 21st century)

Once you've sorted your whole argument into all of its small claims, then you can begin to think: What is the most logical order to address these claims in, so your audience is most easily persuaded by this argument and doesn't lose track of your logic?

While we can't give you an easy answer, we can suggest **some good questions to ask yourself, in order to start organizing:**

Organizing a Rhetorical Claim Sequence: Guiding Questions

- ☐ What ideas does the reader absolutely need to understand in order to fully understand your thesis?

- ☐ How difficult will it be to convince my reader of each of these claims? Are there any claims I can persuade the reader of with few examples, or in very little space?

- ☐ Which claims are necessary for the reader to understand and accept before the reader can understand and accept the more complicated claims?

- ☐ Which claims will I probably need to keep building throughout multiple paragraphs?

Let's take these questions and see how the writer of the above thesis statement could use them to effectively organize her essay.

Giving the Reader Context to Understand Your Argument

In order to write a rhetorically effective persuasive essay, you need to appeal to your audience by giving them sufficient background to understand your argument.

The student whose thesis statement you read above cannot effectively persuade her audience if that audience is not given enough context to understand her thesis's key phrases: "culture of apathy toward what children are allowed exposure to," "picaresque genre convention of a corrupt world" (and the term "picaresque genre," for that matter), and "growing culture of recognition."

This student chose to define the genre convention of a "cruel world" in the introduction to the essay. After the thesis, she included a well-researched paragraph explaining the historical/cultural context of social views, conversations and arguments about the connection between children and media violence. **Starting the essay by using expert evidence to define key terms not only helped the student appeal to her audience, but also established her ethos as a credible rhetor.**

Organizing Your Claims to Guide Your Audience Through Your Logic

You can't persuade your reader if you get him hopelessly tangled in your thought process. In our example essay, the reader absolutely must be convinced of Claim 4: "The novel follows the picaresque genre convention of "a cruel world"" before the writer can even start discussing how that convention helps the novel send its message (Claim 6).

Although you may want to race toward the most complicated or interesting claims in your essay, doing so may not be the most effective way to appeal to your audience. As you write, consider your essay from the perspective of your audience and ask: "Have I successfully and thoroughly persuaded the audience of this point?" To you, a small claim might seem too obvious to require evidence and analysis—however, you have thought more about your own argument than your audience has, and **if you don't convince the reader of all the steps of your thought process, then you will damage your ethos as a credible thinker and, as a result, you will fail in your purpose: persuading the audience.**

Emphasizing Key Claims

As you imagine the shape and logical flow of your argument, consider which claims you might need to keep addressing throughout your essay. **In order to credibly persuade your audience of a particular claim, you may need to support the claim using multiple pieces of evidence or by analyzing a single piece of evidence from multiple perspectives.**

In the thesis statement above, many of the writer's claims (and, ultimately, her whole argument) hinge on her successful argument of Claim 5—that the novel is sending a message about the negative effects that viewing violence can have on children. Because this claim is so central to her argument, the student chose to address it in several paragraphs.

LOOKING TOWARDS THE PORTFOLIO: RHETORICAL ANALYSIS REVISION

Every major essay you write in 39B will undergo revision, and since writing argumentative rhetorical analysis essays is a key skill you will develop in 39B, successful revision of rhetorical analysis drafts is fantastic evidence to deploy in your Final Portfolio. You'll be doing, at minimum, two drafts of this assignment, but further revision is welcome and encouraged—attend office hours to get further feedback from your instructor on subsequent drafts, and/or visit the Writing Center and Peer Tutors to get other perspectives.

The golden rule for revision on an essay like this is: *save everything!* We live in an era of bountiful electronic storage capacity, so there's no reason you shouldn't be saving drafts of your work frequently. Any time you complete a new revision, save it as a unique file before you move to the next revision (and back these files up in the cloud). As you put together your Portfolio, you might decide that you want to include multiple drafts, or sections of multiple drafts, to show the progress of your work and of your skills. If you have separate files for each revision, this is very easy to do!

You should also keep copies of the rubrics you receive from your instructor, your instructor's written feedback on your work, and any written feedback (or other materials) you receive from Writing Center or Peer Tutor personnel. You might want to include these materials in your Portfolio to demonstrate engagement, initiative, and your ability to thoughtfully incorporate feedback.

Another way to get ahead on the work for your Portfolio is to take time for metacognition after each draft, and especially after revisions of earlier drafts. After you finish a draft, take a break. Go outside, take a walk, and maybe have a cup of coffee (or simply pass out where you're sitting, because it's 4AM and you've destroyed your brain). Then, sit down and open a new document. Write, without pressure or expectations, a one to two page reflection on how you approached the draft, and especially how you approached the process of revision if this was not your first draft. What did you learn between earlier drafts and now, and how did you apply it? What feedback did you receive, and from whom, and how did you incorporate it (and how did you decide what feedback to incorporate?). What big lessons do you think this paper taught you, and how do you see yourself improving in certain categories on the Portfolio Rubric? If you write these reflections thoughtfully, you will very likely be able to use them to structure your Portfolio Introduction, and save yourself a lot of work at the end of the quarter when things become hectic!

The Rhetoric-in-Practice Project: Splashing Out on Your Own

The RIP (or: "The Cave of Trials")

Now that you've learned how to analyze the rhetorical situation of a text, and used your understanding of rhetorical situations in order to effectively create your own academic writing, it's time for the no-holds-barred challenge: the Rhetoric-In-Practice Project (aka: The RIP). Despite the ominous name, many students describe this project as their favorite of the quarter. It's not because the RIP is the first time that students get to construct their own rhetoric—we hope that if the rest of this chapter has taught you anything, it's that you've been doing that all quarter long, you savvy rhetor—but it's because the RIP allows for almost limitless formal and rhetorical creativity. In many of the assignments you've written in college and before, you've been given very, very specific limitations about what you are and are not allowed to do. For the RIP, you're the one making the decisions. How many of the decisions? *All of the decisions.*

In many ways, this project prepares you for life after the 39 Series. While you may spend a very small portion of your life formally studying rhetoric, you know that every time you communicate, you are a rhetor, and it is your responsibility to understand the rhetorical situation that you enter when you communicate, so you can do so as effectively as possible. The RIP is a way for you to show your know-how and adaptability as a rhetor.

What Is the RIP?

The RIP consists of two sections: Project and Essay.

The **Project** is a text-based piece of rhetoric (related to the theme of your class) that you will carefully construct in order to target a certain audience and achieve a certain purpose.

The **Essay** is a written document that describes, in close detail, all of the rhetorical choices you made in your Project, regarding each aspect of the Project's rhetorical situation, and how those choices contribute to your Project's effectiveness.

By now, gotten used to thinking about the rhetorical situation for each of the different writing tasks you've been given. Take a look at the rhetorical situation for the RIP Project, and see if you notice a difference:

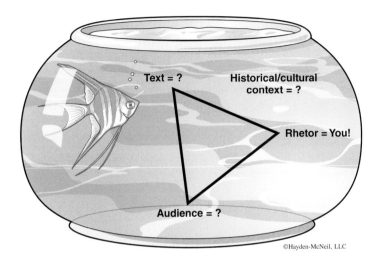

©Hayden-McNeil, LLC

You've probably noticed that the rhetorical situation for this project is *suspiciously empty*. Don't be frightened. Your challenge is to design the entire rhetorical situation surrounding the text you propose to create: you pick the genre, the medium, the audience, the purpose, and the context.

Conceptualizing a Project

In life, the demands made upon us as communicators are rarely as rigid and clear-cut as college assignment prompts—much of your success as a rhetor in the real world depends upon your ability to analyze a broad variety of rhetorical situations and make confident, focused decisions about how to best address those situations. The RIP, then, represents a meaningful culmination of all of the skills taught in 39B: it's your opportunity to apply your skills of critical reading, rhetorical analysis, and effective composition to a free-form project, to demonstrate your adaptability as an everyday rhetor.

The Road to the RIP

Step one: Choose a purpose, audience, and context

Step two: Define genre, medium, and venue

Step three: Research and analyze models

Step four: Compose your RIP project and essay

Step One: Choosing a Purpose, Audience, and Context

The very first step, when making effective rhetorical decisions about a text, is to define your **purpose** and **audience**. In short: what do you want to communicate, and whom do you want to communicate it to? This is the time to get creative and brave. The more unusual your rhetorical situation is, the more difficult decisions you will have to make in order to effectively appeal to the demands of that rhetorical situation, and the more you'll have to say when it comes time to explain your rhetorical decision-making process in the Essay. On the other hand, choosing a rhetorical situation that already exists and then choosing to copy it wholesale will not leave you with many productive opportunities for rhetorical decision-making.

Your **purpose** should be specific and clear. Are you informing? Persuading? Entertaining? **Remember that many texts have several purposes**—after you consider your primary purpose, consider which other secondary purposes might help you achieve your primary purpose!

Your **audience** is possibly the most important part of your RIP project. A nuanced understanding of audience (and the ability to use research to define that audience) can make or break your project. Avoid broad, general audiences ("the public," "men," "scientists,") and get as specific as possible ("single engineers who read *reddit*"). As you move forward with your project, continue to think of ways in which you can further define and narrow your audience, understand the expectations and shared concerns of that audience, and **make focused decisions in order to appeal to that audience's demands.**

Finally, your **context** is very important when it comes to how your text will be received and understood. Is your proposed project going to be released this year? Ten years ago? Five hundred years in the future? Is the culture you are releasing your text into our own (contemporary American) culture? Is it a foreign culture, or an imagined one? What are the values and assumptions present in the context you've chosen, and how will they inform the way that your audience receives your rhetoric? **You need to understand the context of your project so you can determine which ongoing conversations your text will join, and how your text can meaningfully add to those conversations.** Projects taking a past year as their context will benefit from research, and projects taking a future year as their context will benefit likewise from using what we know about today's world (and ongoing trends) to extrapolate what the future might be like.

A NOTE ON AUDIENCE: AVOIDING CIRCULAR REASONING

Since you get to invent the entire rhetorical situation for your RIP, you may be tempted to do a very bad thing. You may have a wonderful idea for a Zombie Cola advertisement.

"Superb," your instructor will say. "That sounds just great. Who is your proposed audience?"

A wily grin spreads across your face and you pull your sweatshirt hood onto your head. "My audience is people who want to buy Zombie Cola."

Your instructor's head has exploded. What's worse is that this type of circular reasoning sets you up to struggle when it's time to write your Essay.

Remember that the Essay asks you to articulate, in detail, why you made the choices you made. The Essay can be seen as a series of implied questions: *How did you use medium to appeal to your audience and achieve your purpose? What was the importance of the context you chose, and how did you work effectively within it? How did you use or subvert conventions of your chosen genre to achieve your purpose?*

So, as you sit down to answer the question of *How did you make your audience want to buy Zombie Cola?*, your Essay will look like this:

I DIDN'T HAVE 2 BECAUSE THEY ALREADY WANTED IT LOL #YOLO.

This Essay is unlikely to receive a high score.

It's important that you develop a nuanced understanding of the rhetorical situation you create, and avoid creating appeals (or a rhetorical situation) that will lead to this kind of simplistic reasoning. This is why an unusual rhetorical situation can work so well for the RIP—you'll need to do more work (and craft more rhetorical appeals) to sell Zombie Cola to impoverished senior citizens on a gluten-free diet than you will need to do to sell Zombie Cola to the Zombie Cola Fan Club (est. 2501 AD).

Step Two: Defining Genre, Medium, and Venue

Once you've determined your audience, purpose, and context, the real fun begins: deciding which medium and genre(s) would be most effective for delivering your message. Which media would most effectively and reliably reach your audience? Where would they be able to find your text? What genre will appeal to them? Once you've chosen a genre, read up on that genre and gather model texts so you can **determine the conventions of the genre and consider how following and/or subverting those conventions will help you effectively communicate your message.**

Finally, make sure you are not underestimating the importance of VENUE: the place your text will appear. **Ask yourself questions about** *how* **audiences will encounter the text, so that you can gather the most helpful possible model texts.** For example, if you're writing a script for a TV show, you might find a venue by asking what channel would the show appear on, and in what time slot. Or if you're writing a blog post: will it be published on Tumblr? On a famous existing blog? Which related websites will link to it?

Step Three: Researching and Analyzing Models

Once you've figured out the rhetorical situation your project will operate within, you must research models that you can use to help shape your text. If you're imitating an existing rhetorical form, venue, genre, or medium, then closely analyzing the rhetorical situations of those model texts will help you understand what audience will expect from *your* text, and how you can effectively satisfy those expectations.

In addition, model texts are invaluable tools for understanding the conventions of the form you've chosen: conventions of the genre, conventions of the medium, and conventions of the particular venue you've chosen. As you analyze your model texts, reread Chapter 2 of *AGWR* to help you spot and track genre conventions of form, style and content.

You can begin your research broadly. For example, if you want to write a newspaper article, you might already know that newspaper articles tend to be printed in column form. But once you gather model texts, you'll realize that it will take a lot more than laying your writing out in columns to create a credible newspaper article—and every paper has its own rhetorical situation, making a series of decisions about content, style and form, in order to achieve its own purpose, for its own audience.

Let's say you decide that *The New York Times* is the best model text for you: it seems to share your purpose and audience, and do so effectively. Now's the time to ask questions about its rhetorical choices. What font does the *New York Times* use, and what effect might that font choice have on audience? (If you're proposing to write an article for the *New York Times*, you'll want to use their font. But if you're proposing to create a fictional newspaper inspired by the *New York Times*, you might choose your own font by deciding what effect the font choice has on the audience, then choosing a font that you think creates a similar effect.) By researching circulation statistics, such as on a website like Alexa.com, you might discover that the *New York Times's* audience is older, more educated, and more wealthy than a median consumer. Look closely at the *New York Times* and try to decide how their diction, syntax, layout, and choice of topics might appeal to this audience directly. What do the articles in the *New York Times* seem to expect their audiences to already know? How explicitly do the articles respond to ongoing conversations in the cultural context? Questions like these will help you best understand the rhetorical situation of your project, so you can act as a credible, expert rhetor.

If you've chosen a more fanciful project—a text that is the first of its kind!—you can still make creative use of model texts to inform your rhetorical decisions.

Let's say you set out to create a commercial advertising Zombie Cola to children. You google "ZOMBIE COLA FOR KIDS COMMERCIALS" and receive startlingly few results. Apart from possibly having gotten yourself added to a government watchlist with this search query, you now realize that there are no model texts in the world that share your exact purpose, audience and message. Instead of looking for something that *exactly resembles* what you want to produce, you can seek out models that can help you with just one aspect of the rhetorical situation you're creating.

In our Zombie Cola example, you might start by finding commercials for other products that are aimed at your target audience: Which rhetorical appeals do these other media use to capture that target audience? What is the effect of those appeals, and why are they effective? Though a commercial for a Pearlescent Pony Princess Playset might not seem to have much to do with your Zombie Cola advertisement, it might be an invaluable model text for helping you better understand one part of your project's rhetorical situation.

Pro Tip: Seek Feedback from Your Audience

As you draft, conduct market research. Seek out people in your life who are used to consuming the type of text you're constructing (your friends who throw Zombie Movie Nights would be a great test audience for the Zombie Cola advertisement) and see how they respond. Or seek out people who are part of your target audience. While their feedback won't be admissible as research in your Essay, you can still use it to gain an outside-the-box perspective on your own work. When you've been staring at the same creative project for weeks, it can be difficult to see every dimension of it without an outside perspective!

Step Four: Composing Your RIP Project

All that's left to do now is to compose your project. If you have a deep understanding of your model texts and have considered at length each aspect of your rhetorical situation, you should be in very good shape.

As you construct your project, you'll demonstrate your rhetorical sensitivity by ensuring that *every* choice you make is purposeful. From font sizes to the placement of the text, from tone and style to diction level and syntactical complexity—every choice should be justified by your purpose, your audience, and the rhetorical situation surrounding your work.

How do you demonstrate that your choices are justified? Why, you write an Essay, of course.

The RIP Essay: Showing Your Work

Successful rhetoric often works so well that it seems invisible. When we try to influence (or, more cynically, manipulate) people, we're more likely to succeed when they don't even know that they're being manipulated. So, if your RIP project is doing its job well, the appeals you're using might seem so natural to your audience that they won't even realize those appeals are present. This is why you write a RIP Essay: to show off all the hard work you put into crafting your rhetoric, and to **demonstrate your awareness of the rhetorical choices you've made**. In this way, the RIP Essay is perhaps more important than the project itself. If we were to fishbowl the RIP Essay, the message you're trying to convey with it is, as always: *I am a rhetorically aware student,* and, in addition: *I am capable of deconstructing my own rhetoric in order to show you that I constructed it thoughtfully in the first place.*

Persuading your reader of this message will require breaking down your rhetorical situation: the demands of that situation (including how you analyzed and came to understand those demands—this means including outside research to establish yourself as a credible rhetor) and *how* you effectively fulfilled those demands. You'll want to be very specific about your purpose and message, and then clearly explain how you achieved them, given what you knew about your audience's shared interests, concerns and expectations. There is room for extensive discussion of genre, medium, venue, form, style, tone, organization, and context. You might also choose to discuss your model texts, in order to demonstrate that you've critically analyzed their rhetorical situations, determined their most effective rhetorical appeals, and demonstrated mastery of those techniques in your own work.

The Final Portfolio: The Ultimate Piece of Rhetoric

This is it: the Final Portfolio, the ultimate piece of rhetoric you will produce in 39B. Maybe you're just beginning 39B and you've flipped to this section to find out what lies ahead (we like the cut of your jib). Maybe it's week 10 and you're skimming this section in a blind, sweaty panic (oh no!). Well, in any case, we're going to do what we do best: break down the rhetorical situation of this bad boy, look at the goals and requirements, and help you think about techniques that will propel you to success.

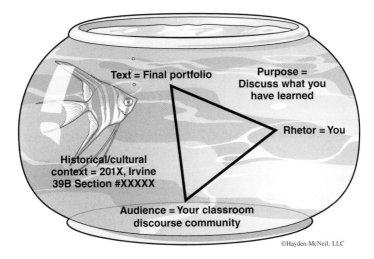

Text = Final portfolio

Purpose = Discuss what you have learned

Rhetor = You

Historical/cultural context = 201X, Irvine 39B Section #XXXXX

Audience = Your classroom discourse community

©Hayden-McNeil, LLC

The audience of your Final Portfolio is the same as the audience of most assignments you have written this quarter: your instructor and your classmates. Over 10 weeks, you should have come to know these people quite well. You should also have become familiar with the specialized terms and knowledge that you share as a discourse community.

You are the rhetor, of course, and the Final Portfolio is the text you're composing. You have a lot of leeway in how you choose to put it together, but in any case, the way that you construct and curate the Portfolio should communicate what you have learned in the course, how that learning took place (using your assembled work as evidence of your development), and anything else you believe your instructor needs to know about your growth as a student over the past quarter.

You should use your accumulated rhetorical knowledge to decide how to best execute the goals of the Portfolio and its Introduction. What evidence will best convince your audience that you've gained the skills you claim to have gained? What tone should you adopt in your Portfolio Introduction and annotations to fit the expectations of your classroom community in this particular situation? How can you provide a richly textured landscape of supporting material to bolster your credibility? The Portfolio is your swan song—the time to bring all of your skills to bear and really prove that you're the rhetor you claim to be!

What to Include?

We use the verb "curate" to describe the way that you put together a portfolio because curation implies thoughtful arrangement and harmony—the idea that all elements of the portfolio work together to persuasively deliver your message.

Requirements for what to include in the portfolio will vary from instructor to instructor, and here it is vital to know your audience. However, we can draw some general guidelines about what you should include in the document. You will certainly include the final draft of every major assignment, but should also include evidence of drafting (both to show your level of engagement in the process as well as evidence of growth from early drafts to more polished work). You will precede these documents with a considered and careful **Portfolio Introduction**, which we will discuss in more detail shortly. You will also find some way to **annotate** the drafts that you include, using these annotations to help direct your instructor's attention to make sure they see what you want them to see and analyze your own rhetorical decisions in your revised work.

There is much space for creativity in the curation of your portfolio, and you may choose to include a variety of artifacts that demonstrate your ownership, initiative, engagement, and awareness, including but not limited to:

- Additional drafts of major assignments
- Low-stakes writing assignments, discussion posts, or freewrites
- Copies of your drafts that your instructor has annotated
- Copies of rubrics you've received from your instructor
- Materials (including written feedback) from the Writing Center or Peer Tutors
- Peer feedback you've given or received

LOOKING TOWARDS THE PORTFOLIO: LOW-STAKES ASSIGNMENTS

Save copies of your discussion posts, low-stakes writing assignments, freewrites, and other small assignments that you complete throughout the quarter. As you assemble your Final Portfolio later in the quarter, you may want to bring in a few of these smaller pieces of writing as evidence of skill development, or as evidence of a way in which you've surpassed benchmarks. You may also find it helpful, after completing a low-stakes writing assignment, to write a short reflection for yourself and save that as well. In that reflection, make some notes about the skills that each assignment helped you to develop. If certain aspects of an assignment (argument, organization, analysis) seem easier for you than they did before, make a note of that too, and try to figure out why! This kind of reflection is fantastic preparation for the metacognitive reflection you'll perform in the portfolio, and doing little bits of it throughout the quarter could save you a lot of time and stress when it's time to begin assembling your portfolio.

The Portfolio Introduction and Annotations

If the materials you present in the portfolio are evidence of your development as a rhetor, the Portfolio Introduction and annotations are the space in which you analyze that evidence to prove the claim that you've done well in the course. Just as you would never put a quote in an essay without taking the time to explain why you've included it (and why it is important), you should not include any written artifacts in your portfolio without explaining how they help demonstrate your aptitude as a rhetor and your success over the course of the quarter.

The Portfolio Introduction and annotations should, ideally, work together to support your argument about your own work, so it makes sense to discuss them together. There are countless strategies for annotation, but what matters most is that you find a way to point out important sections of your work that you'd like to discuss.

One of the main purposes of the Portfolio Introduction and annotations is to demonstrate effective metacognition—that you've been thinking about your own thinking and about your own work. If you've been doing the kind of reflective preparation that was suggested by the "Looking Towards the Portfolio" sidebars throughout this chapter, you'll be in good shape to begin your Portfolio Introduction and annotations, since you will have been recording the development of your own skills throughout the quarter.

As you seek to find a way to convey to your instructor that you've developed the skills that 39B prioritizes, you'll likely want to look at larger-order concerns: effective incorporation of feedback, strong analysis, ownership, initiative, and so on. This often involves using your Portfolio Introduction to directly reference your drafts, and describing sections of the drafts that reflect your mastery or development of these skills. If, instead of looking at larger-order skills that you've developed, you're spending time in the Portfolio Introduction (or annotations) talking about small-scale edits, such as misplaced commas that you've fixed or misspelled words that you've corrected, what message will your instructor take away? Well, they very well might think that you haven't learned very much about what revision entails, and that you're trying to fill up space in the Portfolio Introduction by talking about minor issues.

Be honest with your instructor and with yourself. Your instructor has carefully read your work this quarter and given you feedback on it. Don't stretch the truth when it comes to how you've progressed: if you've dropped the ball in significant ways, don't try to hide it. Acknowledge your shortcomings, and emphasize ways in which you've worked to rectify them. Your instructor wants to know that you've been thoughtfully composing your essays with an eye toward the demands of their rhetorical situations—including this Portfolio Introduction! This is rhetoric about your rhetoric!

Of course, the drafts of your essays are not all that you should discuss: you should also strive to tell parts of the story of your growth as a writer that your instructor does *not* know just from reading your drafts. You should address whatever is relevant about your experience in (and dedication to) the course. Describe the ways in which you've taken charge of your own learning this quarter. Have you come to office hours? Done extra work? Spent time at the Writing Center? Done research you didn't have to do? Revised a paper above and beyond the course requirements?

The most important thing to remember is that **annotations help to direct your audience's attention**. A good annotation tells the reader: "I know that I've handed you a 100-page portfolio, and I know that you've already read a lot of the work in it. I won't make you reread all of it, but please look at this page and this page and this one, because they are important to my argument."

As always, your instructor might have a specific way they want to see your Portfolio put together, or specific artifacts they'd like you to include. But, if you have a creative idea for how you'd like to curate your portfolio, run it by them. The worst that can happen is that they say no. And if they like your idea, you've taken initiative by taking charge of your own learning in order to maximize your potential rhetorical appeal. Basically, you've proven that you know your stuff, and that you care about the work you're doing.

At the end of the day, if you've learned one thing from Writing 39B, it should be this: **all communication is rhetorically situated**—whether you're texting your friends, writing an academic essay, editing a cover letter for your dream job, or drafting the Final Portfolio Introduction here in 39B. And no matter what task you face, the skills that you learn in 39B will help you rise to the occasion by being able to critically read the aspects of a rhetorical situation, then analyzing those factors in order to make decisions that will help you communicate your message as effectively and successfully as possible.

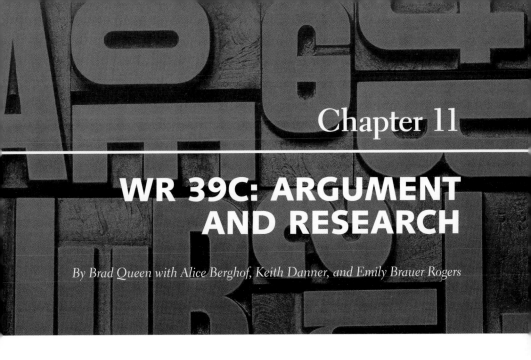

Chapter 11

WR 39C: ARGUMENT AND RESEARCH

By Brad Queen with Alice Berghof, Keith Danner, and Emily Brauer Rogers

This chapter has been written before, many times in fact, in previous editions of the AGWR and before in the Student Guide to Writing at UCI. *Over the years numerous teachers have worked together to write the 39C chapter. Their thoughts linger on these pages, even as this new iteration of 39C recasts them and reshapes the curriculum. The current list of contributors of words and organizational ideas includes Alice Berghof, Keith Danner, Lisa Montagne, Eric Peterson, and Emily Brauer Rogers. My task has been to weave everything together, to synthesize the approaches and values of our teaching community, and to give you a chapter that takes you to the next level as a college-level research writer. Good luck!*

> Education reform. The mass incarceration of African-Americans and institutional racism. Violent rhetoric, obscenity, and hate speech on the Internet, across social media, and in video games. Ethical perspectives on animals. Climate change, resource management, conservation, and the re-design of cities and suburbs. Medical ethics and exploratory science. Upward economic and social mobility for oppressed peoples. Literacy and social change...

Introduction to WR 39C

This list of topics for 39C could go on and on, and it will over the course of the quarter as you and your peers study the various social, cultural, and political problems you see around us today. Your journey through 39C will take you far beyond academic engagement, because at its core this is a course about people and social justice. Your task this term will be to study a social problem in depth, to document and describe its effects on individuals and communities. You'll assemble a body of research to show your readers just how pressing your central problem is today, and you'll locate its historical contexts before analyzing various solutions advocated and debated by experts. Such a rigorous and multi-layered analysis will take you the entire quarter, and all the while you'll stay focused on the people most affected by your central problem, those whose stories need to be told.

On Genre: Fiction vs. Non-fiction

Address these questions in class or in your self-assessment:

☐ What are the differences between fiction and non-fiction as genres?

☐ Why does 39C focus on non-fiction?

☐ Can you list different forms of non-fiction and their differences?

You're probably already getting a sense of the differences between 39C and 39B. They are different, in many ways, but you won't leave 39B behind. The knowledge and strategic know-how you acquired in B—about critical reading, rhetoric, genres, meta-cognitive analysis of your own composing strategies—will serve you well in C as you move into the complicated and interesting world of research writing, as you move from the study of fictional genres into the broad expanse of nonfiction, which is a huge genre that contains many sub-genres within it.

39C teaches you how to become a skillful academic researcher. You'll need such dexterity to locate, select, and then use different kinds of sources, and you'll need various types of evidence to craft and shape convincing arguments, and to answer the questions guiding your research. Understanding *why* and *how* different sources can give you different forms of evidence is a skill called information literacy.

Writing 39C deepens your understanding of rhetoric and communication by teaching you how to conduct research and how to evaluate and use various types of evidence. The reading, composing, and researching practices you'll learn in this course and the various intellectual strategies you develop will help you to succeed in your other courses, prepare you to engage in the university community and in your chosen discipline, and deepen your perspective on current issues and the idea of social justice itself.

Information Literacy

You've learned about information literacy already in the *Anteater's Guide*. What is it?

Here are some questions for you to consider (you might even write out your answers):

1. How is information literacy different from what we think of when we use the word "research"?

2. How does information literacy relate to the broader notion of literacy itself?

Capstone Course

39C is a capstone course, which means it's the culmination of a sequence of courses. As such, you'll put to use what you've learned so far in your previous writing classes and take your learning to the next level. Once you complete 39C, you've satisfied the Lower Division Writing Requirement! Over the course of this quarter, you'll have the chance to generate knowledge about an important and contemporary social problem through research and argumentation. Your research will engage with current scholarship and current debates. At the same time, you'll think alongside your peers, your instructors, and other people within the UCI community as you attempt to convince them that the problem you're studying is important and pressing and the solutions you're evaluating should be taken seriously. Using research and committing yourself to an extended process of drafting and crafting arguments will deepen your credibility as a college-level writer and enable you to take part actively in academic discussions and vital public debates about issues that concern us all.

39C does not ask you to sit quietly or learn passively; it demands that you actively participate in and evaluate academic practices and relevant discussions that shape our cultures and society.

39C TEXTS AND THEMES

Did you know that each 39C section has a central text or a theme? Check them out on our website: http://comp.humanities.uci.edu/courses/wr-39c/

Each core text provides different opportunities that challenge us to evaluate both our personal ethics and the broad spectrum of values that define perspectives of social justice. The arguments and themes from your core text and your research will not tell you **what to think.** You'll need to decide what to argue, what you think, but your texts, sources, and your teacher will give you strategies that show you **how to think.**

When you leave 39C and move on to writing courses in your major, you'll take with you a sense of confidence that you can use the following strategies:

Rhetoric & Composition:

- Recognize forms of rhetorical persuasion and understand the functions of various genres, both academic and non-academic.

- Craft substantive, motivated, and balanced arguments, and use counter-arguments.

- Plan, draft, and revise effectively; develop and skillfully employ a variety of revision strategies that attend to structure, arrangement, pacing, and transitions.

- Read with understanding and engagement across a variety of genres, mediated forms, and discourses.

- Write clear, correct, coherent prose.

- Reflectively evaluate and analyze reading, writing, researching, revising, and organizing processes.

Multimodal Composition & Communication:

- Understand the distinctive rhetorical properties and effects of delivering arguments in written forms, orally, and visually, with particular attention to audience/community, discourses/genres/contexts, and occasions/warrants.

- Arrange, display, and deliver arguments and evidence clearly and coherently.

Research Methods and Ethics:

- Comprehend the importance of information literacy, seen as both the act of researching and the skillful evaluation and use of evidence.

- Understand the definition of information literacy as the ability to discern and critically evaluate source materials of different types, in different media, genres, and discourses.

- Comprehend the communicative and rhetorical intentions of a source and use such understanding to determine a source's value as evidence.

- Learn to locate sources using a variety of tools, methods, and databases.

- Learn research ethics and avoid plagiarism.

Rules of Thumb in 39C: Write to Discover!

☐ Complete all of the ungraded assignments. Embrace the opportunity to make productive mistakes.

☐ Attend every class meeting and participate actively in workshops.

☐ Respond constructively to the work of others and learn to become a fair and rigorous critic.

☐ Talk to your teacher, ask for advice. Go to conferences and office hours. Bring your questions and your insights.

☐ Engage your curiosity and your passions.

HOW TO USE THIS CHAPTER!

The 39C segment of the *AGWR* works together and in close conversation with a number of the other chapters you've already encountered in this book. Your teacher will direct you to specific sections. But you can refer back them on your own and actively consult key strategies and pieces of advice that have already worked for you.

Keep Chapters 5–8 close at hand as you read this one and as you move through your writing process.

Overview of the Quarter

Three major assignments will guide you through the quarter in 39C. They are: 1) The Historical Conversations Project (HCP), 2) The Advocacy Project (AP), and (3) The final ePortfolio (due in that order). You will, however, be expected to work on the ePortfolio over the course of the quarter while you work on and then finish the HCP and while you generate the AP in the second half of the term.

A Tip: Keep the "Meta" in Mind

Remember the definition of meta-cognition from the 39B chapter? Go to page 195 and check it out.

Here's something for you to consider:

Revisit your 39B portfolio and think about how you think you might repurpose specific strategies for the challenges you'll face in 39C.

While the ePort is something quite different from the HCP and the AP in terms of what it teaches you, all three assignments work together to give you a powerful array of communicative, rhetorical, and intellectual strategies. Let's think of the HCP and the AP as the major elements of the writing process curriculum, and the ePortfolio as the major assignment of the reflective or meta-cognitive curriculum. Where the writing process curriculum includes the final and graded compositions of the HCP and the AP, and all of the ungraded assignments you complete along the way—source evaluations, annotations, a research proposal or prospectus, and drafts—the reflection curriculum includes prompts given to you by your teacher over the quarter that ask you to analyze the strategies you're using as you conduct research and invent arguments, and as you draft and revise your compositions. These two curricula work together to teach you how to craft arguments, to deepen your information literacy, and to enable you to understand and master the strategies you use for research-driven writing, rhetoric, and communication.

The Historical Conversations Project

The HCP: a multimodal composition that describes and analyzes a current social, cultural, or political problem and through research locates its relevant historical contexts.

The Advocacy Project

The AP: A multimodal composition (that includes an oral presentation) that develops further the central problem by researching and analyzing possible solutions to it.

Week 1 〉 Week 2 〉 Week 3 〉 Week 4 〉 Week 5 〉 Week 6 〉 Week 7 〉 Week 8 〉 Week 9 〉 Week 10 〉 Week 11

Research & Information Literacy

Throughout the quarter, you'll learn techniques for locating, evaluating, selecting, and using different types of sources and evidence in your compositions. Plan to research steadily, at every step of the process. You'll often find yourself using research strategies as you revise, craft, and deepen your arguments, and as you move from preliminary steps in the early weeks to focused and direct identification of specific evidence for the Advocacy Project in the second half of the quarter.

Your ePortfolio

Your final ePortfolio includes a substantial reflective introduction– another multimodal composition– in which you use selected pieces of evidence to deliver and substantiate arguments about your development as a writer and communicator, and offer a balanced, analytical assessment of your progress over the course of the quarter.

The First Steps

On the first day of class, you'll be assigned the final ePortfolio and the HCP, and given your first writing assignment: A reflective self-assessment. The self-assessment asks you to look backward, inward, and forward as you write this first reflective piece, something that you can use as the first artifact in the ePort you'll assemble and organize over the course of the quarter.

Over the course of the first week or two, you'll work closely with your core text, other readings, and your section's themes for the first time. As you read and engage in class discussion, take note of ideas that interest you and arguments that solicit a reaction from you. When your curiosity is piqued and your emotions engaged, you are ready to articulate your first guiding questions.

Sometime within the quarter's first few weeks, you'll visit the UCI Library and have the opportunity to talk with a reference librarian about the questions you have and how you might begin researching them. These questions serve as the starting points for the first major project.

YOUR SELF-ASSESSMENT

In the self-assessment, you might go back to your portfolio from 39A or 39B, or to reach back even further, to offer some initial thoughts about your experiences with writing, research, and rhetoric, and what you hope to learn in 39C.

Research Tips

Tip #1: Read Widely, with an Open Mind

As you read and explore, write down your questions and your reactions to the things you read. Be mindful of ideas and arguments that make you wonder, or perhaps make you mad. Such reactions and the questions they generate are the first steps toward discovering your arguments. When you begin your research, you will probably have some ideas about what you want to argue, and you will want your essay to support such claims.

LOCATE THE RESEARCH GUIDE FOR YOUR CORE TEXT!

Did you know that each core text in 39C has its own library guide that will help you with your research?

Check it out and explore!

http://guides.lib.uci.edu/w39c

This approach, however, predetermines what you might argue *before* you've engaged with the sources. Remember: There's a difference between a good idea and an idea that is arguable; and the difference comes from the sources. Without sources and evidence, there is no argument. You'll need to push yourself to discover evidence and arguments by finding, reading, and selecting different types of sources—popular and scholarly, for example—that both describe your central problem and give you a sense for what the experts are saying about it.

Approaching your argument with preconceived ideas means you go on a scavenger hunt, picking sources that support your viewpoint and discarding those that challenge or contradict it. You could be wrong. You might have to change your opinions based on knowledge you'll acquire as you research and read.

DISCOVERING RESEARCHABLE QUESTIONS

Write down 3 questions that occurred to you as you did the first readings in your class.

Q: How do you know if your questions are researchable?

Picking only those sources that support your point of view is called "cherry picking," and will probably produce an argument that a reader could dismiss easily because of its inability to acknowledge counter arguments. It would be easy, for example, to find articles supporting my (as yet unproven) hypothesis that Colony Collapse Disorder is caused by pesticides. You could name an obvious culprit: profiteering multinational pharmaceutical corporations that make billions as they poison our ecosystems, land, and food supply. You can see from the rhetoric of the previous sentence that a particular kind of villain is easy to imagine—but such an approach may not be very helpful. Although further research may show that such an assumption is justified, the first task is to get an overview, see where the disagreements are, evaluate sources, and keep an open mind. Conclusive statements come later, after knowledge has been acquired.

Tip #2: Keep Good Notes and Records

One of the important habits you should develop as an academic researcher is to keep track of all your good information and sources. Every time you find a source that you find instructive or valuable, copy the URL or save the URL in your favorites. You can also use tools like *Zotero* that do an excellent job of helping you to organize the research you conduct online. You should also copy and save the keywords you use in various searches.

Tip #3: Look for Academic Sources Early in the Process

Google and Google Advanced Search will help you to find credible sources in both mainstream media and scholarly journals. Such sources can be very useful in helping you show readers that your problem is both current and pressing, and they can help you document people's stories that remind you and your readers of painful and distressing situations. But for an academic essay, the genre you'll be writing in 39C, you'll need to find academic sources that take on the problem with analytical rigor and with scholarly research. These specialized sources are available through Google Scholar and the library's website, both of which give you access to an extensive collection of databases. Your class library orientation will help you become more familiar with these databases and resources available to you.

Academic sources are written by scholars in a particular field for other scholars in that field. This means that these sources are held to a high standard by people who know what they're talking about, and you can trust authors of academic sources to have done their homework. Further, using academic sources lends your own writing credibility. The smooth integration of authoritative, trustworthy, and expert support for your own points is a distinguishing characteristic of strong writing inside and outside the academy.

Advice from former 39C students

"Take your time."

"Don't pick the first source you see. Read it, analyze it, do some background research, then make an educated evaluation of the credibility of the source and how it relates to your topic."

"Try to do some research every day."

"Don't expect to find an excellent source in a matter of minutes. Research takes time! Also, I don't just throw out "bad" sources because even the weakest ones can give you keywords or hints that will lead you to better ones."

"Use sources that would prove both sides in order to strengthen your argument."

Finally, academic sources almost always feature arguments. Scholars develop opinions about their research, and they write academic articles and books to contribute to or change the research in their fields. These academic sources provide not only information, but models for academic argument. As you read them, seek both information and ideas about how to structure and refine your own writing and thinking.

Of course, you should read academic sources critically. You don't have to agree with an author, and you can certainly challenge his or her credibility—especially if you find opposing evidence and arguments in other academic sources.

Tip #4: Remember: Research and Discovery Take Time

All researchers gather some information they end up discarding. It's actually a sign that you're doing a good job exploring if you find yourself pursing a hypothesis and then you conclude later that the evidence you found and the arguments you generated led to focus on more important and telling pieces of evidence. Remember that even if you don't end up using some of the sources you've found, or using them as support for main arguments, the process of finding and reading them has contributed to your journey to becoming an expert on the topic, which then forms a key part of your academic ethos. Be brave and explore when you research and when you write. You never know when that "lightbulb moment" will happen!

The Historical Conversations Project

The Historical Conversations Project asks you to do four things:

1. **define and describe a significant political/social/cultural problem;**

2. **justify and frame this problem** to convince your audience that the problem you're addressing and the questions you're asking are relevant right now;

3. **summarize and critically evaluate conversations and debates** made by credible scholars and organizations about the problem; and

4. **describe the historical contexts of the problem at hand by locating at least 2 pieces of evidence—at least 1 from the past and 1 from the present—**that tie the problem as we see it today to its past.

The HCP asks you to engage with various types of sources that will help you to answer your guiding questions and to describe the problem that sits at the center of your focus.

 A MULTI-MODAL EXAMPLE: "SMOKED OUT"

http://issuu.com/africanhair/docs/national_geographic_usa_2014-08/c/suqy8vi

Another purpose of the HCP is to begin the process of teaching you how to locate, evaluate, select, arrange, and integrate sources into a multi-modal composition. As a genre of communication—and in the case of this assignment, one that frames a problem, delivers arguments, uses evidence, and speaks to a broad audience—a multimodal composition can be a synthesis of various rhetorical positions—visual and written for example—that work together to deepen argumentative positions and claims.

Do you see the URL in the box on the previous page? Type in the URL on your computer to go to an instructive example of a multimodal composition that frames a contemporary problem and engages in a historical conversation.

This piece is called "Smoked Out," and it was published in the August 2014 edition of *National Geographic*. While you are not being asked to create something exactly like this, and your HCP will contain much more textual argumentation than you see here, this example instructs you in a number of ways.

Remember Ch. 5 "Finding Sources: Discovery"?

The "Finding Sources" chapter gives you very good advice for discovering and evaluating key sources, entering scholarly conversations, and framing questions to guide your research. Check out pages 79–98.

It articulates clearly the problem at hand in the explanatory paragraph: "Smokeless options like e-cigarettes—their safety is not yet known, but federal regulation is pending—could be less harmful." Note the analytical question implied by the word "could," and the guiding question about health concerns invited by clause, "their safety is not yet known." Were this an academic composition like the one you have been challenged to create, you would be expected to flesh out the debate or the conversation among experts about whether smokeless cigarettes may or may not be a less harmful substitute for traditional combustible cigarettes.

Also take note of the historical conversation going on between the central problem and its guiding question and the historical context articulated by the use of various historical artifacts delivered in multiple modes. There's the visual advertisement of the medical doctor advocating the health benefits of cigarette smoking, the graphical depiction of the timeline documenting the recent history of cigarette consumption, and then there's the textual description with the phrase, "We've come a long way, baby." Lastly, think about the way the various pieces of evidence are arranged on this page, and how such an arrangement creates an effective synthesis, a composition, that argues in various modes, here visual, graphical, and textual. You can do these same things in your HCP, even if your composition will ultimately look quite different because you are writing, researching, and composing according the expectations of academic conventions.

LOOKING FOR HISTORICAL CONTEXT

Google the phrase, "We've come a long way baby." First, determine the credibility of the web location you're reading. If it's credible, continue reading. Next, figure out what the results tell you about the historical context of the problem articulated in the "Smoked Out" composition?

A question: Can you describe the rhetorical purposes of this phrase in the "Smoked Out" composition?

Try This

1. Choose a keyword or phrase from the sources you are currently working with and conduct research to figure out its historical context. You'll probably have to try various words and combinations of words.

2. After you've searched by using at least 3 different examples, try to answer the following questions in a short reflective analysis:

   • Which keyword searches helped you to discover historical context and why?

   • Why did you choose these particular keywords, and did you make such a choice by understanding the rhetorical context in which you found these keywords?

Questions to Keep in Mind as You Work on the HCP

As you move through the HCP's writing and research process, here are a few questions for you to keep in mind. (You might even write reflectively in response to them.)

• What are the differences between background information and the history of your central problem?

• Locate the historical elements of your HCP. How do they function in your composition to support your description of the problem and your attempt to persuade readers that the problem you're addressing is current, important and pressing?

• What specific aspects of your historical evidence make it historical? Is it far enough back in time to be considered historical? Does it represent significant and meaningful historical changes?

- What are your credible sources saying about your historical evidence?

- How is your historical evidence different from your contemporary evidence? Why are they different? Are they too different to speak to each other to capture historical changes?

- What arguments are you using from my scholarly sources and contemporary research to explain the historical relationship between your two bodies/pieces of evidence?

- What does your thesis look like in the HCP? How has it changed over the course of the process of discovering your guiding questions and your arguments? Is your thesis a rich and descriptive summary of your composition's central problem, one that justifies its contemporary importance?

- How many different types of evidence do you use in your HCP? Can you list these types and describe how they function differently in your composition?

- Explain how the arrangement of your evidence works. Why have you chosen to arrange your multi-modal evidence in the way you have, and how does this arrangement contribute to narrative cohesion and flow, argumentative effectiveness, and analytical depth?

An Interlude on Multimodality

Multimodality sits at the center of all the assignments in 39C. It will help you define your research topics and your guiding questions. It will help you arrange your evidence, develop your arguments, and alter the course of your research. It will deepen and enrich your argumentative style and your rhetorical strategies, both when you write and when you deliver your ideas orally and visually in a presentation to your class.

Multimodality

☐ What examples of multimodality are you using in your class?

☐ What forms of visual evidence are you using in your compositions? Why did you choose these specific pieces of evidence?

☐ What sorts of "artifacts" are you selecting for your ePortfolio? Why are they meaningful to you?

Don't wait until the last minute to find multimodal evidence to experiment with in your drafts and as you assemble your ePortfolio. As you make a case for a problem or a solution or for your learning in your ePort, use your evidence in multi-modal ways to articulate claims and arguments that words alone can't convey. Think about how a video clip, for example, could elicit an important emotional response in your readers; demonstrate to your readers visually striking inequalities that emerge most forcefully in graphs, diagrams, or photographs. When it comes to writing about your own writing, take a multi-modal approach to documenting and analyzing your writing process by taking screen shots of your drafts and the comments you've received from your teacher or your peers, or by using digital photographs of your notes, outlines, and books.

Take a look at the example below from a student's composition. Here you'll see a student summarizing important evidence in a piece about the hot-button issue of net neutrality that advocates government regulation of the Internet in order to give everyone access to publicly beneficial information. What's interesting about this example is that the visual element is a "textual" example that accompanies and deepens the central narrative presentation but does not interrupt it. Notice that the main text interprets the material set aside in the bracketed box by using short and selected elements from it, and that the aside presents contextual information around the selected elements that the reader can choose to pause and read thoroughly.

An Example from a Student's Composition

In 1996, the Rehnquist Court dealt with the question of whether the Communications Decency Act violated the First and Fifth Amendments as the act was broad and vague in defining "indecent" material. The Court ruled unanimously in favor of the ACLU and the First Amendment; in other words, the Court ruled that the First Amendment was violated because the Decency Act enacted "content-based blanket restrictions"—the Act did not define "indecent" material, show that adults would not be impacted, or demonstrate that the "offensive" material had no inherent social value (*Reno v. ACLU*). More important to the matter at hand, net neutrality, is that *Reno* represents the Court's first direct involvement with Internet regulation (Bagwell 137).

Justice Stevens delivers the Court opinion, emphasizing its belief that the Internet is "a unique and wholly new medium of worldwide communication" and is "located in no particular geographical location but available to anyone, anywhere in the world, with access to the Internet" (*Reno v. ACLU*). Additionally, Stevens illustrates how no single organization can control membership and how no "single central" point from a Website or service may be blocked. Thus, it can now be argued that network neutrality's aim—to prevent any single ISP from controlling the Internet's membership and discriminately "censor" websites or services at their discretion, through blocking or throttling outgoing bandwidth—rings synonymously with Justice Steven's thoughts.

From the publishers' point of view, it [the Internet] constitutes a vast platform from which to address and hear from a world-wide audience of millions of readers, viewers, researchers, and buyers. Any person or organization with a computer connected to the Internet can "publish" information. Publishers include government agencies, educational institutions, commercial entities, advocacy groups, and individuals... "No single organization controls any membership in the Web, nor is there any centralized point from which individual Web sites or services can be blocked from the Web." —Justice John Paul Stevens, Majority Opinion, *Reno v. ACLU*.

Questions to Ask

- What other forms of evidence can be used like the quote in the example?

- How is this use of a quote different in its rhetorical effect from quoted material integrated into the flow of the argument on the sentence level?

- How is this use of a quote different in its rhetorical effect from a quote used as a block quote?

- Can you compare your use of multi-modal elements to this example and to "Smoked Out"?

An ePortfolio Moment

☐ You can use your responses to the preceding questions as material for your ePortfolio by capturing screenshots of your use of multi-modality and then by comparing your use to the examples, both textually and visually.

☐ A number of other chapters in the *Anteater's Guide* relate directly to 39C. What have you read so far? How have the strategies helped you? Are you repurposing strategies in 39C that you used in 39B?

☐ What have you read so far that has helped you with your researching and writing processes for the HCP?

☐ What have you learned about locating, evaluating, and selecting sources?

☐ How many different types of sources are you using in your HCP? Can you explain how and why different types of sources can support your argument and give the author (you) credibility?

☐ Have you entered into a discussion among scholars and experts?

☐ Have you used counterarguments? Give examples and analyze them.

An Example from a Student's ePortfolio

Now look at this example from a final ePortfolio. Here we see a student documenting the evolution of his or her outlining strategies. We can see clearly how the act of outlining evolved for this student from a simple method of listing ideas to provide very general guidance when writing a first draft, to become a robust method for inventing arguments, rhetorical positions, and for organizing ideas, sources, and arguments that had already been analyzed thoroughly. Without the visual comparison here, we would wonder whether this student really did become "more selective and conscious" of her or her sources, and whether outlining really did help this student to discover "transition sentences."

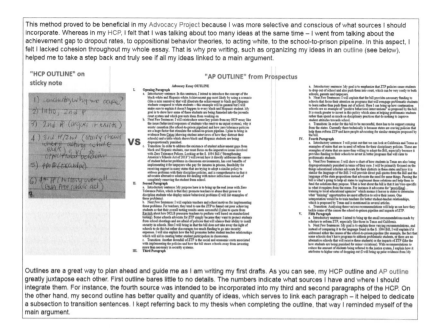

This method proved to be beneficial in my Advocacy Project because I was more selective and conscious of what sources I should incorporate. Whereas in my HCP, I felt that I was talking about too many ideas at the same time – I went from talking about the achievement gap to dropout rates, to oppositional behavior theories, to acting white, to the school-to-prison pipeline. In this aspect, I felt I lacked cohesion throughout my whole essay. That is why pre writing, such as organizing my ideas in an outline (see below), helped me to take a step back and truly see if all my ideas linked to a main argument.

Outlines are a great way to plan ahead and guide me as I am writing my first drafts. As you can see, my HCP outline and AP outline greatly juxtapose each other. First outline bares little to no details. The numbers indicate what sources I have and where I should integrate them. For instance, the fourth source is intended to be incorporated into my third and second paragraphs of the HCP. On the other hand, my second outline has better quality and quantity of ideas, which serves to link each paragraph – it helped to dedicate a subsection to transition sentences. I kept referring back to my thesis when completing the outline, that way I reminded myself of the main argument.

Information Literacy and Working with Sources

Throughout the quarter in WR 39C, you'll find, evaluate, select and use various types of sources to help you understand the issue you are researching and to build informative, credible, and persuasive multimodal arguments. In so doing, you'll put into practice the information literacy skills discussed in the Finding Sources and Using Sources chapters of this guide.

As you research, always be on the lookout for a range of sources, as different types of sources will serve different purposes. For example, news sources will give you information about the most recent developments on your research topic. Such sources often poignantly capture the stories of the people most affected by the problems you'll study, and such human interest rhetoric can help you to meaningfully frame the issue and its relevance for your reader. However, a news article is not a scholarly source, and oftentimes it is not analytical. Such sources offer reports, and the academic expectations of the genres in which you are writing demand rigorous analysis and the use of scholarly sources.

You will encounter many different types of sources in your research process, and good use of these sources in your writing begins with a thorough evaluation of each source. One of the first questions to ask about a new source that you discover is: what **kind** of source is this? What is the genre, and how does that shape the content of the source? Is it popular or scholarly, and if scholarly, what discipline does it come from?

Evaluate Your Sources

Before you use the sources you've found, you need to read them carefully and make sure you understand the information being conveyed. Ask yourself the following questions (explained in more detail in the Finding Sources chapter) as you decide which sources to include in your paper.

- Is the information **RELEVANT** to my topic? Does it further my understanding of important issues, or provide me with a new perspective? If so, how?

- Who is the **AUDIENCE** for the information? Is it written for students, experts, people working in the field, the general public?

- What **AUTHORITY** does the author or organization have to provide information on the topic? What education, training, or experience does the author have that qualifies her to write on this subject?

- What is the **PURPOSE** of the information? Is it to educate, to persuade, to convey factual information, to share opinions, to entertain?

- What **EVIDENCE** does the source include? If the piece is factual, what facts does the author include? Where do the facts come from? If it is an opinion piece, does the author offer sound reasons for his or her opinion?

- How **TIMELY** is the article? When was it written? Depending on the topic and the use you are making of it, some information becomes outdated when new information is available, but other sources that are 50 or 100 years old can be relevant.

- Does the article include **REFERENCES**? Does the author include citations to sources used?

- Is the information **BALANCED**? Does the author or organization acknowledge alternative perspectives?

 SOURCE EVALUATIONS

As you research and when you come across a source you think you will be useful, write down the answers to these questions listed here.

Task: Write 5 source evaluations.

Annotate Your Sources and Create an Annotated Bibliography

After you've evaluated a source and determined that you will find it useful for your project, write an annotation of the source. An annotation refines the information you put together in the source evaluation and reframes it by both summarizing the source and articulating how you are using it for your own argumentative purposes.

- Who are the **author** and **publisher**? What authority does the author have on this topic, and what is the publisher's purpose in publishing this information?

- What kinds of **evidence** does the source draw on? Does it rely on one source of evidence or multiple sources of evidence, and is the evidence cited?

- **When** was the source published? Is this information current, a useful historical artifact, or simply out-of-date?

- How is the source **relevant** to your project? How do you think you might use it? How does it relate to your other sources?

 CREATE AN ANNOTATED BIBLIOGRAPHY

An annotation is the basic entry in an annotated bibliography. Go to the "MLA Formatting and Style Guide" from *The OWL at Purdue* to see examples of annotations and annotated bibliographies:

https://owl.english.purdue.edu/owl/resource/614/03/

Useful Tips
- Make it a practice to write about sources that seem potentially useful, starting with writing out your evaluation of the source, as well as an annotation that summarizes the main ideas or arguments and makes note of key pieces of evidence.

- While writing about your sources before you need to use them in a draft may seem like extra work, and you may be tempted to skimp on or even skip this writing—don't. Preliminary writing about your sources prepares you to use them in some important ways.

- Summarizing a source helps you understand and synthesize the information in that source, which is especially important when working with complex scholarly arguments. After all, successfully paraphrasing a source or introducing and analyzing a quotation requires a solid understanding of the original source.

- Writing down your evaluations helps you achieve new insights about the credibility and relevance of the source that will help you use it more thoughtfully and purposefully in your composition.

- Well-crafted annotations and evaluations create a record of what each source argued, what key evidence was used, and your initial assessment of the source's level of credibility and relevance to your project. Tracking this kind of information so that you can refer back to it days or weeks after you have read a source helps you remember the defining characteristics of sources and the differences between them, and will save you time in the long-run.

- Some of the sentences you draft for your annotations and evaluations will end up in your compositions as part of your analysis.

- Revisit and revise your annotations and evaluations throughout the quarter to keep them up-to-date as your understanding of your sources and their role in your research and writing evolves. You will find that writing about your sources before you use them is actually one of the most important steps in your research process.

Now, Try This!

1. Write a source evaluation following the format listed above for a source published in each of the following sources, all of which you should locate online.

   - Wikipedia

   - A recent article from *The Washington Post*

   - A book review in *The Journal of Popular Culture*

   - A *Time* magazine article published 50 years ago

   - A study published by a governmental organization, such as the EPA or NIH

   - A graph from this study charting data over a 20-year-period

   - An article from *The Journal of American Culture*

Follow-Up Questions:

- When you evaluated the Wikipedia source, did you use a different technique to assess the credibility of a webpage than you did a popular or scholarly article located online?

- How would classify these sources in terms of the genre of each source?

- Explain the relationship between the genre of a specific source and the ways it might be used in an academic composition like the HCP or the AP.

2. Evaluate the Works Cited page of a sample paper, a peer's paper, or even your own Works Cited.

- How many different genres of sources can you locate?

- Does the bibliography contain more of certain genres than others?

- What expectations do you have about the composition and its arguments just from looking at the genres of the sources?

- Now go and read the composition itself and see if you are correct in your prediction.

Techniques that Bridge the HCP and AP

As you develop your AP and its arguments, keep in mind that you are seeking your audience's cooperation. Your audience may be composed of groups or individuals with a range of values and concerns related to the problem and the various and possible solutions. If you take on multiple perspectives when explaining the problem and analyzing various solutions, you will likely succeed in persuading your audience to follow you through your argument, to keep reading, and to consider your arguments seriously. You will probably need to employ a number of argumentative strategies to become a convincing advocate. Your HCP should provide you with a steady foundation on which to stand as you repurpose the knowledge you've gained for the different argumentative purposes of the AP. Here are a few techniques you might use to bridge the HCP and the AP.

Causation

What are the root causes of the problem? Some problems will lend themselves to this type of argument, some will not. Nevertheless, a robust discussion of possible solutions to most of the problems you will be able to address will have to involve analysis of causes and effects of possible solutions.

> **Research Direction:** If while researching for the historical analysis, you found persuasive evidence of particular causes of your problem, research to find further evidence that directly addresses that cause.

Coverage (Comprehensiveness)

Do the potential solutions discussed by scholars and experts satisfactorily address the problem for a significant number of those most affected by the problem?

> **Research Direction:** To support a coverage analysis, you will need to show how many people, or what groups of people, will be affected or have been affected historically; for example, you might present demographic data or studies that quantify the effects of the problem and solution on different groups of people.

Cost/Benefit

Do the benefits of solutions debated by scholars and experts exceed the costs?

> **Research Direction:** To support a cost/benefit analysis, you will need to detail how much a potential solution or solutions may cost to implement, what benefits will result, and how long it will take for benefits to be seen. You will also need to consider what other solutions have been tried in the past and then document and analyze the results. Although this will often take the form of an analysis of financial costs and benefits, other factors—like human well-being—can also be used. For federal policy proposals, the Congressional Budget Office, for example, may have budget estimates available; some think tanks may also have this information.

Feasibility

Are the solutions being debated feasible? Is one or another easy enough to implement without significant negative consequences for other social interests? Does a particular solution have enough support from significant parties to make it likely to be accepted by stakeholders, interested parties, and others in positions to take real action?

> **Research Direction:** To support a feasibility analysis, you will need to present evidence to show that implementation of a particular solution or solutions is feasible in terms of money, time, and support. You will want to offer historical comparisons that tie such feasibility claims to past failures or partial successes. You may also need to show that there is enough political or popular will to support a given solution and/or demonstrate that implementation would not be overly difficult or expensive. You might present budget data, public opinion polls, as well as politicians' statements and voting records on similar proposals.

Comparison

Comparison is usually a type of feasibility argument. To make a comparative argument, you ask: have similar solutions worked well, not so well, or failed in another comparable context? Such a comparable context can also draw from the past, as you may have done already in your HCP.

> **Research Direction:** To support a comparative analysis, you present evidence to show, for example, that a similar policy has worked before in a similar context (i.e., in another city, state, or country, or at some time in the past). In addition, you must show that the other context is comparable to the current circumstances. You may want to look at historical data or policy reviews, for example.

The Advocacy Project

Like the HCP Project, the main assignment of the Advocacy Project is a multi-modal composition that uses various rhetorical positions and different types of evidence to make arguments. This one, however, is a bit different from the first in that over the course of these next few weeks, as you research and evaluate various sources, and as you draft, craft and organize your thoughts and evidence, you will at some point have to make a decision to advocate solutions to your central problem in at least one of the following three ways. 1) **You might advocate one or more specific solutions** to the significant and current political/social/cultural problem that sits at the center of your focus. 2) **You might locate the next steps to potentially solving your project's central problem.** 3) **You might argue for why the current solutions do not work and leave your readers with questions about possible next steps.** By the end of this project, your advocacy positions and arguments will become, after weeks and weeks of diligent engagement, a richly-textured thesis statement, one that deepens your articulation of the problem at hand and argues convincingly for ways to move forward.

Thesis Statements

- ☐ Try to explain the differences between an HCP thesis statement and AP thesis statement.

- ☐ Look at your thesis or the argument from your HCP. How might your thesis or argument for your AP differ?

When we think of the act of advocating and when we imagine a person or an organization who advocates a cause, we think of strongly held opinions delivered with intensity from a rhetorical position that appears unshakable, deeply confident in the ethical rightness of its arguments and the accuracy of its knowledge. If we look at advocacy in such ways, we can understand why it takes time to become a convincing advocate and for an AP thesis to develop and mature.

Academic writers in many disciplines often write with the purpose of advocating solutions to political/social/cultural/environmental problems. When they do so, they are expected to consider and present positions that run against theirs in various ways in order to meet the expectations of their academic audience. These counter arguments help demonstrate their mastery of established arguments and knowledge in areas of discourse and show their recognition of the legitimacy of other perspectives, even if they (you!) seek ultimately to dismiss them.

On Counterarguments

Did you know that using counterarguments can actually strengthen your argument and enhance your credibility?

Tasks:

1. Locate 2 or 3 examples of counterarguments in sources of various types: your core text, an academic article, an article in a popular journal, your own work.

2. Explain the purposes of these counterarguments in each example.

3. Evaluate the rhetorical effectiveness of the counterarguments in each example.

4. Imitate in your own work these argumentative moves.

Remember, there's an opportunity here to create material for your ePortfolio!

Effective advocates deliver strong and impassioned arguments by undermining counterarguments. They do so by choice and with knowledge about the various perspectives and pieces of evidence that may potentially undermine their case. In other words, they have researched, read, and considered positions that run against their own. They use such positions to deepen their own positions. When putting forth arguments in academic or public settings, the most convincing advocates do not simply deliver solutions without first comprehending the informed debates in which these solutions are situated. Rather, successful advocates draw from a deep well of knowledge when carefully selecting the evidence and rhetorical appeals that will make their case about how to address the profound social problems they put before their audiences.

This assignment challenges you to become that strong advocate, one who articulates the depth and complexity of a current and pressing problem and then analyzes various solutions to it. You cannot, in all likelihood, be this advocate at the beginning of the project. You will need to spend time researching and evaluating sources; you will need to explore various arguments and perspectives as you write proposals and drafts. But you will choose an advocacy position at some point, after deepening your knowledge and probably after writing a full draft or two.

As you move through the writing and researching process for the AP, you'll prepare and deliver an oral & visual presentation that will last approximately five minutes. The presentation will then be followed by a short question and answer period. The advocacy presentation gives you an opportunity to try out your arguments and attempt to convince your peers of the legitimacy of your positions and the credibility of your solutions. It also gives you a forum to ask for and receive feedback on your work in progress.

The oral and visual elements of your presentation should work together but not like they do in a conventional presentation in which the visual elements simply restate what you are delivering orally. You can deliver much more information with a couple good visuals than you can possibly talk about in five minutes. So you should make good use of your visual presentation; select important pieces of information and data and create visuals that argue for you without you having to describe all of the details they make visible.

A Multimodal Moment

When you give your Oral/Visual presentation, you'll be hard at work on your AP project.

At this moment, you'll be working on your arguments in 3 modalities at the same time:

1. Written (in your drafts)

2. Oral (presentation)

3. Visual (presentation)

Reflective prompts:

☐ What did you discover about your arguments while you prepared for and delivered the O/V presentation?

☐ Did your advocacy arguments evolve as a result of the presentation? Explain.

Presentation Tips:

1. **Deliver** your presentation with authority and pace yourself. (Stay within the time limit!)

2. **Present** your arguments, thesis statement, or guiding questions clearly and in interesting ways.

3. **Describe and summarize** the significant political/social/cultural problem you're addressing.

4. **Frame** this problem with motives, which are current examples or incidents that show your audience that the problem you're addressing and the solutions you're analyzing are alive and relevant right now.

5. **Document** for your audience the deep foundation of research on which your positions stand.

6. **Demonstrate** how your oral arguments work together with the visual arguments to articulate your arguments or thesis statement.

Questions to Consider

- How did you use and repurpose the knowledge you gained in your HCP?

- In what ways do you think your AP has or will evolve beyond your HCP? How has your evidence and your body of sources evolved?

- How many different types of sources are you now using? Why are you using different types of sources?

 TAKE A STEP BACK

Remember the screenshot in the "Multimodal Interlude" section that we already discussed? This is a tidbit from a student's Reflective Introduction. Notice how the author presents evidence both in the flow of the analysis and in the form of cross references? The embedded links to the "HCP" and the "outline" use the technique of cross-referencing to direct the reader to other sections of the portfolio where the reader will encounter other pieces of evidence.

The Final ePortfolio

Your Final ePortfolio is assigned on the first day of class and due at the end of the quarter. Think of your portfolio as a growing archive that will become full of interesting pieces of evidence as the quarter progresses. You will quickly accumulate artifacts that you can use to document your learning: things like drafts, instructor or peer comments, organizational notes, before and after versions of sentences and paragraphs, and final versions of your compositions. Use these pieces of evidence **to document the work you have done, demonstrate your role in your learning, and articulate your intellectual strategies as they pertain to college level rhetoric, composition, and communication.**

You'll write a reflective introduction to your portfolio. This introduction introduces you as a writer, thinker, and communicator to a community of your peers, and it makes good use of the evidence you've accumulated. You take responsibility for the quality of your work in this document (and in your ePortfolio) by assessing your performance. **The reflective introduction accomplishes two major objectives: (1) it is an analytically incisive introduction that delivers and substantiates arguments about your development as a writer and communicator; and (2) it offers a balanced analytical assessment of your progress.**

Your reflective introduction should be a rigorous multi-modal composition that documents the rich textures of your learning this quarter and perhaps throughout the WR 39 sequence of courses (39A, 39B, and 39C). The introduction should analyze your learning in four areas, which are listed below and followed by prompts that you may use to organize your thoughts. (You may choose to focus on the first three if you cannot address the fourth.)

1. Your Composing Process

- Explain what you have learned about the process of generating a research-based composition.

- What have you learned about arranging the elements of your composition? Have you become more skillful and able to control your presentation of evidence and integrate various pieces of evidence into a coherent and meaningful argument?

- How did conducting research all throughout the drafting process help you to make decisions about the organizational logic of your compositions? In what ways, specifically, did you formulate and reformulate research strategies, framing questions, and guiding claims/arguments by using research?

- Explain how your process of writing drafts, source evaluations, and annotations evolved over the course of the quarter. Did you become more effective at pre-writing tasks?

- Have you experienced moments when the light bulb suddenly illuminated? Can you explain why and how this happened?

2. Rhetoric, Argumentation, and Multimodal Communication

- What have you learned about argumentation and persuasion through the process of generating two multimodal compositions?

- Explain how creating a multimodal composition helped you to articulate your arguments and understand your ethos as the author.

- Can you explain how you arrived at the solutions you chose to advocate? Did you experiment with other solutions before deciding on the one(s) you chose to advocate?

- Was there a specific moment when your thesis became clear to you, and can you explain what you did to arrive at such a moment of clear insight?

- Explain and demonstrate why and how you used various arguments and counter-arguments and numerous and different sources to strengthen your claims.

3. Revision

- Explain your process of revision. How big of a role does revision play in the process of generating and discovering arguments?

- Explain how you used feedback from your teacher and from your peers both in workshops and in conferences or office hours.

- How do you respond to criticism and what sort of critic are you becoming? Use examples of feedback you received on your work-in-progress, your final versions, and in workshops, as well as advice you gave to your peers to address these questions.

- Analyze how you benefit from writing multiple drafts in terms of argumentative presentation, evidentiary support, and narrative development.

- Explain and analyze the types of revisions that benefit you. Do you make broad, conceptual revisions? Do you make structural revisions and reorganize paragraphs? Do you rewrite sentences? Do you make fine word choices? Do you alter your body of evidence through research or omission?

4. Knowledge Transfer

- Now that you have completed the sequence of courses that fulfills the Lower Division Writing Requirement, look back to where you were at the beginning of the quarter, or even at the beginning of your college-writing experience, and look forward to where you would like to be, and assess how your strategies for researching, writing, arguing, and organizing have changed and evolved.

- Have you already applied what you learned in the WR 39 series to writing assignments in other classes? Explain using specific examples, if possible.

- Are you using a variety of strategies to approach your writing assignments in all of your classes? Did the WR 39 series of courses influence your ability to make effective choices about how to approach other writing assignments such as lab reports, memos, blue book exams, short response papers, and any other examples of writing you have been assigned in school?

- Did the WR 39 series of courses influence the ways in which you communicate when you write or communicate outside of school, perhaps in your communities or in your extracurricular activities? Are you using the same strategies in different contexts as you consider the demands of different situations, both in school and out?

ePortfolio Tips

☐ Take a look at other examples of Reflective Introductions

☐ Study examples of other students' final ePortfolios

☐ Work on your ePortfolio all throughout the quarter!

Advice on Reflective Writing

The Reflective Introduction to the Final ePortfolio, the ePortfolio itself, and a variety of exercises along the way will require you to write about your writing process, reflecting on the rhetorical decisions you made throughout the quarter. Keep a writing journal, and save multimodal evidence of your writing and research progress. Self-reflection helps us develop techniques that can improve the rhetorical persuasiveness of our work while increasing our awareness of intellectual strategies and how we as individuals learn from and communicate with the world around us. Reflecting on learning strategies can also build self-confidence.

In 39C, reflective writing is not limited to an after-the-fact review of what we have done. Rather, it is a dynamic method we use throughout the quarter to better understand our work, rhetorical strategies, revision techniques, research methods, work habits…and the list could go on. If we are serious about tracking the progress of our research projects in a weekly self-reflective journal, as well as in a few mid-assignment mini self-reflections, and a brief self-reflective paragraph or two after every major assignment, we will start to become increasingly aware of individualistic learning habits as they pertain, for example, to grammar, syntax, tone, citation format, paragraph construction, topic sentences, transitions, thesis derivation and development, scholarly and multi-modal source analysis, historical and contemporary articulation of a problem, and analyses of solutions.

Frequent and brief self-reflection will lead us to come up with our own ways of analyzing our writing, thinking, and communicating strategies, ways that don't just come down to value judgments like "good" or "bad" or even "strength" or "weakness." We can use self-reflection as a way to challenge our ideas and improve our work, by starting to think about things like the difference between summary and analysis of sources, by asking whether we got at the heart of a scholarly debate or just skimmed the surface of our sources, and by moving from the high school model of writing a report or even a thesis/example/explanation/

proof model of writing, toward a model of research-driven analytical synthesis realized as we progress through the 39C assignments.

Ultimately, everything you write about your composing process can and should end up in your Final ePortfolio in some form, whether in the final reflective introduction to the ePortfolio; in the captions and commentary that introduce, contextualize, and analyze artifacts of your writing; or in the creativity with which you name, organize, and design the various sections of your final ePortfolio.

Here are a few strategies for self-reflective writing, or writing about your writing in 39C:

1. Ask productive questions

Ask yourself a series of questions about what you are trying to achieve when you write self-reflectively. Here are some examples: How and where am I defining and analyzing a problem, and how can I refine the description of the problem I'm studying in order to set up a clearer connection between the HCP and the Advocacy Project? Where in my draft do I simply restate the main points of my scholarly sources and how can I shift toward situating and analyzing debates between groups of scholars? Where are the spots in my writing that define, address, and attempt to persuade a given audience or reach a broader audience?

2. Reflect before, during, and after the assignments

Experiment with the timing of self-reflection. Write a weekly self-reflective journal, but don't forget to keep a running "sideline" commentary open while writing, so you can jot down your plans or impressions. It's important to write a brief, 1–2 paragraph reflection after you finish each major stage of research and each major assignment. Ask your teacher for advice about the timing of such writing and for examples of prompts you might use to get you going.

3. Mix it up

Reflect on a variety of aspects and stages of your research, from topic formulation, through search engine information literacy and search term refinement, all the way to the assessment and analysis of sources.

4. The personal can become the analytical and the political

Use self-reflection as a way to articulate the personal, intellectual motivations behind your research. How are you personally invested in the problems you've studied? Use this occasion to speak out to the world and expand on the larger social, cultural, and political importance of your 39C research projects.

5. Be multimodal

You're making and collecting a series of multimodal artifacts that will serve as evidence for claims you make about your learning in the final reflective introduction to your ePortfolio. Take screen shots of your writing process. Take photos of your notes. Take pictures of places where you write and things that inspire you. What else? It's up to you!

Index